Confessions of Faith
in Early Modern Engla

CONFESSIONS OF FAITH IN EARLY MODERN ENGLAND

BROOKE CONTI

PENN

UNIVERSITY OF PENNSYLVANIA PRESS

PHILADELPHIA

Published by
University of Pennsylvania Press
Philadelphia, Pennsylvania 19104-4112
www.upenn.edu/pennpress

Printed in the United States of America on acid-free paper
10 9 8 7 6 5 4 3 2 1

Library of Congress Cataloging-in-Publication Data

Conti, Brooke.
    Confessions of faith in early modern England / Brooke Conti.
        p. cm.
    Includes bibliographical references and index.
    ISBN 978-0-8122-4575-2 (hardcover : alk. paper)
    1. English literature—Early modern, 1500–1700—History and criticism.
2. Religion and literature—England—History—17th century.   3. Authors,
English—Religious life.   4. Autobiography—Religious aspects.   5. Faith in
literature.   6. Polemics in literature.
    PR428.R46 C66 2014
    820.9'3582   2013038704

For Jim
My fit, conversing soul

CONTENTS

NOTE ON SPELLING AND PUNCTUATION

Although authoritative or scholarly editions have been cited in most cases, at times my analysis depends on early printed texts or individual manuscript witnesses that are not available in modern editions. In transcribing such texts, I have preserved original spelling, punctuation, and capitalization, with the exception of *i/j*, *u/v*, long *s*, and obsolete abbreviations and contractions, all of which have been modernized. When an entire section of text is set in italics in the original, I have reversed italics and roman type for ease of reading.

Introduction

Controversy and Autobiography

In 1642, engaged in pamphlet warfare over the proper form of church government, John Milton took time out from his vivid renderings of the evils of episcopacy to discuss his literary ambitions. A few months later, in another contribution to the same debate, he again interrupted his work's political content with an autobiographical excursion—this one occupying nearly a third of his pamphlet's length and providing his reader with an account of everything from Milton's morning routines to his youthful dedication to chastity.[1] Milton's extended self-reflections in *Reason of Church-Government* and *An Apology Against a Pamphlet* are so well known that their strangeness has often gone unremarked, and there has never been an entirely satisfying explanation for what these autobiographies are doing in the middle of two political pamphlets.[2] Despite the best efforts of scholars, these passages have resisted classification: they are too long and too personal to be called ethical proofs; they involve too little spiritual self-reflection to be regarded as proto-spiritual autobiographies; and although the passage in *An Apology* does respond, at least in part, to an opponent's personal attack, it looks nothing like the self-defenses that appear in other polemics of the period.

But if Milton's autobiographical moments are peculiar, they are far from unique: sudden declarations of belief, assertions of identity, or surprisingly pointed bits of biographical data pop up in controversial religious prose from the reign of James I to that of his grandson James II. In speeches, political pamphlets, and devotional manuals—as well as in more conventionally autobiographical works—writers such as John Donne, Thomas Browne, John Bunyan, and the two King Jameses themselves make much the same move that

Milton does, turning to autobiography at just the moment that they are debating or responding to religious controversy. As in Milton's antiprelatical tracts, these autobiographical moments tend to sit uneasily within their surrounding material, either lacking a clear rhetorical purpose or failing to live up to that purpose. If Milton's self-narratives are too expansive and digressive to properly shore up his polemical positions, something similar might be said about Donne's description of his Catholic upbringing in the prefatory matter to *Pseudo-Martyr* or Browne's account of his heresies in *Religio Medici*.[3] Although Donne's status as a former Catholic seems crucial to his appeals to English recusants to take the Oath of Allegiance, his treatment of his religious history is surprisingly vague: he purports to tell the story of his conversion but elides not only the details of the event itself but also any explanation of what prompted it. Likewise, Browne insists on the triviality of his youthful heresies, but his excuses for them soon grow so numerous and so self-contradictory that it becomes impossible to tell whether or not he eventually abandoned those beliefs. In both cases, the autobiographical details provided by these writers seem to undercut rather than establish their rhetorical authority.

As the examples from Donne and Browne suggest, the problem is not merely that the autobiographical passages that appear in works of religious controversy seem out of place or that they fail to support their authors' polemical ends; even considered simply as narratives they are unsatisfactory, often sputtering into vagueness and incoherence. But if these autobiographical moments are not straightforward, linear narratives, they are also not occasions for deep introspection: they provide neither a detailed account of a writer's religious history nor an examination of his soul. Indeed, it often seems that the more a writer says about his religion the less clear his beliefs or denominational identity become. These puzzling works are what I call confessions of faith: polemically inspired autobiographies that purport to lay bare their authors' beliefs but that tend, instead, to complicate and obscure them.

The name I have given these texts emphasizes their peculiarity and the ways they defy our expectations about what autobiography is and does, whether in the early modern period or in our own. While in literary studies the term "confessional" is usually applied to works marked by raw intimacy and self-revelation (or at least that give the appearance of being so), in religious studies the term "confession of faith," like "creed," refers to a brief series of propositions that sum up the whole of an individual's belief. The works this book examines are poised between these two definitions. They are not confessional in the tell-all twenty-first-century sense of the word, but neither are they bare creedal statements or declarations of corporate identity. Rather, they seem motivated by the essentially creedal impulse to give a coherent public account of their authors' beliefs, but they soon veer off into the idiosyncratic and the particular.

This book argues that the confession of faith is a product of the polemical culture of the seventeenth century. The passages of autobiography that emerge in works of religious controversy seem intended as relatively straightforward professions of belief: a means of aligning their authors with a larger religious position, party, or faction. However, the complicated personal and familial histories of these writers make simple declarations difficult. Their digressions into autobiography are public attempts to probe their individual religious experiences and account for any irregularities; the problem is that an honest accounting—one that acknowledged (for example) that the author was still attached to certain practices from the religion of his youth or still held a heretical belief or two—has no place in the either/or world of religious controversy.

The confession of faith may be guarded or elliptical, but it can nevertheless tell a careful reader quite a bit about its author, and perhaps even more about religious identity and the terms available for its expression in early modern England. As Jesse Lander has reminded us, in the sixteenth and seventeenth centuries polemic was not a kind of religious literature; it *was* religious literature.[4] Nonetheless, polemical culture is a necessary but not sufficient condition for the confession of faith, and the relationship between polemic and autobiography looks quite a bit different in the seventeenth century compared to the sixteenth. English religious polemicists of the sixteenth century—like the polemicists of the early church[5]—frequently write in a strong first-person voice and occasionally include brief snippets of autobiography, but these are not comparable to what we see in the Stuart era. Polemicists such as Thomas More, William Tyndale, and the writers on both sides of the Marprelate controversy may assume a knowing and intimate tone in their works, but they rarely supply unambiguously autobiographical details. When they do, those tend to come in the form of targeted parries or brief self-defenses usually made in direct response to an opponent's personal attacks.[6] Since most sixteenth-century polemicists are writing in defense of what they see as the true church and are assuming a voice that represents that church, we might speculate that autobiographical details were regarded as a liability: to the extent that the particulars of a writer's experience distinguished him from his cause, they could only open him up to attack. But whatever the reason might be, the bio-graphical details that feature in most sixteenth-century polemics belong not to the author himself but to his opponent: the emphasis is on defining one's antagonist, not oneself.

In the seventeenth century that changes, and the writers examined in this book seem eager to supply their readers with personal autobiographical details. The era, to be sure, saw the emergence of many sorts of autobiograph-ical or proto-autobiographical writings. The confession of faith involves a unique *kind* of self-scrutiny, however, one meaningfully different from the self-explorations found in religious verse or in nonfictional prose narratives such as the spiritual autobiography or the self-vindication.[7] I argue that this is a direct result of the unusual pressures of religious life in Stuart England. In an age of oaths of allegiance and civil and religious warfare the need to declare one's beliefs was omnipresent, but the options were generally binary: Catholic or Protestant, conformist or non-. Most of the writers examined in this book do not fit easily into those categories, and thus their autobiographical declara-tions are both longer and less straightforward than polemical engagement would seem to demand, toggling between professions of corporate identity and digressions of a far more idiosyncratic sort. Like much early modern prose, controversial literature is generically fluid, capable of accommodating what appear, to twenty-first-century eyes, to be several quite distinct genres within one work. At the same time, it involves, by its very nature, the taking of sides and delimiting of boundaries. The rigid ideological distinctions and relaxed generic distinctions of controversial prose, taken together, seem to have en-couraged a number of writers to declare their own religious identities along-side their critiques or defenses of their fellow Christians and of their church. Autobiography appears to function for these writers as a forensic device: a way for those in the midst of religious controversy to arrive at and declare the truth of their beliefs. However, as the resulting texts reveal, that truth tends to be more complicated than the terms available for its expression.

Who Do You Say That I Am?

In claiming that religious identity in the seventeenth century was under par-ticular pressure, I am not suggesting that life in the previous century was easy, either for those whose religion put them on the wrong side of the state church or even for those who merely muddled along; three official changes of religion in twenty years would have been, at the least, exasperating and confusing for nearly everyone. But while the Elizabethan Settlement and Elizabeth's long reign meant that, upon James I's succession, England had experienced nearly fifty years of continuity in matters of worship, most people did not yet regard the Reformation as irreversible; some Protestants did not even regard it as completed. At the same time, the rhetoric of intra-Christian religious difference was becoming more rigid. As Alexandra Walsham and Christopher Haigh have noted, the idea of the "recusant"—a self-consciously oppositional or nonconforming Catholic—did not emerge until the 1570s and 1580s, and the same is broadly true for Puritans or nonconformist Protestants.[8] As Elizabeth's reign progressed and Mary's receded from memory, the maturity and increased stability of the Reformed English Church meant that the distinct shape of English Protestantism became clearer, and so too did alternatives to it; with the establishment of a norm the nonnormative becomes thinkable.

Perhaps as important as the later decades of Elizabeth's reign was its end. Anxiety over Elizabeth's successor, and then over the specific nature and biography of that successor, created a different kind of public discussion about religion. By the 1590s it was clear that the shape of religious life in England was not going to change while Elizabeth was on the throne, which mooted certain religious controversies. However, the lack of a clear heir suggested that confessional change after her death was a real possibility. Once the succession of James VI of Scotland was proclaimed, James's complicated religious inheritance gave rise to more specific hopes and fears, all of them matters of heated public debate: would a monarch raised by staunch Presbyterians help England to finish the incomplete work of its Reformation? Or would the son of Mary, Queen of Scots, return England to the Catholicism of his parents and his own baptism?[9]

Many of the period's problems of religious identification are writ large in the lives of the two monarchs whose reigns bookend the texts that I am examining. Each of the King Jameses was baptized into a religion other than the one he would later claim (although James I moved from Rome to Canterbury and James II moved in the opposite direction), and each had an unstable relationship with England's institutional church. Even more than for their forebears and successors, the religious identities of these two monarchs were central to arguments about their legitimacy and inextricable from the ways their actions and policies were interpreted. But while the first King James worked hard, in his confessions of faith, to align the public perception of his

beliefs with the beliefs of his new countrymen, the second King James in-
sisted on the separability of his religious identity from his legitimacy.

The political stakes may have been higher for monarchs than for their subjects, but religious affiliation and its public enactment mattered a great deal at
all levels of society; the very terms most commonly used for Catholics and
Puritans, "recusant" and "nonconformist," highlight their unwillingness to participate in the state church. Although Queen Elizabeth is said to have declared
that it was not her intention "to make windows into men's souls," and her successor said much the same thing, the expectation of external conformity involved a paradox in which outward actions both did and did not reflect internal
states.[10] A subject's external shows were regarded as communicating one kind
of private and otherwise inaccessible truth, that of loyalty, but as being illegible
when it came to another kind of private truth, that of his religious beliefs. Perhaps unsurprisingly, then, the six writers this book considers simultaneously
declare their beliefs and refuse to declare their beliefs, expressing the desire for
transparency alongside a deep skepticism that such transparency is possible.

The pressures placed on both religious identity and the expression of that
identity are discussed explicitly in many of these confessions of faith, but
they are also evident in the works' form and texture. Signs of such pressure
frequently manifest themselves in the fragmentary, elusive, or contradictory
nature of the autobiographical passages themselves: a writer's narrative or
prose style sometimes sputters into incoherence, with suddenly tangled syntax, complicated negative constructions, and the like, when the text starts to
address certain topics.[11] Attending to such disnarrative moments and situat-
ing each work within its political and biographical context can shed light not
only on each individual autobiography but also on the larger textual phenomenon in which they participate—a phenomenon born of their authors' attempts
to articulate an authentic religious identity while negotiating competing political, personal, and psychological demands.[12]

In many ways, these self-narratives reinforce the arguments advanced
by two decades of revisionist historiography on the religious life of early
modern England. The work of scholars such as Patrick Collinson, Brian Cummings, Eamon Duffy, Christopher Haigh, Peter Lake, and Alexandra Walsham
has dismantled what were once thought to be the self-evident categories of
"Catholic" and "Protestant," "Anglican" and "Puritan," helping us to recover
the more complicated reality of post-Reformation lay religion.[13] Whereas
nineteenth- and earlier twentieth-century scholars looked at the intellectual
and spiritual landscape of early modern England and saw rigid denominational

divides, a convincing body of work now suggests that for many English men and women the religious culture was more fluid; those whose beliefs or practices we might now label as Catholic or Puritan did not necessarily see themselves or their neighbors that way.[14]

The confession of faith reflects some of this religious fluidity. The biography of King James I—a man who was baptized a Catholic, was raised a Presbyterian, and later became head of the prelatical English Church—may have been unusually complicated, but it epitomizes the kinds of problems many Britons faced in narrating or defining their religious identities. Many English men and women were baptized into a denomination other than the one they would later claim, and many more underwent subtle shifts in their faith lives, discarding or adopting particular beliefs or devotional practices, sometimes quite casually and incidentally and at other times with great anxiety and soul-searching. The six authors this book considers all have lives or beliefs that they seem to feel require some explanation, excuse, or maneuvering around, and in this way they support a revisionist sense of what early modern religious identities looked like.

But although plenty of Britons may have blended or borrowed elements from both the Catholic and the Calvinist ends of the spectrum—or may have had lives that involved movement back and forth between Rome and Canterbury[15]—the political and polemical culture of early modern England nevertheless painted the world in stark religious binaries. The average Englishman may not have seen his traditionalist neighbors as "papists" or "recusants," but he knew that such people existed, for he heard and read about them with some frequency. Polemical rhetoric infused the public understanding of religious identity, serving, as Jesse Lander has suggested, to both reduce and *pro*duce identities.[16]

In other words, the old dialectical view of the religious life of seventeenth-century England is not wrong so much as it is incomplete. Early moderns did think about religion in binary terms, at least some of the time and in certain contexts, even as they also lived their lives in ways that manifested their tacit and perhaps even their explicit acceptance of more variable and fluid forms of belief and worship. Lay men and women may not have lived in binary categories, but they believed in them. The confession of faith shows us seventeenth-century Britons poised between these two realities: writing in a public realm that tended not to allow for much nuance and that understood religion as an either/or proposition, but attempting to depict an individual history and experience that might not perfectly conform to those expectations.

When given the opportunity or faced with the necessity, what did early modern Christians call themselves? What did they understand those titles to mean or encompass, and how did they explain or defend their application? Most of the historical evidence that has been used to answer these questions comes from church court cases in which those accused of nonconformity (whether Catholic or Protestant) deny those charges despite whatever activities they might have been reported as participating in; these are taken as signs of a possible discrepancy between confessional identity—what one calls oneself—and how others read one's outward behavior or beliefs.[17] But it is difficult to know the truth of the matter, even for those whose irregular lives earned them a spot in churchwardens' reports, and as Judith Maltby and Christopher Haigh have noted, it is still more difficult to know how the mass of generally conforming Protestants defined or explained themselves.[18]

Perhaps most Britons did not have to define or explain themselves. But some did, and a number of those people left written records. The confession of faith may not reveal all or even most of the mysteries of early modern religious identity, but in examining how six early moderns defined and described themselves before an audience of readers, we can learn more about how seventeenth-century Britons actually understood and talked about their religion. Although the recent "turn to religion" in literary studies has demonstrated that religion is a subject worthy of examination on its own terms (rather than simply as a manifestation of state power or as a proxy for political or economic concerns),[19] religion is still too often assumed to be a purely theological or devotional matter: a set of doctrines or practices toted up neatly as if on a ledger, proving one author a Calvinist and another an Arminian. In this book I presume that religion is a category of identity both as central and as unstable as race, subject to continual social and contextual redefinition; the reductive descriptors used by the early moderns failed them, and they will continue to fail us. What the confession of faith demonstrates is that, for many seventeenth-century Britons, it was no simple matter to tell the truth of their religious identity, even to themselves.

Confession and Autobiography

Recent years have seen an explosion of interest in early modern life-writing and a proportionate expansion in the number and nature of those works now regarded as autobiography.[20] As scholars such as Meredith Anne Skura, Henk

Dragstra, Ronald Bedford, and Adam Smyth have argued, early examples of life writing rarely conform to modern notions of how one narrates a life.[21] While earlier studies of the genre naturalized the forms that autobiography assumed in the nineteenth century, seeing as fundamental such features as a coherent narrative arc and an interest in private experience and psychological development, there is now a growing consensus that the category of auto-biography should include a larger and more varied collection of texts.[22] There has also been a movement away from a teleological model that views all life-writing as aspiring to the condition of the nineteenth-century autobiography (and hence sees early works that diverge from that model as somehow imper-fect or defective). Sixteenth- and seventeenth-century autobiographies do not look much like later ones; autobiographical moments occur in a variety of genres and are likely to be fragmentary and fugitive, frustrating those who seek such things as background detail, motivation, and sometimes even just a clear sense of chronological progression. They also reflect early modern as-sumptions about the value and meaning of a life and how one narrates and presents that life. In contrast with the post-Enlightenment belief that subjec-tivity is coextensive with an awareness of an autonomous self, early moderns constructed their selfhood not just through articulations of difference and individuality but also "through a process of identifying . . . with other fig-ures, narratives, and events, and by looking out into the world, rather than within."[23]

Like many of the works examined in recent studies of early modern life-writing, the confession of faith involves autobiographical self-revelations that appear in the middle of works that, properly speaking, belong to some other genre. And like many of those works, the confession of faith also frequently involves the expression of a subjectivity that is as much collective or commu-nal as it is individual. But although this book has benefited from and extends some of the arguments made by recent scholarship on early modern auto-biography, it is not itself primarily a study of autobiography—not even "reli-gious autobiography." It is, rather, an examination of the particular *kind* of autobiographical writings produced by and within a culture of religious con-troversy. The confession of faith dramatizes all the tensions of that culture as well as the fundamental insolvability of those tensions.

The name I have assigned these works highlights their liminal status, poised as they are between an older and a more contemporary model of life-writing and also between two different understandings of the word "confes-sion." If they are not soul-baring, secret-revealing cris de coeur, they are not quite creeds, either. Rather, they are public declarations of faith that slide continually into personal history and private experience. For these writers, the relationship between personal and collective belief requires constant negotiation and assertion. As Jaroslav Pelikan observes in his definitive study of creeds and confessions, Christianity is a religion with a "creedal impera- tive."[24] Unlike the polytheistic faiths of the ancient world and to a greater degree than the other major monotheisms, Christianity has always asserted the intimate relationship between believing and professing one's beliefs; since its earliest days, the church has emphasized the public declaration of belief over and above ritual observance.[25] But alongside this confessional impera- tive lurks an anxiety or uncertainty about just which beliefs must be con- fessed, and creedal statements have, historically, always begotten more creedal statements (dozens in the church's first centuries, and hundreds if not thou- sands overall). For although a creed is meant to be definitive, it is implicitly dialogic. By asserting that *its* propositions are true, a creed acknowledges the existence of contrary propositions even as it invalidates them; there is always defensiveness as well as pugnacity lurking in statements such as "I believe in one God." (If it were self-evident that there was only one God, the faithful would not have needed to say so.)

There is a similar tension between the speaker of the creed and the beliefs he declares. Although in the Western church a creed is most often spoken in the first-person singular, "I believe," it is a corporate declaration of faith. The speaker is not announcing his particular or idiosyncratic beliefs, but using a standard form and formula to align himself with a larger community.[26] Nev- ertheless, the use of the first-person singular still seems to promise delibera- tive, individual choice, and in an age of proliferating options—when there were multiple creeds to choose from or when the precise meaning of the proposi- tions in a common creed were hotly debated—the impression that the speaker of a creed was voicing a considered choice was not necessarily incorrect. Indeed, centuries' worth of catechists stressed the importance of each speaker's understanding and giving active, intellectual assent to every item he recites in his creed.[27]

Only some of the autobiographies that I am examining borrow directly from creedal or catechetical formulae, but all of them exhibit rhetorical fea- tures characteristic of creeds. Their authors seem impelled to sum up and declare their beliefs before an audience; they express affiliation with one group of believers (and/or disaffiliation with other groups); and there is often an uncertain movement back and forth between "I" and "we." None of the authors that I am examining speaks as a Christian Everyman, but in his describing his experiences or explaining his beliefs there is often an uneasy shuttling between private or independent conviction and corporate declaration.

The confession of faith also challenges some of our assumptions about the relationship between religion and autobiography. The older narrative of origins for autobiography linked the genre's emergence to the Reformation, seeing the spiritual autobiographies that emerged among nonconformist Protestants in the middle and late seventeenth century as a natural outgrowth of Protestantism itself. With its abolition of auricular confession and its allegedly greater interest in the inner experience of the individual, Protestantism was long seen as a spur to self-reflection and the subsequent transmission of those reflections to paper.[28] As many scholars in recent decades have observed, however, this narrative of origins for autobiography is problematic, not only for its national and religious chauvinism (autobiographical writings of a similar sort appeared in Catholic countries even earlier than they appeared in England)[29] but also because of its progressivist understanding of the development both of autobiography and of the individualistic self. According to this version of events, the fullest flowering of autobiography occurred in the nineteenth and twentieth centuries, just as human beings in those centuries also attained unprecedented levels of psychological self-awareness and autonomy.

But although this older scholarly narrative has been convincingly challenged, the assumption remains that religious autobiography—whether Protestant or Catholic, Puritan or conformist—designates a work that follows an essentially Pauline or Augustinian model, in which the sinner is saved, the skeptic converted, or the carnal man brought to spiritual truth. To be sure, Paul and Augustine were powerful models for conversion or spiritual regeneration; their presence can be felt not only in the spiritual autobiographies of the mid-seventeenth century but even earlier in the occasional autobiographical passages in Martin Luther as well as in many of the spiritual *bio*graphies in works such as John Foxe's *Acts and Monuments*.[30] But they were not the only or the necessary models for religious autobiography. Indeed, even autobiographies that involve conversion do not necessarily follow the Pauline model: Donne's does not, and neither do the narratives of the two King Jameses. The fact that the confession of faith does not make use of such a readily available framework suggests that something about the Pauline model was inadequate to the task of exploring and explaining the religious identities of many early moderns. Even Bunyan's *Grace Abounding to the Chief of Sinners*, which acknowledges its Pauline framework in its very title, is much more than and much stranger than it has usually been given credit for being. As generations of readers will attest, large portions of Bunyan's narrative are hardly a narrative at all, if by narrative we mean something with a linear story line and a coherent chronology. Rather, as I argue more fully in Chapter 5, it seesaws between past and present, so consumed by the trauma of Bunyan's arrest and imprisonment that it is often difficult to tell when Bunyan is speaking of his conversion and when of his experiences in prison.

The works that this book studies owe less to Augustine's *Confessions* and its progeny than to the early modern creeds, catechisms, and other works of religious didacticism that Ian Green has shown proliferated throughout Renaissance print culture.[31] The autobiographies that I examine are a remarkably heterogeneous group of texts, both in that they occur in a range of primary genres (speeches, devotional manuals, political polemics, and philosophical treatises, to name a few) and in that, *as* autobiographies, they differ tremendously in their narrative structure, strategy, and style. This group of texts supports the current consensus that autobiography is not a genre at all, if by "genre" we mean a collection of works with meaningfully similar formal characteristics. Rather, autobiography is a device or tool that can be used for a variety of different ends; in the confession of faith, it operates as a forensic response to questions of religious identity or assurance. The six authors this book examines make different uses of the tool of autobiography, in part because they are all answering slightly different questions, but all appear to turn to autobiography from a sense of external pressure—in an effort to prove their orthodoxy, their salvation, or simply their belief that God is on their side. As conscious performances and public negotiations of identity, these confessions of faith also challenge the assumption that life-writing is a privileged expression of "inwardness" or "interiority."[32] Although some letters, diaries, and unpublished manuscripts may indeed have some claim (if not an absolute or an unproblematic one) to reflect their author's private realities, published texts such as those I investigate were intended for an audience, and the accuracy of their self-portraits must be treated skeptically.

The fact that the confession of faith is always made before an audience does not mean that it is wholly under the control of its author, however, or that its rhetorical performances are seamless. There are fissures and incoherencies in all of the works this book examines, apparently borne of the pressures of declaring an identity or assuming a role that may not correspond perfectly with biographical or emotional reality—calling oneself a Protestant, for example, while still being deeply attached to one's recusant family, history, and perhaps even certain doctrines and devotional practices. The confession of faith may be intended as a straightforward self-defense, but when the categories provided by a culture of religious controversy do not fit, such defenses are anything but straightforward.

A Century of Confessions

The six writers and public figures this book considers represent very different points on the religious spectrum, and their autobiographies reflect different strategies of religious identification and different problems of self-representation—strategies and problems that change with each man's relationship to the institutional church and with the political climate in which he lived. They also wrote in a range of genres, and not all of their works are as obviously engaged in religious controversy as John Milton's. However, even works as seemingly dedicated to private or personal matters as Donne's *Devotions upon Emergent Occasions*, Browne's *Religio Medici*, and Bunyan's *Grace Abounding to the Chief of Sinners* are also urgent responses to public religious and political upheaval. Such upheavals, as I have suggested, can dramatically change the pressures placed on religious identity and its expression.

In order to chart some of those changing pressures, this book is organized chronologically, in three parts, with each part comprising chapters on two writers whose confessions of faith were published at similar moments and reflect similar strategies and dilemmas. The first part, "Oaths of Allegiance," considers works by James I and John Donne, who, in addition to having a warm professional relationship in their later years, had strikingly similar backgrounds: both men were defined and dogged by their Catholic heritage, their own shifting religious identities, and the Jacobean Oath of Allegiance. Chapter 1 examines the case of James. Born and baptized a Catholic, raised a Presbyterian, and eventually head of the prelatical English Church, James faced an insoluable dilemma. Owing his thrones both to his Catholic parents and to his staunchly Protestant upbringing, James's autobiographical works show him struggling to be loyal to both. Beginning with the letters he wrote to Elizabeth in the period surrounding his mother's trial and execution, this chapter examines James's efforts to negotiate his many conflicting identities. Through *Basilikon Doron* (1599), the preface to the second edition of *An Apologie for the Oath of Allegiance* (1609), and numerous published speeches, I trace the effects of James's dual allegiances on his religious self-representations. James continually slides into autobiography in order to counter either actual or imagined suspicions on the part of his subjects, but the resulting picture of his beliefs—simultaneously Protestant *and* identical to those of his parents—suggests that autobiography could never fully lay those suspicions to rest.

Donne had a similar family background but different personal and political imperatives. If James's confessions of faith refuse to admit to the slightest change in his religious identity, Donne uses his autobiography to foreground his conversion. Both men may have repudiated the religion of their forebears without being entirely able to erase that heritage, but whereas for James rejecting his parents' religion would mean rejecting some of his claim to royal legitimacy, for Donne it is the only way forward. Chapter 2 analyzes the autobiographical aspects of Donne's *Pseudo-Martyr* (1610), a work intimately related to James's *Apologie*, as well as the very different *Devotions upon Emergent Occasions* (1623), a series of meditations on sickness, sin, and death written in the wake of a nearly fatal illness. In *Pseudo-Martyr*, Donne insists upon the fact of his conversion while remaining defiantly reticent about the details (he seems unwilling to identify the English Church by name, much less by its doctrines or practices), but in the *Devotions* he reverses these emphases, alluding obliquely to his conversion while underscoring his dedication to the English Church through repeated references to specific practices. Both works, however, are indelibly marked by the fact of Donne's change of faith. Donne's autobiographies may be narratives of change while James's tell a tale of continuity, but both men's works read like necessary performances of allegiance to the state and conformity to its church.

The book's second part, "Personal Credos," is concerned with John Milton and Thomas Browne. Despite their political and religious differences, both men made striking use of autobiography during the first years of the English Civil War, and their autobiographies reveal similarly personal and idiosyncratic approaches to their beliefs. Unlike James and Donne, for whom alignment with the institutional church is so important, Milton and Browne insist upon the primacy of reason and individual choice. Chapter 3 focuses on Milton's antiprelatical tracts of the 1640s and his *Defences* of the 1650s. Although Milton may not have any doubts about his orthodoxy or heterodoxy, his autobiographies, like those of James and Donne, concern aspects of belief or personal history that seem difficult for him to address directly. Milton's four autobiographies appear at two crucial junctures in his life, and they show him assessing what God wants from him and whether his own ambitions coincide with the divine plan. In the antiprelatical tracts of the 1640s, Milton appears deeply conflicted about setting aside his poetic ambitions in order to serve God with his prose, and in the *Defences* of the 1650s he confronts the possibility that, having allowed him to go blind while defending the Republic, God may not actually want the epic work that Milton always thought would be both his greatest achievement and his greatest gift to the deity. Over the course of these four tracts and the responses they engendered, Milton's faith in autobiography itself seems to be shaken, for in the last of the series, *Pro Se Defensio,* or the *Defence of Himself* (1654), Milton ironically makes the least use of autobiography.

Browne's *Religio Medici*, which shows similar anxieties about the use and misuse of autobiography, is the subject of Chapter 4. First composed around 1635 and revised two more times before its authorized publication in 1643, the *Religio* has often been regarded as a celebration of the English Church's *via media*. However, a careful reading of the work's earliest version—which was circulated in manuscript but never published—indicates that in 1635 Browne was not entirely comfortable within the Laudian church. Rather, the *Religio* presents readers with a Browne who is wrestling with various heterodoxies and heresies, which he appears to have encountered during his medical studies on the Continent. Although even in the *Religio*'s first version Browne claims to have repudiated these heresies (or to have reconciled them to the Church of England), he keeps returning to them almost compulsively. Moreover, an examination of Browne's successive, strategic revisions, in which he gradually erases his work's most revealing autobiographical moments, suggests that Browne was even less convinced of his own orthodoxy than he initially appeared to be.

The book's final section, "Loyal Dissents?" yokes the unlikely pair of John Bunyan and James II, both religious outsiders perceived as a threat to the restored (and Restoration) English Church. Chapter 5 looks at Bunyan's autobiographical writings, beginning with several of his early religious tracts but focusing primarily on *Grace Abounding to the Chief of Sinners* (1666). *Grace Abounding* is closer to a conventional autobiography than any of the other works considered in this book, but I argue that it, too, is deeply involved in a context of religious controversy, being more about Bunyan's current concerns and anxieties than about the youthful conversion that provides his nominal subject. Before writing *Grace Abounding*, Bunyan provided briefer and more fragmentary spiritual autobiographies in some of the tracts published in the years prior to his arrest, but there are crucial differences between those earlier narratives and *Grace Abounding*. The most significant addition, the lengthy account of Bunyan's temptation to "sell Christ for the things of this world," has no precise parallel in Bunyan's earlier autobiographical accounts, but it *does* have a striking parallel in the brief narrative Bunyan gives of his life and emotional state in the weeks and months after his imprisonment. *Grace Abounding* is thus two autobiographical narratives at once, with the story of Bunyan's imprisonment informing, and at times altering, the story of his conversion.

Finally, in a short concluding chapter, I examine James II's autobiographical writings. Like his grandfather, James mentions his religious identity in nearly all of his speeches, but he devotes considerably less attention to the subject than we might expect from a Catholic convert whose religion very nearly lost him the succession (and later arguably cost him the throne). Instead, James's speeches make a case for the separability of his religion and his public role, and they express no apparent sense of tension or anxiety about either his religious beliefs or the relationship between those beliefs and his position as head of the English Church. Moreover, the historical evidence suggests that the majority of James's subjects were willing—at least initially—to have a Catholic on the throne so long as he preserved the Church of England and abided by the rule of law.

This is not to say that the problems associated with conformity ended with James II; the Revolution of 1688 has long been seen as a repudiation of James's religion, and laws restricting the participation of Catholics in English government remained on the books for centuries. In the years after the Restoration, however, the belief that the religion of the average man or woman was a matter of public concern steadily waned, as the works of Bunyan and James II illustrate. It was not that a person's religion did not mean anything to his or her neighbors and fellow subjects; just that it no longer meant everything. The last decades of the seventeenth century therefore mark the end of the autobiography that I call the confession of faith.

But if the confession of faith is limited to the seventeenth century, it also touches on that century's most pressing issues, as well as the topics that most consume scholars of that era today. Sitting at the intersection of literature, religion, and politics, style, self, and subjectivity, the confession of faith demands that we reconsider the relationship among those various subjects and categories of analysis. Despite the increased scholarly attention that nonfictional prose has received in recent years, its specifically literary complexity still tends

to be ignored; too often, such works are used merely for historical or biographical color, or to supplement readings of the era's drama and poetry. However,
as Joan Webber noted more than forty years ago, nonfictional prose "lacks
the protective devices both of fiction and of poetry."[33] Although controversial
prose certainly has artifices and constraints all its own, we would do well to
heed Webber's call for readings of such works that are attentive to their stylistic
and textual richness. As the ensuing chapters show, the confession of faith is
a complex form of self-expression that provides us with a privileged window
into early modern religious identity.

PART I

Oaths of Allegiance

CHAPTER I

James VI and I and the Autobiographical Double Bind

Only a few pages into *Basilikon Doron*, the handbook of advice he wrote for his son Henry, King James VI of Scotland (the future James I of England) gives the prince directions on a number of devotional matters. After treating the proper method of prayer and the appropriate approach to scripture, he abruptly slides into autobiography and then abruptly slides back out: "As for the particular poyntes of Religion," he writes, "I neede not to d[i]late them; I am no hypocrite, follow your Fathers foote-steppes."[1] Although declining to get bogged down in specific points of doctrine may be sensible, by thrusting himself into the discussion the king makes the issue unexpectedly personal: it is *his* religion that readers are invited to contemplate, not the young prince's or their own. No sooner has James focused attention on himself and his religion, however, than he irritably attempts to back offstage. Rather than telling his readers what his beliefs are, James defensively announces what he is not: a hypocrite. This sudden movement toward self-display that is also a refusal of self-display is characteristic of all the autobiographical moments that punctuate James's prose. As with this passage, such moments tend to occur when the subject turns to religion, and specifically to religious controversy; James's impulse toward autobiography is intimately related to his efforts to distinguish and discriminate among Christian denominations.

Although James avoids specifying the "particular poyntes" that Henry should believe or observe, his autobiographical aside introduces James's own religious history as if it were a legible model for his son to follow. But the king's life does not provide a legible model, either in this passage or elsewhere.

Its illegibility is partly due to James's narration—which, as in the above lines, tends to withhold as many details as it supplies—but his elliptical narrative approach is itself the product of the politically complicated facts of James's religious biography. Born and baptized a Catholic in 1566, the same year that Scotland's Reformation was ratified, James was crowned king just a year later, after his mother, Mary, Queen of Scots, was forced to resign the crown in part because of her Catholicism. Given into the custody of Protestant noblemen after Mary's exile and largely raised by his two Presbyterian tutors, the young king was subject to repeated kidnappings and the attempts of different religious factions to gain control over him and his government. James's religious identity was thus a matter of national significance and national debate from the day he was born. Once he became a contender for the English throne this debate intensified, and the pamphlet literature of the day shows keen interest in the question of James's "real" religious sympathies: were they Catholic or Presbyterian? And in either case, how could such a person become head of the English Church? In order to gain and retain his hold on power, James's official beliefs had to shift more than once. This rendered his actual beliefs perpetually obscure, and perpetually the topic of speculation.

If James's beliefs were obscure to his countrymen during his lifetime, they are surely no clearer to us today. But despite the obscurity of James's private faith, the basic facts of his religious biography are well established and were almost universally known by his contemporaries. James's depictions of his religious identity in his prose are therefore not casual or incidental; they would have been written in the knowledge that some portion of his readers would be searching for clues to his beliefs or trying to square what they read with what they already knew of his background. James's autobiographies, born in a context of religious controversy, are what I have described in my Introduction as confessions of faith: conscious attempts to explain or clarify his beliefs that wind up doing very little of either. James's confessions of faith show him struggling to get past the problematic parts of his religious biography—the parts that could give rise to charges either of apostasy or of having at some point falsified his religion—but no explanation appears to be adequate. At times James seems reduced to reciting the barest and most basic of Christian tenets, in a kind of ecumenical creed, to prove his orthodoxy and lack of hypocrisy. Much as he may try to provide a coherent narrative for his shifts in religion, there is no narrative that will permit him to appear as a loyal son and worthy heir to the Stuart line while also appearing a reliably Protestant successor to Elizabeth and ruler of England; the two roles are fundamentally in tension. James's genealogical inheritance made him king of Scotland and a contender for the English throne, but his religious inheritance would have disqualified him from both.

Perhaps unsurprisingly, then, the problem of James's identity suffuses his public prose. In *Basilikon Doron*, in the lengthy preface to the second edition of *An Apologie for the Oath of Allegiance*, and in nearly every one of his published speeches before Parliament, James interweaves an astonishing amount of family history and professions of personal belief. His confessions of faith continually present him as a dutiful, reverent son, attacking the enemies of his parents as his own and virtually eliding any difference between himself and his forebears. When it comes to the specifics of his religion, however, James tries to have it both ways, implying that his beliefs are simultaneously Protestant *and* identical to those of his parents. The tensions between his religious identity and his public role seem unresolvable, and yet his confessions of faith place those tensions on display again and again.

James's textual self-presentations have been the subject of scholarly interest for thirty years now, from Jonathan Goldberg's *James I and the Politics of Literature* to Jane Rickard's more recent *Authorship and Authority*.[2] James's religious identity has been of less interest, at least to literary scholars, and the relationship between James's religious identity and his rhetorical self-presentations has been largely ignored.[3] This chapter argues that the interplay between James's political position and his religious identity is precisely what gives rise to the autobiographical self-portraits that some readers have seen as profoundly disingenuous.[4] As I have already suggested, however, James was in an extraordinary double bind, where he could not tell the truth—whatever that truth might be—without being seen as hypocritical by some portion of his audience. James's confessions of faith thus reveal a writer caught between the need to declare his religious identity and the seeming impossibility of doing so.

His Mother's Son

James's greatest asset and greatest liability as king was his mother, Mary. Thanks to her Tudor and Stuart bloodlines, James was king of Scotland and one of the strongest claimants to the English throne, but as Scotland's deposed queen and Elizabeth's first cousin once removed, Mary had a stronger genealogical claim than James to both titles; moreover, Mary's Catholicism and involvement in plots against Elizabeth caused many Englishmen to regard James himself with suspicion.[5] In Scotland, James's mother's Catholicism was less clearly a liability; it had resulted in her deposition, but it also ensured the loyalty of many powerful Scottish Catholic nobles and at least the provisional interest of strategically useful Catholic princes on the Continent.

Aside from the degree to which Mary helped or hindered James's ambitions, it is difficult to determine his feelings toward her. After the first year of his life James never again saw his mother, and as a child he appears to have had no contact with her; George Buchanan, one of his two tutors, also took every opportunity to abuse and revile Mary before the young king.[6] In his early teens, and under the influence of his French relative and first favorite, Esmé Stuart, James did begin a correspondence with his mother, and he appears to have seriously considered Mary's proposal of an act of "Association" under which she and James would be considered Scotland's joint sovereigns: James would continue to rule as king, but he would do so, officially, in both of their names.[7] In his letters to Mary during his mid-teens, James professes his love and duty toward her in terms that, while formal, occasionally give the appearance of real emotion.[8]

Whatever actions James may have wished to have taken toward effecting the Association, it became a moot issue in 1582, when the sixteen-year-old king was kidnapped by the Protestant Ruthven lords, who were displeased with Esmé Stuart's influence at court. They kept James under a kind of house arrest for nearly a year and forced him to send Stuart into exile. After James's escape, Mary began urging the Association again, but by then James was less supportive; he does appear to have been continuing to negotiate with Elizabeth for an end to Mary's imprisonment, but he was also attempting to repair relations with the English queen, who was increasingly suspicious of Mary and displeased at James's correspondence with Continental Catholic princes and his refusal to turn over English fugitives seeking refuge in Scotland. As James grew more hopeful of a treaty of Anglo-Scottish alliance that would secure his claim to the English throne, he appears to have moved away from his mother and her faction.

In 1586 a Catholic plot against Elizabeth's life was discovered, and Mary was implicated.[9] She was put on trial, convicted, and sentenced to death.

After her sentencing, James attempted to intercede on her behalf. The letters that James sent to Elizabeth and various intermediaries as a part of these efforts show some of his earliest textual struggles to present himself as a worthy heir to both the Stuart and the Tudor lines: he must express outrage at Mary's alleged role in the plot against Elizabeth, while nevertheless acting as a loyal son and a monarch in his own right. These are private letters—no doubt written in the knowledge that they would be read by others, but not intended for a large readership—and they do not explicitly discuss James's own religious identity. Nevertheless, they set up in useful ways the concerns that will occupy us for the remainder of this chapter. In them, we can see the ways that James's conflicting public and personal roles strain his self-presentations, forcing his language at times into fragmentation and incoherence.

Shortly after Mary's conviction, James sent a letter to William Keith, one of his agents in London. In it he expresses outrage at the irregular nature of the proceedings against Mary, although without addressing the specifics of the charges against her or attempting to make a claim on Elizabeth based on Mary's biological relationship to either one of them; instead, he appeals to Elizabeth on the grounds of their equal status and dignity as monarchs. He writes to Keith: "I no way merit at that queen's hands such hard using as to disdain to hear my overture and reasons. . . . Fail not to let her see this letter. And would God she might see the inward parts of my heart where she should see a great jewel of honesty toward her locked up in a coffer of perplexity, she only having the key which by her good behaviour in this case she may open the same" (*Letters* 75). James wishes for Elizabeth to understand the sincerity of his sentiments, but he does not seem to have much hope that she *can* see his true feelings; even if she could "see the inward parts" of his heart, what she would find there would be "a jewel of great honesty . . . locked up in a coffer of perplexity." Although Elizabeth's "good behaviour" has the potential to unlock that coffer and thus reveal James's true sentiments, it is not entirely clear what this good behavior might consist of. (Commuting Mary's sentence? Securing James's title to the English throne?) His words also hint at great personal distress: "perplexity" can mean not just confusion, convolution, or puzzlement but also affliction and torment.[10] The "inward parts of [James's] heart," or his true feelings, are locked in an anguished body.

Jane Rickard has noted that in their correspondence surrounding Mary's conviction both Elizabeth and James stress the depths of their feelings while

lamenting the inadequacy of language to express those feelings, and she comments that it is to the advantage of each to do so; by this means, neither monarch ever has to say anything directly displeasing to the other and can pretend
that any problems stem from the inevitable miscommunications and mis-
understandings of not being able to talk face-to-face.[11] Although this reading
seems generally correct, James's language is vaguer and more agitated than
Elizabeth's throughout the exchange, and I believe this is not merely because
he is in the weaker position politically; rather, this particular crisis, by striking
at the core of James's identity—as son, cousin, heir, and monarch—severely
limits the self-presentations he can draw upon, and therefore the arguments
that he can make.

As the weeks continued, James wrote to a number of people close to
Elizabeth in the apparent hope of influencing her treatment of his mother,
but his language continues to be vague and roundabout. To the Earl of
Leicester he insists that Elizabeth needs to hear his proposals before acting:
"If my overtures and offers be not found reasonable, the Queen may then do
as shall seem to her best; but to proceed before she hear it, could come of no
wisdom." He continues, "My extremity if so should be [i.e., if Mary is exe-
cuted] is greater than I can express" (*Letters* 76). This reference to his "extremity" again points to James's pain and agitation, and it is the closest he
will ever come to a threat; he seems as unwilling to define what he means by
that word as he is to acknowledge that Mary could be executed: "if so should
be" is James's only, periphrastic allusion to the likely outcome of Mary's
conviction for treason.

Elizabeth was apparently displeased by James's back-channel negotiations, and after she responded negatively to the contents of his letter to William Keith, James wrote to her directly, backtracking from his earlier veiled
threats (*Letters* 79). It is hard to know whether James's striving to placate
Elizabeth was motivated primarily by a sincere concern for his mother's life
or primarily by anxiety over his own reputation in Scotland and his future
claim to the English throne.[12] Accordingly, James's final letter to Elizabeth
before Mary's execution has been variously interpreted.[13] The editor of
James's letters describes it as "turgid," while Goldberg elides any mention of
this letter or any other attempts on James's part to persuade Elizabeth against
Mary's execution.[14] However, an attentive reading will reveal how distraught
James seems, as well as his continuing difficulty in expressing himself
directly:

Madame and dearest sister,

> If ye could have known what divers thoug[hts] have agitated
> my mind . . . if, I say, ye knew what divers thoughts I have been
> in and wh[at] just grief I had weighing deeply the thing itself if
> so it should proceed (as God forbid) what events might follow
> thereupon, what number of straits I would b[e] driven unto and,
> amongst the rest, how it might peril my reputation amongst [my
> sub]jects—if these things, I yet say again, were known unto you
> then [doubt] I not but ye would so far pity my case as it would eas-
> ily make you at the first to [re]solve your own best into it.[15] (*Letters*
> 81–82)

Once again, James expresses the wish that Elizabeth could see his inmost
thoughts, but he does not *articulate* those thoughts except in the most opaque
fashion, referring to "the thing itself" (presumably Mary's execution), "what
events might follow thereupon," and "what number of straits" he might be
driven to. Here, where it would seem most essential for James to express himself clearly (whether that clarity represented the actual truth of his feelings
and intentions or a more politic version of them), he opens with nervous
repetition—if ye knew, I say, if ye knew—and soon sputters into incoherence, as if the conflict between what he wants to say and what he can say
forecloses speech almost entirely.

Some of his anxiety James admits to, saying, "I doubt greatly in what
fashion to write in [this] purpose, for ye have already taken so evil with my
plainness," but then he continues, with more assurance, "I have resolved in a
few words and plain to give y[ou my] friendly and best advice appealing to
your ripest judgement to discern t[here]upon" (*Letters* 82). However, rather
than appealing to Elizabeth by revealing the content of the "agitated thoughts"
that he mentioned in the previous passage, or by specifying the consequential
action that he might be provoked to take, James instead shifts his focus to the
impolitic and possibly illegal nature of Elizabeth's proceedings against Mary.
It is *this* more legalistic and diplomatic subject that he characterizes as "plain
speaking": "What thing, madame," he asks, "can greatlier touch me in honour
that [am] a king and a son than that my nearest neighbour, being in straitest
[friend]ship with me, shall rigorously put to death a free sovereign prince and
my natural mother?" (*Letters* 82).

Although James does refer to the "natural" bond between himself and Mary, he does not emphasize it; rather, the legal and procedural issues are what preoccupy him and what seem to constitute the boldness for which he was asking Elizabeth's indulgence just a few lines earlier. This theme is one that James appears to feel more comfortable expanding upon; it removes his own emotions from the discussion and avoids committing him to a particular response if Mary should indeed be executed. And so, warming to this theme, James continues for many long sentences before concluding with the hope that Elizabeth will excuse his "too rude and longsome letter" (*Letters* 83). It *is* a long letter, and a repetitive one, but where some might urge this as evidence that James has no emotional reaction to the prospect of Mary's execution, I would suggest that the amount of space the letter devotes to procedural matters, and the fact that this discussion comes after such a brief and inarticulate expression of James's personal "straits," may actually indicate the degree of James's distress (whether that distress be rooted in his love for Mary or his anxiety about his own dishonor need not concern us). He *cannot* talk about what most upsets him, because doing so could jeopardize his claim to the English throne.

It is difficult to say whether an actual threat from James would have changed Elizabeth's mind, but his previous letter did not, and Mary was executed on February 8, 1587. James's displeasure with Elizabeth and his unwillingness to anger her are both evident in the letter he wrote to her after the event; officially, his words absolve her of blame, but he demonstrates a reluctance to forgive her entirely. Elizabeth, he writes, has purged herself of blame for Mary's execution by means of her "rank, sex, consanguinity, and long professed goodwill to the defunct," as well as her "many and solemn attestations of [her] innocency"—Elizabeth having claimed that she had no hand in the decision, which was made by Parliament (*Letters* 84).[16] However, James implies that Elizabeth still has a few things to answer for: "I wish that your honourable behaviour in all times hereafter may fully persuade the whole world of [your innocence]. And as for my part I look that ye will give me at this time such a full satisfaction in all respects as shall be a mean to strengthen and unite this isle, establish and maintain the true religion, and oblige me to be, as of before I was, your most loving *and dearest brother*" (*Letters* 84–85). As earlier, it is difficult to know how sincerely to take James's words, but his professed desire for a reconciliation that will "establish and maintain the true religion" on their island is worth lingering over. If Elizabeth *can* give James the satisfaction that he desires—and especially if that results in his succeeding her on the English throne—religious differences might perhaps be resolved. In that case, Mary's death would become not a sign of religious conflict but instead a catalyst for the religious reunification of England and Scotland, Protestant and Catholic, Tudor and Stuart.

Basilikon Doron: The Autobiography of Scotland's King

Mary's execution cast a long shadow over James's subsequent self-representations, and in his later life he would repeatedly act to recuperate her image and reputation as he did not act in 1586–1587 to save her life. Although Jonathan Goldberg is surely right that there is a degree of bad faith involved in these latter-day shows of filial devotion,[17] James cannot actually rewrite history or erase the national memory. Indeed, I would suggest that James is well aware of how both his lack of intervention in Mary's execution and his subsequent defenses of her reputation might be read; from the 1590s onward, references to his parents appear almost every time he starts to talk about religion. His confessions of faith are simultaneously works of familial and national history, and they seem at least a semiconscious reflection of the knowledge that he has not acted with entire consistency. James's confessions of faith seem determined to ward off accusations of hypocrisy, but the more he yokes his discussions of his family with discussions of his religion, the more he leaves himself open to such charges.

In numerous places in *Basilikon Doron* (The King's Gift), James explores familial loyalty and its relationship to both religious identity and political success. Composed in 1598 as a handbook of advice to the young Prince Henry, the work was originally intended for a very small audience: its first printing numbered exactly seven copies. Although Jenny Wormald has argued that this limited printing and the fact that the manuscript was written in Middle Scots (rather than the more anglicized Scots that was already relatively common) are signs that James regarded the work as a personal and private one, most of the evidence suggests otherwise.[18] The handsome, elaborately bound copies that James presented to members of his household and select noblemen were clearly given with the expectation that they would be read—and, once received, those copies might have been expected to reach a readership numbering rather more than seven people; the work's seeming exclusivity and the king's authorship would have served to increase rather than diminish its attraction. By 1599 James was no novice, either as an author or as a public

figure; he had been king for more than thirty years and had already published several books, most recently *The Trew Law of Free Monarchies* (1598).
Moreover, although the manuscript was written in Middle Scots, the first
printed edition—the copies that he intended for Henry and other readers—
were printed in anglicized Scots. James had every reason to believe that he
was writing for an audience larger than seven, and as his preface to the work's
second edition testifies, the 1599 edition went even farther afield than he
probably expected, reaching some of his most dedicated political and religious opponents.

But although *Basilikon Doron* is neither James's first published work nor
his first attempt to shape his public image through the printed page, it is the
first to contain any degree of explicitly autobiographical material. Indeed,
from the first page James makes it clear that the entire work is a kind of autobiography, since he and it provide the example that Henry should strive to
follow. As James writes in his dedicatory sonnet:

> LO heere (my Sonne) a mirrour vive [lively] and faire,
> Which sheweth the shaddow of a worthy King.
> Lo heere a Booke, a patterne doth you bring
> Which ye should preasse to follow mair and maire.
> This trustie friend, the trueth will never spaire,
> But give a good advice unto you heare:
> How it should be your chiefe and princely care,
> To follow vertue, vice for to forbeare.
> And in this Booke your lesson will ye leare,
> For guiding of your people great and small.
> Then (as ye ought) give an attentive eare,
> And panse [think] how ye these preceptes practise shall.
> > Your father bids you studie here and reede.
> > How to become a perfite King indeede. (*BD* 1599, 3)

The metaphor of the book as a mirror for the magistrate-reader has a long
lineage, and one interpretation of the first two lines of the sonnet is that
Henry, in looking into this book-mirror, will see reflected his best possible
self, the king that he will someday become if all goes well. However, given
that this book, unlike most in the "advice to princes" genre, is actually written *by* a king, it is difficult to read the "shaddow" (or reflection) "of a worthy
King" that the book supplies as belonging to anyone other than King James

himself.[19] The *Basilikon Doron* is concerned not only with teaching Henry how to behave properly—that is, rightly or morally rather than wrongly—but also with portraying James himself as just such a proper king. In shaping Henry's future behavior, *Basilikon Doron* is also shaping its readers' interpretation of James's past behavior.

The prose epistle to Henry that follows the sonnet makes it even clearer that James envisions his book as his surrogate. He exhorts his son: "Receive and welcome this booke then, as a faithfull præceptour and counsellour unto you: which (because my affaires will not permit me ever to be present with you) I ordaine to be a resident faithfull admonisher of you. And because the houre of death is uncertaine . . . I leave it as my Testament, & latter wil unto you" (*BD* 1599, 8). James does not claim that his book depicts or is directly drawn from his own experiences as king, but in describing it as "a faithful præceptour[,] counsellour . . . [and] admonisher," he emphasizes that for Henry the book is the next best thing to having James by his side: in order to know his father's mind, all Henry has to do is open this volume. But lest Henry or anyone else think that the advice contained within is optional, or merely a collection of wise maxims, James continues, with sudden ferocity,

> [I] charg[e] you in the presence of God, and by the fatherly authority I have over you, that ye keepe it ever with you. . . . I charge you (as ever ye think to deserve my fatherly blessing) to follow and put in practise (as farre as lyeth in you) the precepts hereafter following: and if yee follow the contrair course, I take the greate GOD to recorde, that this booke shall one day be a witnes betwixt me and you, and shall procure to bee ratified in heaven, the curse that in that case here I give you; for I protest before that great God, I had rather be not a Father and child-lesse, [than] be a Father of wicked children. (*BD* 1599, 8–10)

The tonal shift between the opening lines of the epistle and these last ones is striking. Initially, the text is imagined as a "faithful præceptor" that Henry will gladly welcome, but as the fear of filial disobedience creeps in, the book is recast as a collection of fatherly *commands*. The unusual vehemence of these lines seems to register some anxiety on James's part lest Henry not take him and his example seriously enough; such a concern for filial duty and family honor will become a preoccupation of the work as a whole, and one behind which the specter of Mary seems to lurk.

In the work's first edition, the prefatory matter ends here and the body of the text begins. The first of the work's three parts considers a king's duties toward God, followed by parts that concern his duties in his office and then his behavior in "things indifferent." The first part is the shortest of the three, although its position suggests that it treats what James considers the most important aspect of monarchal behavior; as James piously observes, "He [can]not be thought worthy to governe a Christian people . . . that in his own person and hart feareth not, and loveth not the Divine Majestie. Neither can anie thing in his governement succeed wel with him . . . if his person be unsanctified" (*BD* 1599, 24). This is, of course, a period commonplace, but it would be a mistake to think that it is *only* a commonplace—after all, religious identity underlay Mary's deposition and James's accession to the Scottish throne, and at least part of James's claim to the English throne also rested upon his identity as a Protestant prince fit to rule a Protestant nation. Moreover, by the late 1590s James had gone from being a weak and embattled monarch to a relatively powerful one. In telling Henry that the only successful monarchs are God-fearing ones, James is implying that he himself is just such a king, and that his successes are his reward.

A few paragraphs later, in the passage with which I opened this chapter, James does more than merely *imply* that he is orthodox and God-fearing. James has just admonished Henry to read scripture diligently and prayerfully, taking care not to "wrest" the word to his "appetite . . . making it like a bell to sounde as ye please to interpret" (*BD* 1599, 28), when he adds,

> As for the particular poyntes of Religion, I neede not to d[i]late them; I am no hypocrite, follow in your Father's foote-steppes and your owne education therein. I thanke God, I was never ashamed to give accounte of my profession, how-so-ever the malitious lying tongues of some have traduced me: & if my conscience had not resolved me, that al my Religion was grounded upon the plaine words of the Scripture, I had never outwardly avowed it, for pleasure or awe of the vaine pride of some sedicious Preachours. (*BD* 1599, 30)

This passage clearly illustrates James's double bind: although James says that he was never ashamed to give an account of his "profession," and lashes out at the "malitious lying tongues" and "sedicious Preachours" who have apparently called him a hypocrite, he does not—here or elsewhere—actually identify that profession by name; he also refuses to expand on the "particular poyntes" that might clarify his denominational allegiances. James's turn to autobiography seems an attempt to set the record straight and assert his orthodoxy, but he cannot do so in a satisfying way without going into the details of his religious biography—and such details would only open him up to more attacks.

This is not to say that James gives no sense of his religious preferences, simply that he cannot place those preferences in a coherent autobiographical narrative. In the passage above, James's reference to "the plaine wordes of the Scripture" signals his generally Protestant allegiances, and his advice to Henry on matters of private devotion and public policy gives some additional sense of his theological inclinations. James's suspicion of Puritanism is apparent in his urging his son to keep a middle course in his prayers, being "ne[i]ther over strange with God (like the ignorant common sort, that prayeth nothing but out of bookes) nor yet over-homely with him (like som of our vain proud puritanes, that thinke they rule him upon their fingers)" (*BD* 1599, 38). He gives Henry similar advice at the end of the book's first section, when he says that, "for keeping your Conscience sound from that siknes of Superstition . . . yee muste neither laye the safetie of your Conscience upon the credit of your owne conceits, nor yet of other mens humours, how great Doctors of Divinity that ever they be" (*BD* 1599, 46). Instead,

> learne wisely to discerne betwixt poyntes of salvation and indif-
> ferent thinges . . . al that is necessarie for salvation is contayned in
> the Scripture. . . . And when any of the spiritual office-bearers in the
> Church, speaketh unto you anything that is wel warranded by
> the worde, reverence and obeye them as the Heraulds of the most
> high God: but (if passing that bounds) they would urge you to
> embrace anye of their fantasies in the place of Gods word, or
> would colour their particulars with a pretended zeale, acknowledge
> them for vaine people passing the boundes of their calling. (*BD* 1599,
> 48–50)

James's suspicion of Puritanism seems to be less about doctrine than about decorum—although the two charges often overlapped in seventeenth-century religious polemic.[20] The Puritans' lack of respect toward God in their prayers and their reading of scripture is connected to their lack of respect toward their monarch in attempting to advance their own agendas, and both mark them as James's enemies.

That James is speaking from his own experience in warning Henry against Puritanism and its apparently associated lack of respect for both God and king becomes clearer as *Basilikon Doron* continues. In the work's second section, which lays out "a kings dutie in his office," James seems especially preoccupied with his family history and obligations, which he transfers sternly to his son in much the same way he did in the work's prefatory epistle. In explaining the king's responsibilities as the judge and chief minister of justice, James identifies several unpardonable crimes, among them "Witch-crafte, wilfull-murther, Incest . . . Sodomie, Poysoning, and false coyn" (*BD* 1599, 64). But there is yet another crime that James urges his son to consider unpardonable—although he acknowledges that he might be considered a biased party: "the unreverent writing or speaking of [against] your Parents and Predecessors" (*BD* 1599, 64).[21] James continues: "I graunt we have al our faults, which (privatly betwixt you & God) should serve you for examples to meditate upon and mende in your person, but should not bee a matter of discours to others; sen ye are come of as honorable Predecessoures as any Prince lyving, *Sepeliatur synagoga cum honore* [the synagogue may with honor be suppressed]: and I praye you, how can they love you that hate them whome of yee are come?" (*BD* 1599, 1:66). It is not at all clear that the "unreverent" writing or speaking that James refers to need be untrue to merit punishment—just irreverent. He shows the same anxiety about unauthorized interpretation here as he has earlier in describing himself as "no hypocrite" and in warning his son not to rely on divines who have only their own interests at heart. Moreover, James clearly expects religion to be the basis for the irreverencies that Henry might hear spoken of his forebears, as his Latin quotation indi-cates: the passage comes from a history of the early church and refers to what the author regards as the justified suppression of Jewish communities in those days.[22] Given that the term "synagogue" was often used in post-Reformation Britain to describe illegitimate Christian denominations, it appears that James is again referring to the interference of Scottish Puritans during his parents' reign and his own.[23] Further evidence that James is urging his son to antici-pate (and punish) malicious gossip based on James's religious identity comes just a moment later. He claims that he saw "the judgments of God . . . fal upon all them that were chiefe traytoures to my Parents," and affirms that the only subjects who constantly bode by *him* in his troubles were those who also stood by his mother (*BD* 1599, 66). Being a traitor to James's parents did not require that one be a Protestant or object, specifically, to their Catholicism—but the two were usually allied.[24] Once again, James's slide into autobiography is occasioned, but also complicated, by his personal and familial religious history.

As the work progresses, James continues to warn his son against his own old enemies—those clergymen who, during Scotland's Reformation, "begouth to fantasie to them selves a Democratik forme of government" (*BD* 1599, 74)— and as before this quickly leads him to autobiography. He writes: "There never rose faction in the time of my minority, nor trouble sen-syne, but they [the Reformists] were ever upon the wrong end of it, quarrelling me (not for any evil or vice in me) but because I was a King, which they thoght the highest evil: & because they wer ashamed to profes this quarrel, they were busie to looke narrowlie in al my actiones: and I warrant you a moat in my eye, yea, a false reporte was matter ynough for them to worke upon" (*BD* 1599, 74–76). This past experience could provide an explanation as to why James declined to discuss the particular points of his religion in that earlier passage, and why he sounded so defensive. And yet for someone who seems so vexed by the presumption of those who would "look narrowlie in[to] al [his] actions," he seems almost to have an autobiographical compulsion; the fact that he forecloses any self-revelation almost as soon as such revelation begins does not negate his apparent impulse to explain, to clarify, or to set the record straight. Here as elsewhere in *Basilikon Doron* James's discussion of religious controversy—even when it is future religious controversy that he imagines his son confronting—leads him immediately and inevitably to his own autobiography, and almost as immediately to the cessation of that autobiography.

Although James's anger at the Scottish Puritans amounts to an admission that religious conflict lay behind some of his and his parents' political struggles, he consistently refuses to acknowledge that their own religious identity might have been problematic. Instead, as we have seen, he emphasizes the hostility of Puritans to monarchy (and their associated irreverence toward God). Later, James produces another explanation for his parents' difficulties, and one that removes responsibility even further from the sphere of religious conflict. In the course of advising Henry on the importance of making a good marriage and keeping himself free from lust and fornication, James provides the cautionary tale of his grandfather and Henry's great-grandfather, James V, whose "harlotrie" was repaid by "the suddaine death at one time of two pleasant yong Princes; and a daughter only borne to succeed to him" (*BD* 1599, 124). Although James then resumes giving Henry more practical advice about how to marry well and how to treat his wife, after only four paragraphs he abruptly returns to his grandfather's adultery and the rebellion it bred through the agency of his bastard son Bothwell. Although James may well have believed that his parents' misfortunes were God's punishment for James V's sexual incontinence, it is striking how this explanation manages to elide any mention of his parents' own behavior or religious identities.[25]

As James has already indicated, his early political struggles have led him to realize how easily his actions might be misconstrued even when there is nothing *to* misconstrue. Nevertheless, and somewhat paradoxically, he insists that his son needs to live in a thoroughly honest and transparent way, for it is not enough simply to make good laws and to rule well. Rather, he tells Henry, "let your owne life be a Law-booke and a mirrour to your people, that therein they may read the practise of their own Lawes; and . . . see by your shaddow what life they should leade" (*BD* 1599, 104). Elsewhere James will seem to amend this advice, suggesting that it is less how Henry truly lives than how he *appears* to live that matters, for "the people that see you not within, can not judge but according to the out-ward appearance of your actions and companie" (*BD* 1599, 108–10). A while later he will repeat this point with the aid of a different metaphor: "IT Is a true olde saying, That a King is as one set on a skaffold [i.e., a stage], whose smallest actions & gestures al the people gazingly do behold: and therefore although a King be never so precise in the dischargeing of his office, the people who seeth but the outwarde parte, will ever judge of the substance by the circumstances" (*BD* 1599, 1:162). While Jonathan Goldberg has read passages such as these as cynical assertions that appearances matter more than reality, and that a mere show of transparency is sufficient for a ruler's credibility,[26] it is possible to see these statements, instead, as expressing a frustrated awareness that no matter how honest one is or what good intentions one may have, the truth cannot always be presented in terms that one's audience will understand. These statements might almost be read as a gloss upon James's autobiographical method and the peculiar way he seems to expect whatever personal information he reveals to be transparent and self-explanatory. Despite past experience to the contrary, James acts as though autobiography were the last word on a given subject, and by asserting what he is or does or believes he closes down discussion. In fact, given the intractable conflict between James's family history and public identity, any details he provides only open him up for further scrutiny.

Basilikon Doron was indeed closely scrutinized as readers other than the seven original intended recipients got hold of it, and it attracted criticism almost immediately from the Scottish Kirk for its strong words against Puritanism and its seemingly "Anglo-pisco-papistical Conclusiones."[27] Accordingly,

James made a number of changes before he reissued the work in 1603. The new edition was printed in both Edinburgh and London just before Elizabeth's death (this fortuitous timing may or may not have been coincidental), and it soon went through at least eight editions in England as James's new subjects snatched up copies in an attempt to get a glimpse of their new monarch.[28] The most notable alteration to the work is the addition of a lengthy epistle "TO THE READER" just after the original dedicatory epistle to Prince Henry. One reason for this epistle was simply to better frame the work for a much wider audience, one that would now include Englishmen as well as Scots.[29] Another purpose of the epistle, however, was to respond to criticisms made by those who had either read the earlier edition or heard detailed accounts of its contents.[30]

James begins the epistle with a characteristic insistence upon his own honesty and transparency. "CHaritable Reader," he writes,

> it is one of the golden sentences, whiche Christ our Saviour uttered to his Apostles, that there *is nothing so covered, that shall not be revealed, neither so hid, that shall not be knowne*. . . . Whiche should move all godlie and honest men, to be very warie in all their secretest actions, and what so-ever middesses [means] they use for attayning to their moste wished endes: least otherwayes howe avowable soever the marke be, where-at they aime, the middesses being discovered to be shamefull . . . it may turne to the disgrace both of the good worke it selfe, and of the authour thereof: since the deepest of our secrets, can not be hid from that al-seeing eye. (*BD* 1603, 12)

James initially appears concerned with truth and transparency for ethical and religious reasons: the ends do not justify the means; God knows all; and to think that one can escape his notice and judgment is both foolish and sinful. However, as James develops this theme in the next paragraph, his argument to the public starts to sound more like the one he previously made to his son: "As this is generallie true in the actions of all men, so is it more speciallie true in the affaires of Kings. For Kings being publike persons, by reason of their office and authoritie, are as it were set . . . upon a publicke stage, in the sight of all the people; where all the beholders eyes are attentivelie bent, to look and pry in the least circumstance of their secreatest driftes. Which should make Kings the more carefull, not to harbour the secretest thought in their minde, but suche as in the owne time they shall not be ashamed openlie to avouch"

(*BD* 1603, 12). This second paragraph implies that kings should always be aware of their actions and conscious of being observed, *not* because they are ultimately accountable to God (much less their subjects) for those actions, but because their onlookers are prepared to "look and pry in the least circumstance of their secretest drifts." The pragmatism of this explanation and James's obvious distaste for those prying eyes are in striking contrast to the apparent piety of the previous paragraph, but James still seems to be saying that behaving openly and honestly will allow one to triumph over any potential enemies; the possibility of misconstruction when one is actually being honest is not acknowledged. As in the first edition of *Basilikon Doron*, James's impulse toward autobiography seems motivated by the need to control interpretation—a desire predicated upon the simultaneous awareness that interpretation cannot be controlled and the rejection of that awareness.

Indeed, the fact that James goes on at such length about the danger of "secret" thoughts suggests that he might not simply be assuring his readers of his current transparency but obliquely be acknowledging that something about the 1599 *Basilikon Doron* either was or could be interpreted as deceptive. He never expresses this possibility outright, however, and instead says quite the opposite: since his work was not intended to be made public, it must be taken "for the true image of my very minde" (*BD* 1603, 22). Still, he hastens to address those criticisms that he has caught wind of. "The first calumnie," which has to do with James's religious identity, resulted from "the sharp & bitter wordes, that [*Basilikon Doron*] used in the description of the humours of Puritans" (*BD* 1603, 14). Although James acknowledges his dislike of Puritans, he expresses astonishment that anyone could doubt his religious beliefs, especially since in his book he has "so clearlie made profession of my Religion, calling it the Religion wherein I was brought up, and ever made profession of, and wishing [Prince Henry] ever to continue in the same, as the onely true form of Gods worship; that I woulde have thought my sinceare plainnesse in that first part upon that subject, shoulde have ditted the mouth of the most envious *Momus*" (*BD* 1603, 14). Of course, neither his initial confession of faith, where he assured Henry that he was "no hypocrite," nor this one is unambiguous. But while it is difficult to believe that James is not aware that he is leaving himself open for misinterpretation, his insistence upon his own honesty is, I think, a sign of strain and an indication of his awareness that there are certain things he cannot talk about openly, even if he wished to. This is a characteristic of the confession of faith as I have defined it: the move toward autobiography seems to be a movement toward self-declaration and self-definition, but the autobiographical details the author provides turn out to be inadequate. James's difficulty is that he cannot define himself with any specificity without losing control over his self-definition.

1603 and Onward: The King upon the English Stage

James continues to profess his desire to be transparent before his subjects in nearly every one of his subsequent published works, with his religious identity the subject that most frequently prompts such declarations. Just as in *Basilikon Doron*, so in his later works James sounds both wistful and defensive, as if the need to explain himself were something he resented having to do because such explanations were continually misunderstood. Of course, his uncertain religious identity was central to many of the hopes and fears that he inspired in his new subjects, and his writings and actions were scrutinized every bit as closely as he seems to have expected. However, he proved less able to control interpretation than he might have wished. The English Catholic community had not been wholly in support of his claim to the throne before the fact—the Spanish Infanta was a Jesuit favorite—but after his accession many dared to hope that he might return to the faith of his fathers.[31] The hopefulness of these Catholics was not entirely unfounded: in the years before Elizabeth's death James had also been in contact with foreign Catholic princes (up to and including the pope himself), to whom he had allowed it to be hinted that he might consider converting in exchange for political or military support for his claim to the English throne; the recent example of Henri IV of France made the possibility of James's conversion seem all the more plausible.[32] Quite a few English Catholics found additional encouragement in the autobiographical passages in *Basilikon Doron* where James asserts his love for those who remained loyal to his parents as well as his distaste for Puritanism.[33]

By contrast, those same passages were read with more apprehension by those within the English Church who felt that it had not yet experienced a full reformation. However, these subjects, too, hoped that James might lend a sympathetic ear to their complaints. While Elizabeth had repeatedly thwarted the hopes of would-be reformers, they thought that a new monarch with a solidly Presbyterian upbringing and a demonstrated interest in theology might be willing to support their cause.[34] As it happened, both groups had some of their hopes met and some of them dashed. In the first months of his reign,

James did slacken the antirecusancy laws and gave every sign of being willing to leave peaceable lay Catholics unmolested—but he did not extend the same toleration to the missionary priests in his country and certainly showed no inclination to return either himself or his new nation to Rome.[35] At the same time, in response to petitioning from reformist clergy and laypeople, James convened the Hampton Court Conference in order to give their complaints full airing. Although most historians no longer see the conference as a rout for the prelates, but conclude that the reformers emerged from the conference with a number of their concerns addressed, the episcopal hierarchy and the prayer book remained firmly in place, and discontentment lingered.[36]

This discontentment is addressed by James in his first speech before Parliament on March 19, 1603/4, just two months after the Hampton Court Conference. James also took the unusual step of having this speech published shortly after its delivery—a sign of how eager he was for his words, including his autobiographical self-portraits, to reach his subjects.[37] On his arrival in England, James says, although he "found but one Religion . . . which by my selfe is professed, publikely allowed, and by the Law maintained: Yet found I another sort of Religion, besides a private Sect, lurking within the bowels of this Nation."[38] The "other sort of Religion" is, of course, Catholicism, and the "sect" is Puritanism. In accordance with his dismissive terminology, James wastes no time on the latter, but he devotes quite a lot of space to recusants and his own relationship to them. "For the Papists," he writes,

> I must put a difference betwixt mine owne private profession of mine owne salvation, and my politike government of the Realme for the weale and quietnes thereof. As for mine owne profession, you have me your Head now amongst you of the same Religion that the body is of. As I am no stranger to you in blood, no more am I a stranger to you in Faith. . . . And although this my profession be according to mine education, wherein (I thanke God) I sucked the milke of Gods trewth, with the milke of my Nurse, yet do I here protest unto you, that I would never for such a conceit of constancy or other prejudicate opinion, have so firmly kept my first profession, if I had not found it agreeable to all reason, and to the rule of my Conscience. (*PW* 138)

As he has in *Basilikon Doron*, James hedges about the exact nature of his "profession." Although this passage would have assured an early modern reader of

James's Protestantism, it leaves unaddressed any possible differences among his Presbyterian upbringing, the prelatical English Church, and the specifics of his own current religious beliefs. He is also careful to note that his profession is the result of his "education," and that it was sucked in "with the milke of [his] Nurse," rather than claiming that he was born into it or owed it to the tutelage of his parents—which would, of course, have been false. But at the same time that he emphasizes the earliness of his instruction in the faith, he also emphasizes that his religion is not *merely* the result of his upbringing but rather a considered choice; his profession is in accordance with both his conscience and his reason.[39]

But if James's Protestantism is staunch, he insists that it is also reasonable, and for "the weale and quietness" of his realm, he can tolerate Catholics in a limited way. The passage continues: "I was never violent nor unreasonable in my profession: I acknowledge the Romane Church to be our Mother Church, although defiled with some infirmities and corruptions, as the Jewes were when they crucified Christ: And as I am none enemie to the life of a sicke man, because I would have his bodie purged of ill humours, no more am I enemie to their Church, because I would have them reforme their errors" (*PW* 138–39). James concedes a remarkable amount to the Catholic Church, his language going beyond what might be thought necessary either to convince his Protestant audience to support limited toleration for Catholics or to reach out to his recusant subjects (and indeed, comparing Catholics to the Jews who crucified Christ is not a simile likely to endear him to the latter population). It is not, I think, too fanciful to suggest that James has his own mother, Mary, at the back of his mind when he discusses Catholicism as his "Mother Church . . . defiled with some infirmities and corruptions." Mary, too, like the Jews in James's analogy, sought the death of someone she ought not to have, and although James's language makes it clear that he does not condone that action or agree with the tenets of Roman Catholicism, unlike Elizabeth, James is determined, as he says a moment later, not to "straight the politique Governement of the bodies and mindes of all [his] Subjects to [his] private opinions" (*PW* 139).

After asserting that he is no persecutor and that those recusants who are loyal subjects need not fear, he returns to the nature of his own faith by way of suggesting that all of his subjects can depend upon his governance in church matters: "As my faith is the Trew, Ancient, Catholike, and Apostolike faith, grounded upon the Scriptures and expresse word of God: so will I ever yeeld all reverence to antiquitie in the points of Ecclesiasticall pollicy" (*PW*

140). This impromptu creed can be taken almost any way a reader or audience member likes. Coming immediately after his clarification of his attitude toward English Catholics, it is quite evident that James is not aligning himself with Rome but rather implying, as most Protestants did, that his faith is *more* authentic than that of the Catholic Church, being grounded in scripture (and presumably in scripture alone); however, in saying that he "yeeld[s] all reverence to antiquity" in matters of ecclesiology, James is leaving open the question of exactly what "antiquity" endorsed: prelacy or Presbyterianism? Or something else entirely?[40]

James's ambiguous language and the fact that he was a masterful politician can lead one to believe that in passages such as this he is deliberately obscuring his beliefs in order to appeal to as wide an audience as possible; it is also true, as Brian Cummings has noted, that James and the English Church under him restricted or forbade the open discussion of many theological points, especially those surrounding predestination.[41] We need not assume, however, that James's vagueness is calculated—or that, if it *is* calculated, it is deliberately deceptive. Rather, James's ambiguity seems to reflect the limitations placed on how he can describe his religious identity: presenting himself as a loyal son is in permanent tension with presenting himself as a thoroughgoing Protestant, and both are in tension with the historical record. In all his confessions of faith James has difficulty expressing himself (perhaps even *to* himself) without exposing the fault lines within his narratives of familial, national, and religious continuity.

*   *   *

However tolerant James may have intended his policies toward recusants to be, his leniency was tested by the Gunpowder Plot and its aftermath. The plot to blow up the Houses of Parliament while its members and the king and queen were all assembled was discovered on November 5, 1605. On November 9, James gave a previously scheduled speech before Parliament—but after the events of the preceding days he altered the first part of his speech in order to address the crisis.[42] After giving thanks to God for preserving him, his family, and the nation, James reflects on the many plots against his life that he has endured and survived, having, as he says, "ever bene subject unto [dangers], not onely ever since my birth, but even as I may justly say, before my birth: and while I was yet in my mothers belly"—an apparent reference to the assassination of David Rizzio, Mary's secretary and rumored lover, which occurred in front of the pregnant queen and which many feared would result in a miscarriage (*PW* 148).[43] He then congratulates himself for having (as he claims) almost single-handedly discovered this plot, before turning to the nature of the plot's would-be perpetrators. As he has in *Basilikon Doron* and his first speech before Parliament, James makes a careful distinction between those recusants who are nevertheless faithful citizens—being merely "blinded . . . with some opinions of Popery, as if they be not sound in the questions of the *Reall presence,* or in the number of the Sacraments, or some such Schoole-question"—and those enslaved to "the trew grounds of Popery," which for James means loyalty to the pope before one's rightful monarch. James has always tolerated the first group and despised the second, and he declares that he has no intention of changing his policies toward either group in any fundamental way (*PW* 152).

But while James's recusancy policies did not greatly change in the wake of the Gunpowder Plot, the enforcement of those policies *did* change.[44] Most immediately, James gave orders for the expulsion of all Catholic priests, and he oversaw the institution of the Oath of Allegiance, which required recusants to swear allegiance to James and promise to serve him and deny aid to any foreign lord who might act against him.[45] The Oath of Allegiance was to be administered only to those whose loyalty was considered suspect, and, like the Tudor Oath of Supremacy, the Oath of Allegiance expected its subscribers to recognize their sovereign's sole jurisdiction over church and state. However, it also included several paragraphs that many Catholics considered inflammatory: the oath taker was to vow that he or she would "doe my best endeavor to disclose and make knowen unto his Majestie . . . all Treasons and traiterous Conspiracies, which I shall know or heare of," and to swear, further, that "from my heart [I do] abhorre, detest and abjure, as impious and Hereticall, this damnable doctrine and Position, That Princes which be excommunicated or deprived by the *Pope,* may be deposed or murthered by their Subjects, or any other whatsoever."[46] James himself seems to have regarded the oath as an entirely uncontroversial way of identifying those recusants who were *not* loyal subjects, but as William Patterson points out, although the oath officially dealt only with matters temporal, its reference to impious, heretical, and damnable Catholic doctrines seems either accidentally or deliberately to prevent the more innocuous interpretation that James claims he intended.[47] Consequently, Catholic opinion on the oath was split. Many recusants took the oath, including George Blackwell, the head of the English Catholic mission, but others, from Pope Paul V on down, saw it as a violation of conscience. They urged their coreligionists to refuse the oath, assuring them that, if they were executed, they would die martyrs' deaths and enjoy rewards for their fidelity in heaven.[48]

Pamphlet warfare on the subject began almost immediately. In 1607 James fired off a salvo of his own, *Triplici Nodo, Triplex Cuneus, or an Apologie for the Oath of Allegiance.* Although James wrote the work anonymously, in the persona of a loyal gentleman at court, the veil over his authorship was rather thin; the frontispiece, for example, bears his coat of arms. He seems to have believed that anonymity would strengthen his work's persuasiveness, allowing his arguments to speak for themselves rather than arriving with the implied threat of a royal command. As he explained later, "I thought it not comely for one of my place, to put my name to bookes concerning scholastick *Disputations;* whose calling is to set forth *Decrees* in the Imperative moode."[49] His strategy backfired, however, when Catholic polemicists seized on his unacknowledged authorship as proof that he had something to hide.[50] Many of them also made much of his Catholic heritage, branding him an apostate, a hypocrite, and one not to be trusted by Christian subjects of any denomination.[51]

James responded with a new edition of the *Apologie* in 1609, this time published in the royal voice and under his own name. The most significant alteration to the work, however, was the addition of an enormous preface longer than the entire original work.[52] Addressed to Prince Rudolph II of Germany "And to all other right high and mightie Kings; and right excellent free Princes and States of Christendome," its ostensible purpose is to convince James's fellow rulers (Protestant and Catholic alike) that they should take the controversy surrounding the oath seriously, for if subjects in England would not swear their loyalty to James, those in other countries might be provoked by the forces of Rome to similar disobedience or outright treason (*Apologie* 2r–v). In fact, however, James dispatches this part of the preface in the first fifteen pages, and from there he moves swiftly into an autobiographical refutation of his opponents' attacks, giving a detailed account of his religious upbringing and the specifics of his current beliefs. Although this preface constitutes James's most sustained confession of faith, it has received virtually no scholarly attention; many editions of James's works do not even include the preface with the text of the *Apologie.*[53] As we shall see, however, the preface is a compelling literary and political document, and one that reveals much about James's complicated religious position.

As in *Basilikon Doron,* in the preface to *An Apologie* James's account of his religious beliefs is bound up uneasily with professions of filial piety. To the papal charge that he is an apostate, James replies that he can be no such thing, for "not onely having ever beene brought up in that Religion which I presently professe, but even my Father and Grandfather on that side professing the same . . . [I] cannot be properly an Heretike . . . since I never was of their Church" (*Apologie* 33). James thus begins his self-defense with his usual evasiveness, refusing to specify just *which* religion he presently professes and ends with what is at best a half-truth: both his father and grandfather were born, raised, and spent most of their lives as Catholics—though each at various times declared himself a Protestant for political advantage.[54] As for his mother, James apparently realizes that he cannot evade or falsify *her* religion, but he does attempt to minimize its significance: "As for the *Queene* my Mother of worthy memorie," he writes,

> although she continued in that Religion wherein she was nourished, yet was she so farre from being superstitious or *Jesuited* therein, that at my *Baptisme* (although I was baptized by a Popish *Archbishop*) shee sent him word to forbeare to use the spettle in my *Baptisme*; which was obeyed, being in deed a filthy and an apish trick, rather in scorne then imitation of *CHRIST*. And her owne very words were, *That shee would not have a pockie Priest to spet in her childs mouth.* As also the Font wherein I was Christened, was sent from the late *Queene* here of famous memorie, who was my Godmother; and what her Religion was, *Pius V.* was not ignorant. (*Apologie* 33–34)

James admits that his mother was a Catholic and that she had him baptized by a Catholic archbishop—but he quickly downplays the importance of this act by noting first that his mother forbade the traditional Catholic baptismal practice of spitting in the infant's mouth (a symbolic allusion to Jesus's healing of the deaf and mute man in Mark 7:31–34) and then that his godmother was the irreproachably Protestant Queen Elizabeth; moreover, he tells his reader, his baptism took place in a font specially provided by Elizabeth.[55] This attempt to gloss over his apparently Catholic baptism by supplying a host of dubiously mitigating circumstances (does a Protestant font cancel out a Catholic priest?) only serves to suggest how uncomfortable James finds the subject of his religious identity and how close to the bone his opponents' charge of apostasy must have struck. A similar excessiveness continues in the next several lines, as James assures his readers that his mother "was not superstitious" and that "in all her Letters (whereof I received many) she never made mention of Religion, nor laboured to perswade mee in it" (*Apologie* 33). In fact, he says, her very last words were a message to him that he should not change his religion "except my owne Conscience forced mee to it" (*Apologie* 33).

In presenting his mother as a tolerant and broad-minded sort of Catholic, James contradicts the popular narratives about Mary and her last days. In the years after her execution, Catholic and Protestant propagandists fought to retell Mary's story, but they were generally agreed on her staunch commitment to the Roman religion.[56] This is not James's only rewriting of Mary's last days; as John D. Staines has noted, James pressured the historian William Camden to provide a broadly sympathetic account of Mary's tragic fall in his *Annales*, which significantly downplays Mary's Catholicism.[57] Here in the *Apologie,* James entirely omits any reference to his mother's imprisonment for her alleged role in Catholic conspiracies against Elizabeth or to his own inaction during her trial and execution. Nevertheless, this attempt to rehabilitate Mary's image—she is not a superstitious fanatic, and he is not a disloyal son—seems a tacit acknowledgment of the historical reality even as James rewrites that reality.

From here James moves to his own beliefs, implicitly responding to the attacks of Persons, Bellarmine, and other Catholic polemicists: "Neither can my Baptisme in the rites of their Religion make me an *Apostate*, or Heretike in respect of my present profession . . . since we . . . [are] all baptized *In the Name of the Father, the Sonne, and the holy Ghost*: upon which head there is no variance amongst us" (*Apologie* 33–34). As in his first speech before Parliament, James seems to turn from narrative autobiography to simple, broadly Christian creedal statements when his family history gets too convoluted. But if a belief in a triune God is about as basic a Christian belief as one can have, James is willing to be more specific. He believes, he says, in the three main creeds (Apostles', Nicene, and Athanasian); he accepts the first four general councils; he reveres the saints but does not worship them; and so on (*Apologie* 35, 37). Sometimes James's intentions seem sincerely ecumenical, as if he really wishes to smooth over the differences between the Protestant and Catholic churches. He speaks respectfully of the Virgin Mary, for example (though he believes she has better things to do in heaven "then to heare every idle mans suite and busie her selfe in their errands"), as well as of the devotional use of religious images; he also insists that he has consistently shown more favor toward Catholics than toward Puritans (*Apologie* 37–38, 40, 45). At one point, James goes so far as to say that he would be willing to regard the pope as the greatest of all the bishops and the head of the Western church, but he cannot accept that the pope's dominion is other than spiritual or that he has any jurisdiction over temporal princes or their lands (*Apologie* 46–47). At other times, however, James jeers at Catholic practices and beliefs. Of purgatory he says, "It is not worth the talking of. . . . Onely I would pray [Cardinal Bellarmine] to tell me; If that faire greene Meadow that is in *Purgatorie,* have a brooke running thorow it; that in case I come there, I may have hawking upon it" (*Apologie* 43). And once he concludes the explicitly autobiographical portion of the preface, James moves immediately and without any clear transition into an extended proof that the Catholic Church is, in fact, the Antichrist (*Apologie* 51ff.).

As with the Oath of Allegiance itself, in this defense of the oath James spoils his gestures of conciliation and ecumenism by swinging abruptly into unexpectedly mocking language. It is as if he felt the need to undercut any moderation, lest it raise questions about his Protestant credentials or his commitment to the cause of true religion. Throughout his published works, as we have seen, he repeatedly attempts to ward off charges of hypocrisy even as he repeatedly claims that he is of the same religion as both his parents and his subjects. It is possible that what he means is that he believes himself to be Christian in a broader sense, but even had he made such a claim, it would not have answered the underlying questions that his subjects had about his religious identity: *both* Protestants and Catholics believed themselves to be "Christian in a broader sense" (their opponents were the narrow ones).[58] James is therefore in an untenable position, forever trying to silence his critics with autobiographical evidence whose very nature ensures that the charges of hypocrisy will either continue or resume from a different quarter.

As William Patterson has argued, one of James's fondest desires was to use his position as king of England to effect the reunion of Christendom. In the first two and a half years of his reign he worked ardently to bring about an international ecumenical council, and although the Oath of Allegiance controversy meant that his communications with the papacy soured, James was still not significantly daunted.[59] Throughout the 1610s he had scholars such as Isaac Casaubon and Hugo Grotius making his case for a general council, and he was widely celebrated by Continental Protestants (and some moderate Catholics) for his dedication to the cause of Christian unity.[60] There are surely multiple reasons for his interest in reunifying the church, but his confessions of faith, filled as they are with contradictory claims, familial metaphors, and snippets of family history, suggest that one of his motives was deeply personal: to restore his family's honor and bridge the gaps between them, himself, and his nation.

*   *   *

As I have noted, in his speeches before Parliament after becoming king of England, James frequently expresses the wish that his people could see his heart—in much the same way that in 1586, facing the likelihood of his mother's execution, he told William Keith that he wished Elizabeth could see it. In his speech after the discovery of the Gunpowder Plot, he assures his people that he has no intention of changing his policies toward Catholics, and as a sign of his sincerity, he says that he wishes, along with "those ancient Philosophers, that there were a Christall window in my brest, wherein all my people might see the secretest thoughts of my heart" (*PW* 153). In another speech, given in 1610 and also dealing, in part, with the treatment of recusants, he says: "I [have] now called you here, to recompence you againe with a great and a rare Present, which is a faire and a Christall Mirror . . . as through the transparantnesse thereof, you may see the heart of your King" (*PW* 179). Unlike in his letter to Keith, where James depicted himself as needing Elizabeth's assistance in order to show his true feelings, here he insists that he *can* show his heart to his people. As in that letter, however, the metaphor of the crystal breast usually signals an abortive attempt at autobiography, and it also usually accompanies a discussion of his religious policies.[61]

    Of course, to tell the *whole* truth of James's religion would entail acknowledging that it had undergone some shifts. James may well have believed that these were not meaningful shifts—all Christians being, as he says in the *Apologie*, baptized in the name of the Father, the Son, and the Holy Ghost—but he surely knew that they could seem problematic to others, and so his confessions of faith provide a narrative of continuity even though such a narrative does not perfectly fit the facts. He does not see himself as a convert or an apostate, as is made clear in a 1610 speech in which he describes those who have left the Church of England for Rome. Such people have "forsaken the trewth, either upon discontent, or practise, or else upon a light vaine humour of Noveltie, making no more scruple to seeke out new formes of Religion, then if it were but a new forme of Garment" (*PW* 200). To James, to be a convert (at least from Protestantism to Catholicism) is to be a frivolous and dangerous seeker of novelty. That a conversion could represent a true and profound change of heart is not acknowledged, and neither does James account for the possibility of experiences like his own: a gradual change in one's beliefs, practices, and even denominational labels over time. Naturally, he cannot acknowledge that his religion has ever undergone a change if he is both to remain true to his parents and act as the champion of the English Church. The stakes are higher for James than for most English men and women, and the drama of his religious life played out on a much larger stage than theirs. The *nature* of that drama, however, is remarkably similar to that enacted by the more private individuals examined in this book. Like them—and like so many less remembered Britons—in his confessions of faith James appears to have struggled to articulate his religious identity and to make it conform to the demands of the times and his position.

CHAPTER 2

Conversion and Confession
in Donne's Prose

If even the king of England seemed unable to declare the truth of his religious experience in a straightforward fashion, it should be no surprise that many of his subjects were similarly cautious or similarly conflicted. The Thirty-Nine Articles and the Oath of Allegiance may have spelled out the essentials of an Englishman's faith and expected his assent, but under James the English Church forbade the explicit discussion of more divisive points of doctrine, such as predestination.[1] Although preachers were the immediate targets of such edicts, many English men and women seemed to share a sense that the specifics of their beliefs were simultaneously vitally important and best not described in too much detail. John Donne is an exemplary case. Like James I, Donne was a Protestant from a staunchly Catholic family who remained troubled by the aftereffects of the Reformation, and like James, in his prose Donne is prone to cagey first-person explanations and defenses of his religious identity.

I suggested in my first chapter that James's vague and contradictory confessions of faith are occasioned by political imperatives that their author finds as urgent as they are impossible to address; a similar phenomenon is at work in Donne, whose *Pseudo-Martyr* and *Devotions upon Emergent Occasions* simultaneously declare Donne's allegiance to the Church of England and reveal his difficulty coming to terms with his conversion. But although the future dean of St. Paul's would eventually become closely associated with James and his church, the differences between the self-presentations of sovereign and subject are as important as their similarities. Both men may have repudiated the religion of their forebears without being entirely able to erase their Catholic heritage, but whereas rejecting his parents' religion would for James mean rejecting some of his claim to royal legitimacy, for Donne it is the only way forward: he cannot *persevere* in his parents' religion and still achieve the advancement he seeks. Thus, while James declines to admit to even the slightest change in his beliefs—asserting that his religion is the same as both his parents' and his subjects', and that the faith in which he was raised in Scotland is the same as the one he defends in England—Donne uses his confessions of faith to foreground his conversion.

That conversion is treated most fully in *Pseudo-Martyr*, Donne's first published work. Like the second edition of James's *Apologie for the Oath of Allegiance*, *Pseudo-Martyr* is both a contestant in the debate over the Oath of Allegiance and its author's confession of faith. Although James's autobiography offers a narrative of continuity and Donne's one of change, both read like necessary performances of allegiance to the state and conformity to its church. The difference is that while James, as king, has the luxury of simply declaring that his beliefs have not changed, Donne must both say and show how his *have*. Accordingly, *Pseudo-Martyr* lingers over Donne's Catholic upbringing and his long process of deciding between Rome and Canterbury—but while the text makes clear that Donne has left the church of his youth, it elides most of the details of his conversion and gives few positive specifics about the church he has since joined. More than a dozen years later, with *Devotions upon Emergent Occasions*, Donne will publish another work declaring his loyalty to the Stuarts and their church, but this time with fewer explicit references to his conversion and a much more ostentatious performance of his allegiance to the church of which he is by then a minister. In both works, however, Donne leaves out the event at the heart of his story: the conversion itself.

Like James's confessions of faith, Donne's purport to narrate (or at least explain) how their author got from his Catholic past to his Protestant present, but also like James's, Donne's never quite succeed in doing so. Although the sixteenth and seventeenth centuries certainly had models for conversion narratives—in addition to Paul, Augustine, and Luther, the sinner's path to salvation was told in countless funeral sermons and in works such as John Foxe's *Acts and Monuments*—the confession of faith does not follow this model. Rather, as I have suggested, it is a fundamentally *disnarrative* genre: one produced by a conflict between what the author wishes to say and what he can say. The constraints of polemic and polemical culture do not permit the kinds of detailed autobiographical investigations that they seem to inspire.

Pseudo-Martyr and the *Devotions* may be Donne's only explicitly autobiographical works, but nearly all Donne's works are strikingly performative,
full of the first-person pronoun and monologues that can sound downright
confessional. Donne's poems in particular have long tempted readers to interpret them autobiographically: surely *this* poem must have been written
to his future wife, Anne More, or *that* one on the eve of his ordination.[2] At
the same time, Donne shifts so rapidly from one posture to the next—and
the textual history of most of his poems is so vexed—that few scholars today
would argue that each poem must have a precise analogue in Donne's life.
Even apart from the problems of context and chronology specific to Donne's
poems, lyric poetry is simply less autobiographical than nonfictional prose.
As Philip Sidney asserts in his *Defence of Poesy*, the poet "never lieth," because
he "nothing affirmes."[3] Poetry may depict *a* truth, but it is a truth that can
exist outside narrative or causal logic; the parts do not all have to add up or
be readily explicable. As Molly Murray's work on Donne suggests, poetry allows Donne to inhabit a state of religious indeterminacy.[4] Nonfictional prose,
however, carries other expectations and makes more truth claims, and the
prose of religious controversy all but demands a coherent articulation of religious identity. So while it should not surprise us that Donne's *Holy Sonnets*
and *Satyre III* are slippery and evasive when it comes to the specifics of Donne's
theology, it *should* surprise us that a work such as *Pseudo-Martyr* winds up
being similarly evasive. *Pseudo-Martyr* positions itself within the debate over
the Oath of Allegiance and foregrounds its author's Catholic upbringing
and adult Protestant identity, but it withholds the kind of autobiographical
detail that would seem most essential to shoring up Donne's polemical
authority.

Pseudo-Martyr and the Oath of Allegiance

Pseudo-Martyr is nearly the only source of information about the occasions or
motives behind Donne's conversion, which remains one of the great mysteries
of his biography. Many scholars, following Izaak Walton's lead, place Donne's
conversion somewhere in the 1590s, but even this approximate dating is disputed, and no immediate catalyst for Donne's change of faith is known.[5] Most
critics agree that, whenever and however it occurred, Donne's conversion was
not a dramatic, road-to-Damascus moment but rather a gradual process that

likely sprang from a complex set of motives and concerns. However, scholarly interpretation of the meaning and significance of this apparent fact have varied tremendously. Given Donne's descent from Thomas More and his upbringing in a family that seems to have had More's example ever before them (Donne's two Jesuit uncles were exiled, one after having served time in the Tower of London, and his younger brother Henry died while in prison for having harbored a priest in his rooms at the Inns of Court),[6] some scholars have read Donne's conversion as apostasy and naked careerism. In this account, Donne was ambitious above all else, desirous of the kinds of patronage unavailable to recusants, and prepared to sacrifice the faith of his fathers rather than risk any future advancement.[7] Other critics are more sympathetic, noting that throughout his later career Donne articulates a sustained and coherent critique of the post-Tridentine Catholic Church; they argue that, far from turning his back on his recusant family, he blamed their sufferings on a papacy that, in the wake of the Council of Trent, he found newly absolutist and authoritarian.[8] *Pseudo-Martyr* does not resolve the tensions between these two interpretations of Donne's conversion; indeed, it has sometimes functioned as Exhibit A for those who see Donne as a calculating careerist. But although establishing the fact of Donne's conversion seems to have been one of *Pseudo-Martyr*'s primary purposes, a careful reading of its autobiographical passages indicate that even as late as 1610 Donne may not have considered himself fully Protestant, even if he no longer identified as Catholic.

By the time *Pseudo-Martyr* was published in 1610, the controversy over the Oath of Allegiance had been raging for years. In a 1609 letter to his friend Henry Goodyer, Donne expresses his dissatisfaction with the shoddy scholarship of one recent defender of the oath, William Barlow, bishop of London, who had taken on the task of responding to the Jesuit polemicist Robert Persons.[9] Donne tells Goodyer, "I looked for more prudence, and humane wisdome in [Barlow], in avoiding all miscitings, or misinterpretings, because at this time, the watch is set, and every bodies hammer is upon that anvill."[10] But although Donne is aware of the oath's high political stakes and he expresses the wish that Barlow had made a stronger case for it, in the same letter to Goodyer he expresses what seem like reservations about the Oath of Allegiance itself: "In the main point in question, I think truly there is a perplexity (as farre as I see yet) and both sides may be in justice, and innocence; and the wounds which they inflict upon the adverse part, are all *se defendendo* [in self-defense]."[11]

Given the ambivalence about the oath that Donne displays in this letter, it is somewhat unexpected that *Pseudo-Martyr*—which was in the hands of the printer less than eight months later—should come out so unequivocally in support of the oath.[12] In the work's more than four hundred pages, Donne uses examples from recent and ancient history and his training in canon law to argue that God does not permit disobedience to one's sovereign, and that true martyrdom can never come from it, only the dishonorable death of a traitor. Donne's dismissal of Rome's position, combined with the work's apparently swift composition and its dedication to King James, have led scholars such as John Carey and Arthur Marotti to conclude that *Pseudo-Martyr* was primarily a bid for patronage: whatever Donne's personal feelings about the Oath of Allegiance may have been, he saw an opportunity to gain James's favor, and he took it.[13]

Pseudo-Martyr may indeed have been written for careerist reasons, but that does not mean that it is a cynical or calculated production—one in which Donne is falsifying his "real" beliefs for personal gain. It is clear from his letter to Goodyer that Donne was concerned that the oath receive the best defense possible, and his observation that its opponents might be operating in good faith is not the same thing as his endorsing their position. Several recent readings of *Pseudo-Martyr* have argued that the work is not as unequivocally supportive of the oath or as unsympathetic to English Catholics as was once thought. In contrast with Jonathan Goldberg and Debora Shuger's influential readings of Donne as a natural-born absolutist, Annabel Patterson, Rebecca Lemon, and Douglas Trevor have emphasized signs of Donne's independence from James.[14] Lemon, for example, highlights the importance that *Pseudo-Martyr* places on following one's own conscience rather than external authorities (whether those authorities be popes or kings), while Trevor reads the work as reluctant to intervene in matters of religious opinion or enforce religious conformity.[15] These more generous interpretations of Donne's work sometimes imply a subversive, or at least resistant, motive: their suggestion is that Donne resented having been pressured (if he was pressured) into writing *Pseudo-Martyr* or that he was ambivalent about the expansion of state power represented by the oath, even if he believed in its goals.

Although these readings have, among their other virtues, the advantage of making Donne a more sympathetic figure, we do not need to imagine a covertly oppositional Donne in order to explain his authorship of *Pseudo-Martyr* or to see him as a complex and conflicted individual. I would argue that a different possible explanation for Donne's composition of *Pseudo-*

Martyr emerges in the work's dedicatory epistle to King James. Donne tells his sovereign that, when he saw "how much your Majestie . . . vouchsafed to descend to a conversation with your Subjects, by way of your Bookes," he "conceiv'd an ambition, of ascending to your presence, by the same way."[16] Although this is conventional flattery—the patron inspired the work—it is not only conventional. By James's "descent" Donne probably means his condescending to explain the logic behind the Oath of Allegiance to his subjects; however, the greatest "descent" in *An Apologie* is surely James's confession of faith: his decision, in the preface to his 1609 revision, to lay bare so much of his religious background and beliefs.[17] As we saw in Chapter 1, James's background has broad similarities to Donne's own, and so do the two men's confessions of faith. I have argued that the controversy over the Oath of Allegiance both prompted James's autobiography in *An Apologie* and ensured its elliptical nature, but James's autobiography, in turn, seems to have prompted Donne's. With its articulation of a fundamentally moderate Christianity whose only quarrel with Rome is over the matter of supremacy, James's confession of faith may even be partly responsible for Donne's decision to write in support of the Oath of Allegiance. We know that Donne was carefully following the debate over the oath, and the second edition of James's *Apologie* might well have convinced Donne both that he could support the oath and that his personal history would make him a valuable spokesman. As we shall see, the *Apologie* and *Pseudo-Martyr* have much in common, not only in the kinds of autobiographical material that their authors present, but also in the unstable and shifting attitudes they express toward English Catholics.

James's influence on *Pseudo-Martyr* may be referenced on the work's very first page, but the biographical similarities between the two men are never mentioned by Donne, who reveals his own religious history only gradually over *Pseudo-Martyr*'s extensive prefatory materials. In the dedicatory epistle to James, Donne says nothing about his Catholic background, describing his book as simply the natural tribute of a loyal subject to his king: "For, the equall interest, which all your Subjects have in the cause . . . gives every one of us a Title to the Dignitie of this warfare. . . . For this Oath must worke upon us all; and as it must draw from the Papists a profession, so it must from us, a Confirmation of our Obedience" (*PM* 3). By referring to an "us" set in opposition to the Papists, Donne implicitly identifies himself as a Protestant, but it will not be until the subsequent "Advertisement to the Reader" that he suggests that this has not always been the case. In the "Advertisement" Donne announces to his audience, by way of explaining his reasons for writing

Pseudo-Martyr, that he has the greatest respect for *true* martyrdom, "hav[ing] beene ever kept awake in a meditation of Martyrdome, by being derived from such a stocke and race, as, I beleeve, no family . . . hath endured and suffered more in their persons and fortunes, for obeying the Teachers of Romane Doctrine" (*PM* 8).

While his identity as a former Catholic is essential in establishing that Donne understands the arguments made by his onetime coreligionists, given that he has since rejected that faith, his lingering over the sufferings of his famous recusant family is somewhat puzzling.[18] His words suggest pride in his family history, but such pride runs counter to the aims of *Pseudo-Martyr.* Donne cannot express admiration for the sufferings of his family members, since those sufferings, although ultimately due to "obeying the Teachers of Romane Doctrine," are more immediately the result of conflict with England's church and crown. Even if Donne believed (as David Norbrook has suggested) that his ancestor Thomas More's martyrdom was fundamentally different from the martyrdom that England's missionary priests were urging their disciples to embrace, he could hardly boast about belonging to a family with a long tradition of resisting monarchal power in a work whose explicit purpose is to encourage English Catholics to *support* their monarch.[19] What this confession of faith shows, then, is the conflict between Donne's intended use of autobiography, as a way to shore up his polemical position, and the messy emotional backstory that his autobiography carries with it. Donne may now be a Protestant, but he is also (apparently) still proud of his Catholic heritage. These two positions are not inherently contradictory, and they might be held simultaneously by an actual person; however, for a polemical persona, they *are* at odds, and they sit beside each other in *Pseudo-Martyr* in uneasy irresolution.

Donne's expressed attitude toward his Catholic upbringing remains conflicted in the lengthy "Preface to the Priests, and Jesuits, and to their Disciples in this Kingdome" that follows the "Advertisement." Donne begins this preface on the defensive, claiming that he expects personal attacks from Catholic controversialists but insisting that his intention in entering the debate over the Oath of Allegiance is not "*Ostentation,*" nor "*Provocation,*" nor yet "*Flattery* to the present State" but a simple desire for the "unity and peace of [Christ's] Church" (*PM* 12). One of the calumnies Donne seems to anticipate from his opponents has to do with his change in religion, so he quickly turns to autobiography in order to prove the slow and deliberate nature of his conversion. He writes:

I used no inordinate hast, nor precipitation in binding my conscience to any locall Religion. I had a longer worke to doe then many
other men; for I was first to blot out, certaine impressions of the Romane religion, and to wrastle both against the examples and against
the reasons, by which some hold was taken; and some anticipations
early layde upon my conscience, both by Persons who by nature had
a power and superiority over my will, and others who by their learning and good life, seem'd to me justly to claime an interest for the
guiding, and rectifying of mine understanding in these matters.
(*PM* 13)

Although this passage purports to describe Donne's conversion, its language
tends to obscure rather than clarify his current religious sympathies. Donne
is apparently writing *after* having "blotted out" the early impressions made
on him by the Catholic Church, but the term "locall religion" is oddly reminiscent of the Catholic charge that the very name of the English Church
precludes its claims to universality.[20] It seems unlikely that Donne is consciously disparaging the Church of England, but his use of this term suggests
discomfort with the fragmentation of the Christian church, and thus at least
some potential ambivalence about his new religion. Insofar as the Church
of England has helped to blot out Donne's earlier, mistaken allegiance to
Catholicism, its influence must be positive, but as a merely local religion—and
one that demands the "binding" of his conscience to it—the English Church
seems to receive only lukewarm approbation from Donne.

Similarly, although Donne speaks of needing to wrestle against his
Catholic upbringing, he does not explain why he felt this need or what compelling arguments were offered by the Protestant side. Instead of giving reasons for his conversion, he gives excuses for its tardiness, and along the way
he gives a detailed and even sympathetic account of his Catholic friends and
family members; this passage compares favorably, for example, with the description of his upbringing that he gives in the preface to *Biathanatos*, his
posthumously published tract on suicide, in which he speculates that his
morbid affection for suicide might be the result of having had his "first breed-
ing and conversation with men of suppressed and afflicted Religion, accustomed to the despite of death, and hungry of an imagin'd Martyrdome."[21] By
contrast, in *Pseudo-Martyr* Donne presents his first teachers not as the lean
and hungry men depicted in *Biathanatos* but instead as people whose "learning and good life" inclined him toward their beliefs more than did their

power as his elders. Indeed, not only does he speak neutrally of the "examples and reasons" they provided in support of Catholicism, he describes them as "rectifying" his understanding—a word choice that suggests some reluctance, even in 1610, to regard their instruction as flawed.[22] While his account of his upbringing seems offered by way of an explanation for his subsequent prolonged period of religious indecision, the sensitivity with which he describes his family and its claims upon him—and the complete absence of any similar sense of the attractions of Protestantism—makes the religion he has rejected more vivid than the one he has adopted.

As the passage continues, Donne underscores how careful and deliberate the process of his conversion was: "And although I apprehended well enough, that this irresolution not onely retarded my fortune, but also bred some scandall, and endangered my spirituall reputation, by laying me open to many mis-interpretations; yet all these respects did not transport me to any violent and sudden determination, till I had, to the measure of my poore wit and judgement, survayed and digested the whole body of Divinity, controverted betweene ours and the Romane Church" (*PM* 13). But despite his claim to have "surveyed and digested the whole body of Divinity, controverted between ours and the Romane Church," Donne never quite says what the outcome of this survey was, or what specific doctrines or arguments changed his mind. This is in striking contrast to most polemical conversion narratives, which readily identify by title and author the books that changed their writers' hearts or reproduce the arguments that convinced them of the error of their ways.[23] The reader has every reason to believe that Donne is a member of the Church of England, but, like James, Donne is cagey about identifying his religion too precisely; although he refers continually to "our" church, placing it in implied contrast with that of the Catholics, he never mentions a single defining characteristic of that church.[24] It is true that *Pseudo-Martyr* is written, at least ostensibly, for a Catholic audience, but Donne's vagueness about his religion does not seem to be in the service of such readers' imagined sensibilities; after all, he regularly uses words such as "Papist" and is not stinting in his attacks on the priests and Jesuits who are his immediate addressees. Rather, for all his anger at Bellarmine and other Catholic controversialists, he seems not yet entirely to have detached himself from his upbringing or able to look on it with the distance he claims to have achieved.

Despite his apparent unwillingness to go into specifics, Donne nevertheless insists that a conversion has taken place, and *Pseudo-Martyr* becomes his proof of that change in faith: "For, to have always abstained from this decla-

ration of my selfe, had beene to betray, and to abandon, and prostitute my
good name to their misconceivings and imputations; who thinke presently,
that hee hath no Religion, which dares not call his Religion by some newer
name then *Christian*" (*PM* 13–14). By "this declaration of [him]selfe" Donne
seems to be referring to the autobiographical account he has just given—or
perhaps to the whole of *Pseudo-Martyr*, which, in making a case for the Oath
of Allegiance, might be taken as an earnest of his loyalty to James and the
Church of England. However, this declaration itself does no more than the
previous sentences to clarify with which church his allegiances actually lie,
and its tortuous syntax only further confuses the issue. Although "some
newer name than Christian," like "locall religion," sounds like a typical
Catholic disparagement of Protestantism, Donne cannot be identifying himself as a Protestant in this passage, for he seems to be allying himself with the
"hee" who *dares not call* his religion by some newer name than Christian.[25]
The sentence would make considerably more sense if Donne were writing as
a Protestant convert to Catholicism: such a person might well be displeased
by the charge that he hath no religion if he dared not call that religion by
some newer name than Christian. But of course, a reader knows this not to
be the case. The only way to make sense of this passage is as Donne's defense
of his refusal to choose between the two: he is not Catholic *or* Protestant,
simply Christian.[26] Such a nonidentity might be useful in allowing Donne to
speak to both sides of the Oath of Allegiance debate, but it is unlikely to
satisfy either one for very long. Donne himself seems uncomfortable with his
unsettled status, for he obfuscates his meaning through the passage's complicated negative constructions and a switch from the first to the third person,
as if unwilling to identify himself with this man of a faith so general as to be
virtually meaningless.

Perhaps realizing the unsustainability of this (non)position in a controversial work, two sentences later Donne will abandon his autobiographical
use of the first person entirely. For all his struggles, he seems reluctant to call
himself a Protestant—and if he no longer considers himself a Catholic, neither does he appear to have fully detached himself from that identity. Like
James in *An Apologie*, Donne may have supplied this brief confession of faith
with the intention of providing a straightforward ethical defense: proof that
he is a conforming member of the Church of England. But if so, the gaps and
tangles in Donne's rhetorical performances betray just how complicated his
religious identity really is. However, while James's autobiography in *An Apologie* is also evasive as to the exact nature of *his* religion, James's confession of

faith is, as we have seen, at least a positive, declarative one: he is of the same religion as his parents and the same religion as his people; he was baptized in the name of the Father, the Son, and the Holy Ghost; he believes in the Apostles', Nicene, and Athanasian creeds; and he has never wavered in those beliefs.[27] Donne, on the other hand, insists upon his conversion but lingers over his recusant past and his protracted period of religious indecision; there is no positive articulation of his current beliefs—except insofar as his authorship of *Pseudo-Martyr* proves his willing conformity to James and his church.

Doubt and the *Devotions upon Emergent Occasions*

Although James apparently urged Donne to take holy orders in the aftermath of his entry into the Oath of Allegiance controversy, some five years would pass between the publication of *Pseudo-Martyr* and his joining the ministry.[28] Many biographers attribute this gap to the even longer work they presume Donne had to do, post conversion, in order to feel committed to the Church of England. Whether or not this is true, the conversion that seems only partly complete by the writing of *Pseudo-Martyr* shaped the rest of his personal and professional life. Although there is no evidence that he imagined a career in the ministry until King James all but thrust it upon him, by the time the fifty-one-year-old Donne fell gravely ill in late 1623, he had been a minister in the Church of England for nearly nine years and dean of St. Paul's for two, and his reputation as a preacher was well established.

Devotions upon Emergent Occasions, which Donne wrote and published while still not fully recovered from his illness, is as different from *Pseudo-Martyr* as it is possible for two nonfictional prose works to be: the subject of the *Devotions* is not political controversy but the stages of Donne's sickness, which the work transforms into a series of meditations on the sinful nature of man. Nevertheless, the two works can be read as companion pieces, for both are confessions of faith that emerge from a climate of religious controversy, and both draw a contrast between their author's Protestant present and his recusant past. Whereas in *Pseudo-Martyr* that past was foregrounded and Donne's membership in the Church of England only implicit, in the *Devotions* Donne's dedication to his adopted church is repeatedly emphasized and his recusant past referenced more obliquely. In both works, however, the autobiographical content is elliptical and problematic, resisting the demands of straightforward narration.

Although the *Devotions* is clearly an autobiographical text, critics have long had difficulty deciding just how autobiographical it really is. On the one hand, Donne published the *Devotions* just weeks after his nearly fatal illness, and the work appears to follow the actual course of his sickness: each of the twenty-three devotions has a Latin and English heading that identifies a discrete stage of the disease, such as "The Patient takes his bed," "the Physician is sent for," or "I sleepe not day nor night," while the devotions themselves are usually in the first-person singular and seem to give Donne's personal reflections on the deeper meaning of each stage of his physical and spiritual decline and recovery. On the other hand, apart from the specifics of his illness, Donne says little about his life, and he often seems to be speaking more as a Christian Everyman than in his own voice. Although his sickness may have inspired the work, the *Devotions* itself, with its highly artificial structure (twenty-three devotions, each divided into a Meditation, an Expostulation, and a Prayer), can appear so generalized as to make it impossible to recover either the exact circumstances or the personal significance of his illness. Perhaps for this reason, the work's autobiographical features have not received much attention in recent years,[29] and most scholarship on the work's genre or form have focused instead on its possible indebtedness to one or another meditative or devotional tradition.[30] Although these efforts, usually undertaken as part of the search for Donne's religious sympathies, seem to have reached an impasse (surely a work that can be argued to be indebted to *both* Ignatian and Calvinist sources is not meaningfully one or the other), the long-standing assumption that the *Devotions* reveals Donne's theological or devotional proclivities is not entirely wrongheaded, for the work places Donne's religious identity on constant display. Indeed, more than his illness, that identity is the *Devotions*'s primary autobiographical focus.

Apart from his sickness, nearly the only life event that Donne mentions in the *Devotions* is his ordination, and his relationship with both the royal family and the Church of England are constant preoccupations of the work.[31] Having dedicated *Pseudo-Martyr* to James, he dedicates the *Devotions* to Prince Charles, and his dedicatory epistle establishes the work at its outset as a gesture of loyalty to the monarchy and the state church. In the epistle (which I examine more fully at the conclusion of this chapter), he describes James's role in his ordination; alludes to his presentation of *Pseudo-Martyr* to James as a reason for dedicating the *Devotions* to Charles; and expresses the hope that he will "live . . . to see the happinesses" of Charles's reign and experience the continuing favor of the Stuart family.[32] In the body of the work he has much less to say about the royal family, but he continues to emphasize his professional identity. He frequently addresses his readership as though speaking to his usual audience at St. Paul's, and, even when he is engaged in seemingly private colloquies with God, his outpourings more often than not involve his working through and then staunchly reaffirming his church's position on issues and practices that were a matter of some controversy in the 1620s. Throughout, Donne appears determined to present himself as an unfailingly orthodox member of the English Church. This might seem an unnecessary gesture on the part of the dean of St. Paul's, but it grows more explicable when set alongside his repeated references to relapsing into sin and his allusions to recusancy. In that context, Donne's constant reassertion of his orthodoxy reads as a defensive strategy: the action of a man working hard to counter any suspicion of continued adherence to—or backsliding into—the old religion.

The clearest expression of this anxiety comes at the very end of Donne's work. In the twenty-third devotion, having apparently weathered his life-threatening illness, Donne is warned by his doctors of the danger of relapsing. He meditates on the various meanings of "relapse," moving from considering the term in relation to his sickness to considering its spiritual implications. At first he appears to be concerned with human sinfulness in general, but it soon becomes clear that he has a specific sin on his mind. "Shall *I alone*," he asks the Trinity,

> bee able to overthrow the worke of *all you,* and *relapse* into those *spirituall sicknesses,* from which your infinite *mercies* have withdrawne me? Though thou, O my *God,* have filled my *measure* with *mercie,* yet my *measure* was not so *large,* as that of thy *whole people,* the *Nation,* the *numerous* and *glorious nation of Israel;* and yet how often, how often did they fall into *relapses?* And then, where is my *assurance?* how easily thou passedst over many other sinnes in them, and how vehemently thou insistedst in those, into which they so often *relapsed;* Those were their *murmurings* against thee, in thine *Instruments,* and *Ministers,* and their turnings upon other *gods,* and embracing the *Idolatries* of their *neighbours.* (*Devotions* 123)

Although the "spiritual sicknesses" Donne speaks of have frequently been interpreted as simple doubts about God's mercy, his reference to the Israelites points in another direction.[33] In his account, the nation of Israel did not simply complain about God's ways, they complained, specifically, about his religious institutions. "The *Magistrate* is the *garment* in which thou [God] apparellest *thy selfe*," Donne will write a few lines later, adding, "when they would have *other officers*, they would have *other gods*" (*Devotions* 123). While the Israelites' sin of doubting God through their doubts in his "instruments and ministers" seems an unusually specific crime, Donne's interleaving his discussions of their sins with allusions to his own (which he does throughout this section) suggests that he sees an explicit connection between the two; a moment later he will assert, "I have *had*, I have *multiplied Relapses* already" (*Devotions* 124), and for a good thirty lines after that he will meditate upon the awfulness of the Israelites' relapses—which are, always, relapses into idolatry.

Given that "idolatry" in seventeenth-century England was virtually synonymous with "Roman Catholicism," this could be his oblique way of admitting that, on what Donne thought would be his death bed, he experienced doubts about his conversion to the Church of England.[34] Certainly the rest of this Expostulation supports the argument that he is motivated by something more than ordinary uneasiness about his salvation, and anxiety about having had such a close call would answer the perpetually vexing question of what prompted him to rush his work into print while still under doctor's orders to neither read nor write.[35] Elsewhere in the work Donne evinces a similar concern with both his own forsakings (or near-forsakings) of God and with the safety provided by God's church: he demands whether God will not stay for Donne's repentance, as he stayed for the Israelites'; asks to be defended against those who would "undermine [him] in [his] *Religion*"; and condemns those who would "make *new friends* by changing [their] *old religion*" (*Devotions* 12, 28, 74). Donne also describes God's "*Church* and . . . *Word,* and . . . *Sacraments,* and . . . *Ordinances*" as hills of safety from sin; claims to find God's "*voice, in [his] Ordinances*" and repeatedly asks God to send him comfort through his "*Institutions,* and . . . *Ordinances*" and "the *Seales* of [his] *Church*" (*Devotions* 109, 113, 18, 24). Taken together, these passages present a man whose fears about the enormity of his spiritual failings are assuaged only by the perceived stability of the institutional church.

Several other critics have also read passages such as these as expressions of anxiety about Catholicism, but they have understood them primarily as encoded warnings to Prince Charles about the danger of leading England back to Roman Catholicism.[36] While it is certainly possible that some political advice may be embedded in the *Devotions*, I agree with Richard Strier that the work's most sustained political agenda is its investment in the more ceremonial or "Arminian" aspects of the English Church.[37] This political agenda, however, seems to me more personal than polemical: Donne expresses concerns about *his* idolatry and *his* relapses, and he craves shelter for *his* sins in the institutions that God has ordained. In my reading, Donne's speaker is not waging a campaign on behalf of the English Church so much as he is insisting on his own alignment with it. Anxiety about his spiritual fidelity and the permanence of his conversion are what account for Donne's dramatic performance of religious orthodoxy throughout the *Devotions*.

Such performances take different forms in the three parts of each devotion—Meditation, Expostulation, and Prayer—and so for the remainder of my examination of the *Devotions* I consider each part separately. In the Meditations Donne reflects in a general way on the brevity and vanity of human life, usually using his circumstances only as an example of a general principle and making few references to God. Nevertheless, although the Meditations are commonly described as the most "secular" section of the *Devotions* and may initially seem the least personal,[38] in them Donne proves himself to be extremely aware of his audience, even at times employing the second-person pronoun in ways that suggest he is addressing his readers directly. In Meditation 2, for example, Donne describes how even "*Man . . .* the noblest part of the *Earth,* melts so away, as if he were a *statue,* not of *Earth,* but of *Snowe.*" Then, as if anticipating an interjection, he adds, "And how quickly? Sooner then thou canst receive an answer, sooner then thou canst conceive the question" (*Devotions* 11). In Meditation 14 Donne appears to envision an audience that is similarly engaged. Musing upon the futility of assigning dates and hours to events, he writes: "Howsoever [*Tyme*] may seeme to have three *stations, past, present,* and *future,* yet the *first* and *last* of these *are* not (one is not, now, & the other is not yet) And that which you call *present,* is not *now* the same that it was, when you began to call it so in this *Line,* (before you found that word, *present,* or that *Monosyllable, now,* the present, & the *Now* is past)" (*Devotions* 71). Donne seems to be imagining his audience reading his words aloud or speaking them along with him. The fact that Donne hastened his work into print and dedicated it to Charles suggests that he does not think of his devotions as purely private, and the language in Meditations such as these supports the idea that he is both seeking out an audience and self-consciously performing before it.[39] In arguing for Donne's Arminian sympathies, Strier notes that "for Donne, legitimate devotion must be public."[40] Strier may be right about Donne's Arminianism, but the public nature of Donne's autobiography is also typical of the confession of faith, which always demands an audience. As I argued in the Introduction to this book, the confession of faith is not a work of private self-exploration but a public declaration of religious allegiance.

By contrast with the Meditations, in the Expostulations and the Prayers Donne directs his words explicitly and it would seem exclusively to God— but these anguished and ostensibly private moments still depend upon an audience. Although the Expostulations have often been described as the emotional center of the *Devotions*, Donne's expressions of what Joan Webber has called his "questioning, rebellious love" are only partly about his relation-ship with the divine or his sense of his own sinfulness.[41] To a surprising de-gree, the concerns that Donne raises have to do with the shape of the Church of England itself, and nearly half of the Expostulations include an evaluation of beliefs and practices on the fault line between the churches of England and Rome. Donne questions God about the logic behind, among other points, a Christian's duty to his king (Ex. 8); the observance of holy days (Ex. 14); the appropriateness of funeral bells (Ex. 16); the respects due to the dead (Ex. 18); the relative importance of faith and works (Ex. 20); and confession (Ex. 4, 9, 10, 13, and 20). Other issues raised more obliquely are the place of scripture and its right interpretation (as allegory, metaphor, or literal truth) (Ex. 19), religious images (Ex. 16 and 18), and, of course, idolatry (Ex. 23).

In other words, Donne's Expostulations are performed assessments of issues of theology, ecclesiology, or devotional practice under debate within the English Church. Some of these issues he raises only immediately to solve, as in Expostulation 8. Having spent the preceding Meditation discussing the mortality of kings, Donne begins the Expostulation with an apology for his presumptuousness in speaking so boldly of his monarch (who, after all, has just sent his own physician to Donne's bedside). Within a few lines, however, Donne has satisfied himself that he is not being disrespectful in God's eyes, and he shifts the focus to those who *do* speak "negligently, or irreverently" of God by criticizing their king: "Though *Kings* deface in themselves thy [God's] first *image,* in their owne *soule,* thou givest no man leave to deface thy second *Image,* imprinted indelibly in their *power*" (*Devotions* 42). There is really no issue to debate here: Donne asserts that kings are to be obeyed at all times, regardless of their behavior or the nature of their rule.

At other times, as in Expostulations 16 and 18, where Donne deals with funeral bells and the respect due to the dead, he seems more conflicted, re-solving his perplexity only by concluding that the issues are *adiaphora*, things indifferent to salvation. He begins Expostulation 16 by saying, "My *God*, my *God*, I doe not expostulate with *thee*, but with *them*, who dare doe that: Who dare expostulate with *thee*, when in the voice of thy *Church*, thou givest allowance, to this *Ceremony* of *Bells* at *funeralls*" (*Devotions* 83). Donne criticizes those reform-minded members of his church who would do away with ceremonies such as bell-ringing on the grounds that they are Popish or pagan relics. He admits that the funeral bell may occasionally have been an object of superstition, but since God has given "allowance" to the practice it should not be fussed over.

Even when Donne cannot arrive at an entirely satisfactory answer from God—in Expostulation 18 he never satisfies himself as to why God forbade priests to officiate at funerals in Leviticus—he always, and often rather ostentatiously, submits himself to the dictates of the church. As he declares in Expostulation 7, he seeks God's "great *Helpe*, thy *Word* . . . not from *corners*, nor *Convenventicles* [*sic*], nor *schismatical singularities*, but from the assotiation, & communion of thy *Catholique Church*, and those persons, whom thou hast alwayes furnished that *Church* withall" (*Devotions* 39).[42] Nevertheless, as Strier notes, Donne does no more than pay lip service to the idea that issues such as bell-ringing are matters of indifference, and the work makes clear that Donne's personal preferences lie with a more rather than a less ceremonial church.[43] In Expostulation 16, for example, Donne follows his criticisms of the anti-bell faction with his impassioned support not only of bell-ringing but also of religious images—on the grounds that "wee cannot, O my *God*, take in too many *helps* for religious *duties*" (*Devotions* 84). He soon draws back from this position, but only at length and with some show of effort: "I know I cannot have any better *Image* of *thee*, than thy *Sonne*," he writes, "nor any better *Image* of *him*, than his *Gospell*: yet must not I, with thanks confesse to thee, that some *historicall pictures* of his, have sometimes put mee upon better *Meditations* than otherwise I should have fallen upon? I know thy *Church* needed not to have taken in from *Jew* or *Gentile*, any supplies for the exaltation of thy *glory*, or our *devotion*; of *absolute necessitie* I know shee needed not; But yet wee owe thee our thanks, that thou hast given her leave to doe so" (*Devotions* 84). In these Expostulations Donne seems to be simultaneously endorsing and resisting the logic of "things indifferent": he repeatedly asserts that bell-ringing and religious images *are not* necessary, but their very unnecessity, and his apparent attraction to such unnecessary adjuncts to worship, seem to make him nervous. As often as he declares that images are not essential, just as often he turns around and reasserts their devotional value, as if struggling to justify his own fondness for both images and church bells—perhaps made uneasy by their residual association with Catholicism.

In other Expostulations Donne manages to defend a more ceremonial English Church only by changing the terms of the question. Expostulation 14 finds him preoccupied with the appropriateness of feast days and their observance. It begins,

> My *God,* my *God* wouldest thou cal thy selfe the *Ancient of dayes,* if we were not to call our selves to an account for our *dayes?* . . . When thou reprehendest the *Galatians* by thy Message to them, *That they observed dayes, and Moneths, and Tymes, and Yeares,* when thou send-est by the same *Messenger,* to forbid the Colossians all *Criticall dayes, Indicatory dayes, Let no Man Judge you, in respect of a holy-day, or of a new Moone, or of a Saboth,* doest thou take away all Consideration, all destinction of *dayes?* Though thou remove them from being of the *Essence* of our *Salvation,* thou leavest them for *assistances,* and for the *Exaltation* of our *Devotion,* to fix our selves, at certaine *periodicall,* & *stationary times,* upon the consideration of those things, which thou hast done for us. (*Devotions* 72–73)

His debate with God over this matter of church observance goes on for a while as Donne produces scriptural text after scriptural text arguing for the importance of holy days. By the end of the Expostulation, however, he has essentially abandoned the argument. He converts the issue of holy days into a metaphor for the stages of his life, and especially of his illness: "Thou [hast], O my *God,* made this *sicknes,* in which I am not able to receive meate, my *fasting day,* my *Eve,* to this great *festival,* my *dissolution*" (*Devotions* 75–76). After his resurrection and final judgment, Donne will celebrate "my *Seventh day,* my *Everlasting Saboth* . . . where I shall live as long, without reckning any more *Dayes* after, as thy *Sonne,* and thy *Holy Spirit* lived with thee, before you three made any *Dayes* in the *Creation*" (*Devotions* 76). By celebrating the signs that God sends him of each discrete stage in his life and salvation, Donne does several things at once: he sidesteps the issue of institutionalized holy days by focusing on his own particular "critical days"; he implicitly up-holds the logic behind the church's holy days by showing that God operates in the same way in his own life; and he suggests that all such observances are temporary—and thus presumably not worth quarreling over—as they will last only until the Second Coming and the end of chronological time.

As all of these examples from the Expostulations suggest, the *Devotions* is as much a work of controversial as of devotional prose. Its two elements— autobiographical meditation and controversial discourse—are mutually consti- tutive. As in *Pseudo-Martyr* and in James's works, the autobiographical elements in the *Devotions* are intertwined with the process of defining and distin- guishing between Christian denominations; elaborating on the differences between churches is also a way of defining and articulating one's own beliefs, or attempting to do so. The *Devotions* may seem to belong to a genre very dif- ferent from *Pseudo-Martyr* or James's speeches and political writings, but as confessions of faith they have a great deal in common: they are all public performances of religious identity whose autobiography is more declarative than narrative. Donne never explains or describes his conversion; instead, he demonstrates his allegiance to the English Church and all its ordinances and institutions.

If the Meditations indicate that Donne is performing for the benefit of an audience, and the Expostulations reveal that performance to be an enact- ment (however nervous) of English Church orthodoxy, in the Prayers Donne hints at the motivation behind the performance. Although the Prayers, un- like the Expostulations, do not show him challenging God on points of reli- gious practice, they are still deeply involved in at least one of the touchy issues raised in the other section: the confession of sins. Confession is the only controversial topic that Donne considers more than once, doing so in five separate Expostulations (numbers 4, 9, 10, 13, and 20) and adopting an unmistakably confessional pose in at least two Prayers (numbers 10 and 15). Donne frets over the subject, unable definitively to assert the necessity of confession—perhaps because the Church of England does not recognize it as a sacrament—but seemingly equally unable to get past it. In Expostulation 20 he writes, "If it were meerely *problematicall,* left meerely indifferent, whether we should take this *Physicke,* use this *confession,* or no, a great *Physitian* ac- knowledges this to have beene his *practise, To minister many things, which hee was not sure would doe good, but never any other thing, but such as hee was sure would doe no harme.* The use of this spirituall *Physicke* can certainly doe no *harme*; and the *Church* hath alwaies thought that it might, and doubtlesse, many humble *soules* have found, that it hath done them *good*" (*Devotions* 108). The "if" that begins the passage suggests that confessing one's sins is *not* "left meerely indifferent" by the church, but by the end of the quotation Donne has drawn back to the assertion that confession only "might" do the individ- ual some good. This kind of equivocation is familiar from his other Expostulations, but the insistent way in which Donne continually returns to the subject is unusual. He claims repeatedly that the confession of sins is a sort of "physicke" for spiritual ills, describing its healing effects in an address to God in Expostulation 13: "Till wee tell thee in our sicknes, wee think our selves whole, till we shew our *spotts,* thou appliest no *medicine*" (*Devotions* 69); in Expostulation 10 he uses similar language: "As *Phisicke* works so, it [confession] drawes the *peccant humour* to it selfe, that when it is gathered together, the weight of it selfe may carry that humour away" (*Devotions* 54).

Although Donne has related other matters of church doctrine or practice to his illness, the relationship has never been this immediate. To take holy days as a representative example, he begins Meditation 14 with a discussion of the critical days of his sickness, which leads him to reflect on the futility of dividing time into particular units. Then, in the Expostulation, his thoughts turn to the church's feast days and fast days. In other words, the primary function of the subject seems to be as a *metaphor* for Donne's illness—and a somewhat awkward one at that. By contrast, Donne seems to imagine confession as not just a metaphor for the medical remedies used by his doctors but as itself a treatment for what ails him. In his notes to the passage in Expostulation 20, Anthony Raspa observes that the analogy between confession and medical purgation goes back at least to Galen, who recommended purgation as a cure for spiritual ills (*Devotions* 182). Donne, however, seems to be doing the opposite: envisioning confession as a cure for *physical* sickness. Although Donne appears to believe that his spiritual and physical states are interrelated, the nature of that relationship is not made totally clear. Does Donne think that his sinfulness brought on his illness? Is his spiritual anguish a sin occasioned by his physical pain? Or has Donne's bodily ill-health simply reminded him, forcibly, of his spiritual weakness?

An answer is not forthcoming from the Prayers, where, despite placing himself in a confessional posture, Donne remains safely in the realm of generalities. Prayer 10 provides a representative example. Donne begins his confession confident that he is doing what God wishes: "Though thou knowest all my sins, yet thou knowest them not to my *comfort,* except thou know them by my telling them to thee" (*Devotions* 54–55). But then he continues, with mounting concern, "How shall I bring to thy knowledg by that way, those sinns, which I my selfe know not? . . . If I confesse to thee the *sinnes* of my *youth,* wilt thou aske me, if I know what those sins were? I know them not so well, as to name them all, nor am sure to live houres enough to name them al" (*Devotions* 55). As Donne attempts to confess, he is continually brought up short by the impossibility of enumerating his sins except under very general names—sins of his youth, sins of omission, sins against his neighbor—and he lists every conceivable category up to and including "sins against the laws of that *Church,* & sinnes against the lawes of that *State,* in which thou hast given mee my station" (*Devotions* 55). Finally, as if exhausted, he concludes, "If the naming of these *sinnes* reach not home to all mine, I know what will; *O Lord* pardon me, me, all those *sinnes,* which thy *Sonne Christ Jesus* suffered for, who suffered for all the sinnes of all the world; for there is no sinne amongst all those which had not been my sinne, if thou hadst not beene my *God,* and *antidated* me a pardon in thy *preventing grace*" (*Devotions* 55). With this final statement Donne undoes the entire work of his confession. Not only has he managed to accuse himself of every known sin without specifying any, he has effectually rendered the whole idea of confession beside the point. If a person is fundamentally guilty of all sins—including those he has not actually committed and those he is not aware of (and especially if God has already pardoned him ahead of time)—confession would seem to serve no purpose.

But as Prayer 10 is far from the last time Donne will argue in favor of confession or assume a confessional pose, he clearly has more at stake than simply showing the act to be a matter of personal discretion. Although each attempted confession ends with the claim that confession has been rendered irrelevant by Christ's crucifixion, Donne nevertheless returns, almost obsessively, to a confessional posture. Moreover, while he never gets especially detailed about his sins in these Prayers, several seem to point toward recusancy: in Prayer 10 there is that otherwise puzzling claim to have sinned against the laws of church and state; in Prayer 15 he cites the "wilfull absteining from thy *Congregations,* and omitting thy *service*" as another grave transgression; and in Prayer 23 he speaks of his "*Spirituall Fornications*"—a phrase that the *Oxford English Dictionary* defines as "idolatry" (*Devotions* 55, 81, 126).

Donne's treatment of confession is not exactly unorthodox, for the English Church did retain confession as a part of the prayer book and as a prologue to the sacrament of Communion, even though by the seventeenth century it had become a decidedly collective act.[44] However, Donne's focus on the practice emphasizes the long shadow cast by his early Catholicism. Donne still seems drawn to a sacramental understanding of confession, which he abandons only, and with noticeable effort, midway through each confessional passage. And if the sin he most wanted to confess were a sense of continuing attraction to aspects of the Catholic Church, his confessional impulse would become doubly suspect as a manifestation of that very sin.

By the end of the *Devotions* Donne appears to have moved away from this impulse, for his final Prayer, although it alludes to his transgressions, is not a confession: he *begins* it with the conviction that he has been forgiven. The work does not leave him at peace, however; it leaves him worried about the possibility of again relapsing into the "*Spirituall Fornications . . .* which have induced thy former judgments upon me" (*Devotions* 126). In the end, it is unclear whether Donne's belief in his forgiveness stems from certitude in God's mercy—or from the belief that the publication of the *Devotions* constitutes, if not a confession, then at least a satisfactory confession of faith.

Whatever actual heterodoxies may still exist in his religious thought, the *Devotions* presents Donne as a sincerely conforming member of the Church of England. One especially strong witness to his loyalty to the state church comes in the work's dedicatory epistle to Prince Charles. Donne begins the epistle with a radically abbreviated autobiography: "*I* Have had three *Births*," he writes, "One, *Naturall*, when I came into the *World*; One *Supernatural*, when I entred into the *Ministery*; and now, a *preternaturall Birth*, in returning to *Life*, from this *Sicknes*" (*Devotions* 3). Donne's account of his three births— his biological birth, his ordination, and his recovery from his sickness— seems a rewriting of his own history. Each birth represents a potential starting point, and taken together the three could form a rough narrative of one version of his life. As it develops, however, the history Donne provides grows decidedly strange. He continues: "In my *second Birth*, your *Highnesse Royall Father* vouchsafed mee his *Hand*, not onely to sustaine mee *in it*, but to lead mee *to it*. In this *last Birth*, I my selfe am borne a *Father*: This *Child* of mine, this *Booke*, comes into the world, *from* mee, and *with* mee. And therefore, I presume (as I did the *Father* to the *Father*) to present the *Sonne* to the *Sonne*; This *Image* of my *Humiliation*, to the lively *Image* of his *Majesty*, your *Highnesse*" (*Devotions* 3). Presumably at his first birth, which he does not describe, Donne was a child, but at his second birth he portrays himself as the woman in labor, with King James assuming the role of either midwife or father: he holds Donne's hand in childbed after having first led him to it. Even the exact issue of this birth is unclear. Although the epistle's first sentence leads us to believe that it will be Donne himself, reborn as a minister, the actual description of this birth never presents him in that role.[45] Indeed, the only individual specifically assigned a familial role is King James, whom Donne refers to as "your"—that is, Charles's—father. The apparent absence of father and child in Donne's second birth and their ready presence in the relationship between James and Charles confuses the connections among all three men. If it is in fact Donne who was (re)born with the aid of James, are he and Charles brothers? Or is Charles somehow the son of James and the feminized Donne? Both possibilities are suggested by the passage, but they are only suggested; to do more would be as presumptuous as it is absurd. Nevertheless, by blurring genders and genealogies Donne succeeds in intimating a relationship between himself and the royal family that is deeper than one of mere patronage.

In his third birth Donne mysteriously changes sex and family position yet again: not child, not mother, but father. Although in the first line of the epistle he explained his third birth as a "returning to *Life*, from this *Sicknes*," his real interest seems to be the birth of "this *Child* of mine, this *Booke*"; it is only as a byproduct of *this* birth that Donne himself is born into a new role, that of father, or author, of the *Devotions*. With this final familial shift Donne moves into a position of agency: there is no one holding his hand in childbed now, and he seems to give birth to his book entirely by himself. He and his work form a complete family unit, and it is one that may be in competition with the father-son unit of James and Charles. By making Donne a father—and a self-regenerating father at that—Donne's third birth implies an alteration in his relationship with Charles and James, and potentially quite a radical one. Donne's language of fathers and sons suggests not only James and Charles and Donne and his book but also the heavenly father and *his* son. Like God the Father and God the Son, Donne and his book are coeternal: as he describes it, in language that seems to echo the Nicene Creed, the *Devotions* comes "into the world, *from* mee, and *with* mee." Although Donne surely is not claiming an equivalency between himself and the Almighty, his language does suggest that, as an artist and a man of God, he is both independent from and in some ways more privileged than the king himself.

But while his description of this third birth may reveal that Donne has conflicted feelings about his dependence upon the royal family, by the end of the epistle he has arrived at a happy reconciliation: intermarriage between these two "families." He expresses to Charles the wish that he, Donne, might "see the happinesses of the times of your *Highnesse*," but he claims that this can only come to pass "if this *Child* of mine, inanimated by your gracious Acceptation, may so long preserve alive the *Memory* of . . . JOHN DONNE" (*Devotions* 3). In asking Charles to "inanimate" his child, Donne is, on one level, simply hoping that Charles's patronage of him and his book will lead to its public success and thus keep alive Donne's memory. However, his choice of the word "inanimate"—synonyms for which include "quicken" and "infuse with life"—suggests that he is imagining Charles's own participation in a fourth birth. Perhaps Donne is casting Charles as his coparent for this formerly spontaneously generated book, or perhaps he envisions him as the father of some new issue, born of him *and* the book (whose figurative womb he, Charles, will inanimate). In either case, whether it is Donne's child or grandchild, the resulting offspring will be a coheir of both the Donne and the Stuart lines—a genuine merging of Donne's identity with that of the royal family and their church.

By multiplying the numbers of fathers and sons (which eventually come to include Hezekiah and Manasseh, as Kate Frost has argued)[46] and continually changing his own role within these pairs, the dedicatory epistle suggests an extreme instability in the parent-child relationship. Indeed, the most striking thing about the epistle's abundance of family members may be that, among all those possible relatives, Donne's own biological family is entirely absent. In contrast with the autobiographical prefatory matter to *Pseudo-Martyr,* in which Donne's Catholic family makes such a prominent appearance, neither in its dedicatory epistle nor anywhere else does the *Devotions* so much as hint that Donne might have parents or children of his own.[47] Donne seems to be signaling the replacement of his biological family with the Stuart family and the replacement of his allegiance to the Catholic Church with allegiance to James. No matter what residual emotional attachment Donne may have to Catholic practices, his devotion to his king is also a demonstration of loyalty to the English Church. In the *Devotions,* as in the confession of faith more generally, declarations of fidelity can substitute for other narratives that are simply too complicated to tell.

PART II

Personal Credos

CHAPTER 3

Milton and Autobiography in Crisis

Alexander More, whom John Milton vilified in the *Second Defence of the English People,* is the first person known to have remarked on the autobiographical passages in Milton's prose. "In this very *Second Defence* of yourself or the people," More writes, "as often as you speak for the people your language grows weak, becomes feeble, lies more frigid than Gallic snow; as often as you speak for yourself, which you do oftener than not, the whole thing swells up, ignites, burns."[1] More may have held a grudge against Milton, but his observations are shrewd: in the four political tracts in which Milton provides some kind of autobiography, once he starts talking about himself he seems hardly able to stop. The autobiographical material in *An Apology Against a Pamphlet,* for example, amounts to fully a third of a work whose chief purpose is arguing against episcopacy. More does not conclude that Milton believes his own press, however, and his suggestions about the psychological underpinnings of Milton's confessions of faith should give us pause: "You picture yourself dear to God, but do not believe it. . . . How handsome you are, in your own opinion, when you imagine that you have painted those things for eternity which you have only painted for a while, and, as you are drawn by four white horses, imagine that all nations everywhere are transfixed with admiration for you, that all the centuries applaud you. This is a vain delusion."[2] More implies that the versions of himself that Milton presents to his audience mask his fear that he actually is *not* dear to God. "Hence," More will say later, rolling his eyes as Milton calls God as his witness, "that really too anxious protestation."[3]

Although Alexander More is far from a reputable character and his own self-defenses are often ludicrous, he is nevertheless a more perceptive reader of Milton's confessions of faith than many later critics have been. There is no

question that Milton's autobiographical excursions in the antiprelatical tracts
and the *Defences* are well known; few passages of his prose are more familiar.
The scholarly analysis they have received, however, has been exceedingly limited. The central question would seem to be: What are Milton's autobiographies *doing* in the middle of these four political tracts? The conventional
explanation for these passages has long been that Milton is "giving his credentials for speaking," but this explanation raises more questions than it answers.[4] Why does Milton turn to autobiography in these four tracts, and not
in his many others? Why at these two moments in his career? And why do
Milton's autobiographical passages take such expansive and digressive forms?
Not only have scholars not answered these questions, they have also, by and
large, not examined the autobiographical passages themselves with any degree of care and detail.

As we have already seen in the confessions of faith of James I and Donne,
religious polemic is surprisingly hospitable to autobiography, but its argu-
mentative and ideological demands simultaneously spur self-declaration and
serve to limit those declarations. Milton seems more consciously interested in
the forensic possibilities of autobiography than James or Donne, and he also
provides far more autobiographical material than either of those two authors;
he uses his confessions of faith to present his reader with what seem to be full
narratives of his history and motives. However, a closer look reveals that, like
James's and Donne's, Milton's confessions of faith are nervous and evasive,
dealing with aspects of his personal history and belief that seem difficult for
Milton to address directly. Whereas James's and Donne's confessions of faith
show their authors attempting to make their messy lives conform to a norma-
tive, orthodox religious identity, Milton's depict a man struggling to discern
his political, spiritual, and literary vocation—categories that for Milton are
profoundly interrelated. But while Milton's religious identity is highly idiosyncratic and individualized, his self-explorations are no more private or merely
personal than James's or Donne's; his anxieties may not concern denominational identity or institutional allegiance, but they are still provoked by and
dependent on a public audience.

Although Milton's confessions of faith involve intensive self-scrutiny, they
do not have a great deal in common with the Puritan spiritual autobiography
as we normally conceive of that genre.[5] As Stephen Fallon has detailed, Milton's autobiographical writings lack nearly all of the markers of the spiritual
autobiography: there is no early sinning, no hearing the call, resisting the call,
believing, doubting, and finally arriving at a full conviction of salvation.[6]

Indeed, although Milton's works may be autobiographical and written from a more or less recognizably "Puritan" perspective, they have almost nothing else in common with the later genre. Milton's autobiographies, written right in the messy middle of life, also lack the distance of the typical spiritual autobiography, in which the real story is always in the past and told retrospectively. Instead, Milton's autobiographical passages show a man deeply anxious about both present and future, hoping for great things but half convinced that they will pass him by.

Milton only rarely admits to this uncertainty, and acting to counter these few indications of insecurity is virtually everything else he says about himself, which promotes the popular image of him as a man of unparalleled self-confidence. No matter how thoroughly *in medias res* Milton finds himself, he always acts as though he were surveying his life from a remote distance (this often requires that he project himself into the future, which he happily does). He admits no doubts and recognizes no setbacks, presenting himself as a man with an unshakable conviction in himself and his calling, who has never altered in the least: it was not Milton who changed his mind about the ministry—it was the church that changed under the prelates; Milton has not abandoned poetry—he's just deferring it while his country calls. Christopher Hill has said that Milton himself is the worst enemy of Milton biographers, and often he is the worst enemy of Milton critics too: even readers with a healthy amount of skepticism are frequently taken in by Milton's self-presentation in these passages.[7] But while there is no disputing that his confessions of faith nearly always assume a tone of overwhelming self-confidence, if Milton were really so certain of his literary election (which is, to a large degree, inseparable from his spiritual election), it would seem that he would not need to declare it so insistently or at such length.

As the quotations from Alexander More suggest, it seems to be Milton's sense of vocational unease and uncertainty that produces autobiographical passages that say nearly the opposite. Sometimes his autobiographies are prompted, in part, by the attacks of other pamphleteers, but Milton never confines himself to answering specific insults, and there are several examples of published attacks that Milton fails to answer (or fails to answer in a personal vein).[8] Rather, his confessions of faith seem to emerge from a sense of uncertainty about his mission or when the attacks of his opponents hit closest to those uncertainties. Milton produces his first confessions of faith in the early 1640s, as he reluctantly sets aside his poetic ambitions in order to serve God with his prose, and he produces the others a decade later as he confronts the possibility that, having allowed him to go blind while defending the Republic, God may not actually *want* the epic work that Milton always thought would be both his greatest achievement and his greatest gift to the deity. As a careful close reading of these passages will show, Milton's stridency in his confessions of faith seems intended to convince himself of the truth of his literary-spiritual destiny as much as to convince his readers.

The Antiprelatical Tracts, 1641–1642

Milton's first published prose works are a series of five antiprelatical tracts, the last two of which, *The Reason of Church-Government* and *An Apology Against a Pamphlet,* contain half of Milton's total autobiographical output. With these pamphlets Milton was joining a debate about the proper form for Protestant ecclesiastical government which extended back as far as the English Reformation, but which had gained new momentum since the 1633 appointment of William Laud as archbishop of Canterbury. Those who opposed episcopacy found the hierarchical structure of the English Church dangerously close to papacy, prone to corruption, and indifferent to the spiritual needs of the common worshipper. In the 1620s and 1630s the kind of outspoken opposition to prelacy found in Milton's tracts inspired swift and brutal punishment: for Alexander Leighton's 1628 *An Appeal to the Parliament; or Sions Plea Against the Prelacie* (a work that was to inspire more than a few aspects of Milton's *Of Reformation,* including the arresting image of the bishops as a poisonous wen on the head of the state)[9] Laud had Leighton arrested and whipped, his face branded, his nose slit, and one ear cut off.

If never without risk, by 1641 the political climate was safer for pamphlet writers. In November 1640 the Long Parliament met, beginning a session that was to last through the following September and include a concerted assault upon the bishops. In December 1640 the Root and Branch Petition, signed by fifteen thousand Londoners asking for the destruction of episcopal government and "all its dependencies, roots and branches," was delivered to the House of Commons, and the following February Archbishop Laud was charged with treason, impeached, and eventually imprisoned. At the same time, the Long Parliament had significantly loosened the restrictions on the press, and a flood of pamphlets on issues of church and state washed over London. While Bishop Joseph Hall was chosen by the Church of England to defend episcopacy in this war of polemics, one of his principal opponents was a group of reform-minded ministers whose initials spelled their pseudonym, Smectymnuus. The two sides had been exchanging ever-longer and more tediously entitled pamphlets for several months when Milton decided to enter the fray with *Of Reformation* (1641), siding with his former tutor, Timothy Young (he who put the "TY" in Smectymnuus) and Young's associates.[10]

Over the next year Milton would contribute four more antiprelatical tracts to the debate. These differ from those of the other contestants in the controversy in a number of ways—including their disinclination to rely upon church fathers or to delve too deeply into historical disputes—but perhaps their most striking difference lies in the strange autobiographical passages that occur in the last two of the series. Scholars have sometimes "explained" these autobiographical passages by pointing out that *Church-Government* is the first of Milton's tracts to bear his name, and thus might have seemed to Milton to mandate a public proffering of credentials.[11] However, while a relationship surely exists between the presence of Milton's autobiography in *Church-Government* and his decision to sign his name to the work, there is no more reason to think that putting his name on the title page prompted Milton to provide some autobiographical background than that writing an autobiography inspired him to stake an authorial claim. (Moreover, the notion of any easy connection between name and autobiography is immediately thrown into question by *An Apology*, a work that contains autobiography but does not bear Milton's name.)

The autobiographical passage in *Church-Government* is simply too long and too complex to be explained away as easily as it often is, whether as an ethical proof, a proto-spiritual autobiography, or Milton's attempt to model himself on the prophets of the Hebrew Bible. Although there are moments in which Milton is indeed writing within one or another recognizable tradition, the design of the passage as a whole is ad hoc. The fact that Milton supplies a lengthy autobiographical account in *this* work, and not in his three previous ones (or in the many polemics of the 1640s that will follow *An Apology*), suggests that something other than adherence to literary convention is at work. It is, in short, a confession of faith, and like the other confessions of faith that we have examined, it has its roots in that which cannot be spoken: not simply Milton's feeling of literary unpreparedness or reluctance to take the public stage, but a deeper uncertainty about God's plans for Milton's life—and whether or not Milton's own ambitions coincide with the divine design.

Milton's confession of faith in *Church-Government* appears at the work's halfway mark, in what is commonly referred to as the preface to its second book. Milton begins by lamenting the burden of knowing spiritual truths and the lack of welcome that the bearer of disagreeable information often receives. But, he writes, "If the Prelats have leav to say the worst that can be said, and doe the worst that can be don . . . no man can be justly offended with him that shall endeavour to impart and bestow without any gain to himselfe those sharp, but saving words which would be a terror, and a torment in him to keep back. For me I have determin'd to lay up as the best treasure, and solace of a good old age, if God voutsafe it me, the honest liberty of free speech from my youth, where I shall think it available in so dear a concernment as the Churches good" (*YP* 1:804). Milton's autobiography thus begins on a relatively impersonal note, but it swiftly takes a turn to the particular. Given the present crisis, *any* man might be justified in entering the polemical fray, so long as his conscience impels him and he is doing so without hope for gain. As Milton turns to his own situation, however, he seems to discard the image of terror and torment for a more pragmatic motive: he is speaking boldly *now* so that in his senescence he might look back on his life with contentment. His description of himself as a shrewd long-term planner does not seem to have much in common with the opening image of a man whose writing is motivated not by the hope of "gain to himselfe" but by holy terror. Although the proximity of those two images suggests that both motives might be Milton's, the shift from third to first person distances Milton from that first, anxious writer, as if to emphasize the control he has over both himself and his work.[12]

This same pattern is repeated throughout the tract's autobiographical section: a half-formed expression of uncertainty is quickly followed by an assertion of confidence. Even when, as with his next lines, Milton seems on the verge of self-scrutiny—"For if I be either by disposition, or what other cause too inquisitive or suspitious of my self and mine own doings, who can help it?"—he rushes on: "But this I foresee, that should the Church be brought under heavy oppression, and God have given me ability the while to reason against that man that should be the author of so foul a deed, or should she by blessing from above on the industry and courage of faithfull men change this her distracted estate into better daies without the lest furtherance or contribution of those few talents which God at that present had lent me, I foresee what stories I should heare within my selfe, all my life after, of discourage and reproach" (*YP* 1:804). Milton sandwiches his brief admission to some feelings of self-doubt between two strong declarations of what he is "determin'd" to do, and he has hardly begun to consider the reasons for his uncertainty (is it his natural disposition? or something else?) before he dismisses the entire discussion with a shrugging "who can help it?"

No one may be able to help Milton's tendency to overanalyze himself and his actions, but he quickly transforms the habit from a possible weakness into a strength: with an extraordinary act of projection he abruptly casts his narrative into the future, imagining a scenario in which he has chosen *not* to pen his antiprelatical tracts. Some critics have argued that, with his insistence upon his own foresight, Milton is styling himself as a Hebrew prophet.[13] However, while he does occasionally ventriloquize those voices crying out in the wilderness, this comparison is not wholly accurate: for one, the only thing that he "foresees" is his own spiritual and emotional state, and he makes no bets as to whether the church will be brought out of danger by the work of faithful men or whether their absence and neglect will lead to its oppression. Whatever concern Milton may have for the church's welfare, in this passage his focus is less upon the institution's fate than upon his own. Thus, in reproducing for his reader the voice of his conscience (as he imagines it speaking to the version of himself who has declined to write pamphlets in God's service), Milton supplies a rebuke for both possible outcomes. First, envisioning a church imperiled, he has his conscience scold, "Timorous and ingratefull, the Church of God is now again at the foot of her insulting enemies: and thou bewailst, what matters it thee for thy bewailing? . . . when the cause of God and his Church was to be pleaded, for which purpose that tongue was given thee which thou hast, God listen'd if he could heare thy voice among his zealous servants, but thou wert domb as a beast" (*YP* 1:804–5). Then Milton considers the other possibility:

> Or else I should have heard on the other eare, slothfull, and ever to be set light by, the Church hath now overcom her late distresses after the unwearied labours of many her true servants that stood up in her defence; thou also wouldst take upon thee to share amongst them of their joy: but wherefore thou? where canst thou shew any word or deed of thine which might have hasten'd her peace; what ever thou dost now talke, or write, or look is the almes of other mens active prudence and zeale. Dare not now to say, or doe any thing better then thy former sloth and infancy . . . what before was thy sin, is now thy duty to be, abject, and worthlesse. (*YP* 1:805)

Far from conceiving of himself as a voice crying out in the wilderness, Milton expresses anxiety about all the *other* voices that might be raised without his joining the chorus. In recounting this period of his life in the *Second Defence,* he will say, similarly, that the bishops "had become a target for the weapons of all men," and "all mouths were opened against them" (*YP* 4:623, 621). Whether or not the church recovers from her enfeeblement, there is glory to be won, and Milton, terribly aware that he is a latecomer to this particular vineyard, seems oppressed by the fear of missing out on it entirely. (And indeed, the very same month that Milton published *Church-Government* the bishops were ousted from the House of Lords.)

But although Milton appears genuinely concerned about his belatedness, and speaks slightingly of his own effort and courage—describing his actions as "this litle diligence" and only "something more than wish[ing] [the church's] welfare" (*YP* 1:805–6)—soon a new explanation for his uneasiness emerges: *this* sort of writing is really not what he has prepared himself for. He hopes, however, that he will meet with an understanding reader:

> To [the reader] it will be no new thing though I tell him that if I hunted after praise by the ostentation of wit and learning, I should not write thus out of mine own season, when I have neither yet completed to my minde the full circle of my private studies, although I complain not of any insufficiency to the matter in hand, or were I ready to my wishes, it were a folly to commit any thing elaborately compos'd to the carelesse and interrupted listening of these tumultuous times. Next if I were wise only to mine own ends, I would certainly take such a subject as of it self might catch applause, whereas this hath all the disadvantages on the contrary. . . . Lastly, I should not chuse this manner of writing wherin knowing my self inferior to my self, led by the genial power of nature to another task, I have the use, as I may account it, but of my left hand. (*YP* 1:807–8)

Milton never makes a claim but he deletes or emends it, seemingly torn between asserting the value of his current work and denying its artistic pretensions. The subject of his tract may be "no new thing" to the learned reader, but if Milton were seeking praise for his work—which he could gain if he wanted to!—he would not be writing while his studies are still incomplete. On the other hand, if he were better able to produce something that he felt was a true work of both learning and art, that, too, would be unseasonable:

the age is too restless and distractable for such a thing. The upshot of all of this seems to be that Milton's polemical efforts should be taken as evidence of his sincerity and selfless intentions: since the work cannot redound to the glory of his craftsmanship or talent, it must speak only to his sense of duty.

As earlier, however, Milton seems eager to leave the muddle of the present behind. Rather than dwelling on what he might or might not be able to do right now, he quickly turns first to his past and then to his future: "And though I shall be foolish in saying more to this purpose, yet since it will be such a folly, as wisest men going about to commit, have only confest and so committed, I may trust with more reason, because with more folly to have courteous pardon. For although a Poet soaring in the high region of his fancies . . . might without apology speak more of himself then I mean to do, yet for me sitting here below in the cool element of prose . . . to venture and divulge unusual things of my selfe, I shall petition to the gentler sort, it may not be envy to me" (*YP* 1:808). Although Milton acknowledges the oddity of focusing so much of his writing upon himself, he excuses it with the vague assertion that "wisest men" have done the same. Unusually for him, he does not name any of these men, although he does suggest that he surpasses them by divulging yet more autobiography than they; a moment later he claims that he is *still* not going as far as he might if he were writing verse. The opening of this passage shows the same uncertain back-and-forth motion as the previous one, but it soon disappears as the passage continues: "I must say therefore that after I had from my first yeeres . . . bin exercis'd to the tongues . . . it was found that . . . [whether] in English, or other tongue, prosing or versing, but chiefly this latter, the stile by certain vital signes it had, was likely to live" (*YP* 1:808–9). Once Milton begins his account of his early years, his narrative suddenly has a shape, with all its events tending toward one end: the emergence of Milton as a great poet. It is precisely *because* he is a poet—although he has as yet shown few signs of it to the outside world—that Milton claims indulgence for his polemic's unusual excursions into autobiography.

Milton now gets to what most readers would regard as the meat of his autobiography, what Louis L. Martz has called "that surprising and rather embarrassing revelation of Milton's poetical hopes and dreams."[14] Fueled equally by the encouragement of his friends and his own "inward prompting," Milton came to believe that, "by labour and intent study . . . joyn'd with the strong propensity of nature, I might perhaps leave something so written to aftertimes, as they should not willingly let it die" (*YP* 1:810). Skipping over the uncertainty of the present, he imagines his future as a linear continuation of his past—or at least the version of his past that he gives here; as John Shawcross and Richard Helgerson note, there is little evidence that he envisioned a poetic future for himself until he was nearly twenty, and he here conveniently omits any mention of his early intention to enter the ministry.[15] For all his confident, prophetic language, what he actually predicts is quite vague: at some undetermined point in the future his literary talent will manifest itself in some undetermined way. He asserts that he will write in his native tongue for "God's glory by the honour and instruction of my country" (*YP* 1:810–12), but otherwise he does not know what form his great work will take; instead (and despite his protestation that "time servs not now" to discuss the specifics of his literary ambitions), he devotes several dozen lines to considering, by turns, suitable subjects for an epic, tragic, or lyric celebration of his nation and its God.

After this discussion Milton apologizes again for presenting himself to the public eye before he can do justice to his talent: "The thing which I had to say, and those intentions which have liv'd within me ever since I could conceiv my self any thing worth to my Countrie, I return to crave excuse that urgent reason hath pluckt from me by an abortive and foredated discovery" (*YP* 1:820). This time Milton is excusing himself not simply for coming forward as a writer before being ready, or even for doing so in a format that he believes to be inferior, but rather for having been *forced* to tell his audience of his long-term literary ambitions before he is able to deliver on them. With this he sets aside the matter of church government: no longer is he simply providing evidence of his reluctance to enter the polemic fray; now he makes plain what seems really to have been bothering him: his lack of poetic progress. He continues,

> the accomplishment of [these ambitions] lies not but in a power above mans to promise; but that none hath by more studious ways endeavour'd, and with more unwearied spirit that none shall, that I dare almost averre of my self. . . . Neither doe I think it shame to covnant with any knowing reader, that for some few yeers yet I may go on trust with him toward the payment of what I am now indebted, as being a work not to be rays'd from the heat of youth, or the vapours of wine . . . but by devout prayer to that eternall Spirit who can enrich with all utterance and knowledge . . . to this must be added industrious and select reading, steddy observation, insight into all seemly and generous arts and affaires, till which in some

measure be compast, at mine own peril and cost I refuse not to sustain this expectation from as many as are not loath to hazard so much credulity upon the best pledges that I can give them. (*YP* 1:820–21)

While early Milton criticism regarded Milton's "covenant" as proof of the poet's unswerving sense of his life's mission (if not an outright demonstration of his prophetic powers), more contemporary scholarship has tended to doubt this. Although recent critics are correct in pointing out that Milton could not possibly have known what he would do in twenty-five years, and that, moreover, the audience for his polemics probably could not have cared less about his poetic ambitions, they have not arrived at a satisfactory answer as to *why* he makes this contract with his reader. One suggestion, advanced in different ways by John Guillory and Kevin Dunn, has been that Milton is not so much promising to deliver a specific work as he is demonstrating that he possesses sufficient literary and moral authority for his antiprelatical arguments to be taken seriously: not only does Milton, as a poet, have the right to act as a spokesman for his party, but by sacrificing something of great personal value he has proven his fitness to serve that party.[16] Whatever the merits of this argument, it seems inadequate in light of the sheer volume of information that Milton provides about his literary plans. Even if his audience does not care about his poetic dreams, Milton does, very much—to the point that they are almost all he can talk about.

More than trying to convince his readers, I suggest, Milton is trying to convince himself. Much as James's and Donne's confessions of faith show them struggling to assert their orthodoxy despite their more complicated past and present allegiances, *Church-Government* shows Milton struggling to bring his poetic and spiritual vocations into alignment. He claims that his literary talent is God-given, "a power above mans to promise," and elsewhere he equates the power of poetry with that of the priesthood (*YP* 1:820, 817). Despite his years of study, however, his abilities have borne only occasional fruit, and now that he feels compelled to serve God in polemic warfare Milton may be doubting whether he will ever have the opportunity to return to his poetic studies; more crucially, he may be doubting whether God even wants him to continue those studies, and whether God values the offering Milton vaguely hopes someday to make. In Milton's impassioned defense of poets and poetry, one can hear him trying to justify the value of a literary life (to himself? to God?) in much the same way that he once attempted to justify it to his father in *Ad Patrem*. The covenant with his readers, then, is really a covenant with himself, made in the public eye to give it more weight and make it that much harder to renege on.

*   *   *

Milton's final antiprelatical tract appeared two or three months later. As its title suggests, *An Apology against a Pamphlet Call'd A Modest Confutation of the Animadversions upon the Remonstrant against Smectymnuus* is a direct response to the pamphlets of Joseph Hall and the Smectymnuans (as well as a partaker of their tradition of unwieldy titles), but it is also a defense of Milton himself. In an earlier tract, *Animadversions upon the Remonstrants Defense against Smectymnuus,* Milton had mocked Bishop Hall for everything from his opinions on church government to his writing style; moreover, Milton strongly implied that there was a relationship between Hall's pro-prelatical position and his weak transitions, infelicitous metaphors, and faulty logic.[17] Such taunts, in turn, provoked a new work from an unknown pen: *A Modest Confutation of a Slanderous and Scurrilous Libell, Entituled, Animadversions.*[18] Although most of the *Modest Confutation* is devoted to vindicating Hall and advancing his episcopal arguments, its author also rebukes the anonymous Milton for his unseemly language and allegedly equally unseemly behavior. Milton's *Apology* is thus a response to a response, and as such does not cover a great deal of new ground with its ecclesiastical arguments. Milton does not merely refute the Confuter's personal attacks, however; he provides an elaborate confession of faith that reveals his developing sense of himself as a writer and outlines the relationship he believes to exist between an author and his work.

Even taking into account the Modest Confuter's attacks upon Milton, *An Apology* contains an astonishing amount of self-disclosure: of the fifty-nine pages of the original tract, the first twenty pages may be regarded as autobiography of a greater or lesser degree. Although there are no records of what Milton's original audience thought of this extraordinary feat of self-contemplation, it certainly is not typical of writers of the period. Among the hundreds of other tracts on the subject of church government published from 1640 to 1642, virtually none contains more than an autobiographical sentence or two. By the mid-1650s, when Milton writes his Latin *Defences,* his opponents will themselves return autobiography for autobiography and one personal defense for one personal attack, but in the antiprelatical debates this does not happen: when maligned by Milton, neither Joseph Hall nor the

Modest Confuter speaks up in his own defense. As with the confession of faith in *Church-Government*, this one tells us a great deal about Milton's preoccupations, as much through what Milton does not say as through what he does.

Despite the personal nature of so many of the tract's pages, Milton left the work anonymous. It probably would not have been difficult to track him down as its author—and he provides so much information about himself that he can hardly be too concerned with keeping his identity a secret—but in leaving his name off the title page he appears reluctant to take the same kind of credit for it as he did for *Church-Government*.[19] Perhaps he felt it unwise to go on the record maligning a bishop as prominent as Hall, or perhaps he was faintly embarrassed by the nastiness of some of his own rhetoric. I suspect, however, that part of the explanation may lie in Milton's uneasy sense that his belief in the close relationship between a work and its author may not reflect entirely well upon *him*. As Milton attacks the Modest Confuter and his writing, he posits a direct correspondence between a writer and his work, insisting that he knows everything he needs to know about the Confuter (not to mention Joseph Hall) based upon his book. However, not only has the Confuter painted a very unflattering portrait of Milton based—he says—solely upon what he has found in the *Animadversions*, but, in the immensely long autobiographical portion of *An Apology*, Milton proves that he is far from willing to let his works speak entirely for themselves.

Although his confession of faith in *An Apology* comes at the very beginning of the work rather than in the middle, as it does in *Church-Government*, the two sections begin in much the same manner: after a general statement about the burden of knowledge and the difficulty of acting morally upon that knowledge, Milton enters into his autobiography by way of discussing the duty he feels toward God and his church—a duty that requires him to take on the somewhat uncomfortable task of writing in his own defense: "Now against the rancor of an evill tongue . . . I must be forc't to proceed from the unfained and diligent inquiry of mine owne conscience at home (for better way I know not, Readers) to give a more true account of my selfe abroad then this modest Confuter . . . hath given of me" (*YP* 1:869–70). Even though Milton has already freely given an account of himself in *Church-Government*, he now depicts the task as one to which he has been driven only reluctantly, and only in self-defense. As in *Church-Government*, however, Milton again seems less interested in external reality—vindicating himself with *proofs* of his virtuous deeds and lifestyle—than with the internal: the results of an "unfained and diligent inquiry of [his] owne conscience." In the earlier pamphlet he focused on the future rather than the present, the speculative or desired rather than the verifiable, and a similar pattern is evident here: he privileges what he thinks and feels over whatever actions his antagonist may have alleged him to have taken—without first bothering to prove those allegations false.

Milton acknowledges that he might have followed the examples of many illustrious men by suffering in silence, but "when I discern'd [the Confuter's] intent was not so much to smite at me, as through me to render odious the truth which I had written, and to staine with ignomiy that Evangelick doctrine which opposes the tradition of Prelaty, I conceav'd my selfe to be now not as mine own person, but as a member incorporate into that truth whereof I was perswaded . . . . . Whereupon I thought it my duty, if not to my selfe, yet to the religious cause I had in hand, not to leave on my garment the least spot, or blemish in good name" (*YP* 1:871). Milton's argument is that his self-defense is not *really* a self-defense, since the Modest Confuter's target is not really Milton but the antiprelatical faction as a whole. This is a reasonable enough claim, but it is one that the *Modest Confutation* itself does not quite bear out. In the letter to the reader that prefaces the work, the Confuter writes, "If thou hast any generall or particular concernment in the affairs of these times, or but naturall curiosity, thou art acquainted with the late and hot bickering between the *Prelates* and *Smectymnuans*: To make up the breaches of whose solemn Scenes, (it were too ominous to say Tragicall) there is thrust forth upon the Stage, as also to take the eare of the lesse intelligent, a scurrilous *Mime,* a personated, and (as himself thinks) a grim, lowring, bitter fool."[20] Although Milton is attacked as a scurrilous fool, it is the style and method of Milton's writing, not the substance of his views, that the Confuter decries. Indeed, he gives the opinions of the Smectymnuans exactly as much respect as those of the prelatical faction, using the same images for the works of both sides: they are (somehow simultaneously) "hot bickerings" and "solemn Scenes." Later the Confuter will say that Milton's greatest concern in *Animadversions* is not the proper form of church government but rather private and personal spleen, "the other businesse being handled but by the by, or not at all: and where it is, in such a wretched, loathsome manner, as once I did almost doubt me, whether or no you did not jeer at both sides, at Religion, and God, and all."[21] While the Confuter makes no bones about his own political and religious sympathies and will spend the last third of the work arguing for episcopacy and a set liturgy, his personal attacks on Milton occur only in the first part of his tract, and only have to do with Milton's lack of decorum (and perceived related lack of virtue). He does not malign the other Presbyterians, and while he may indeed intend for his readers to extrapolate from Milton's character to the validity of his cause, it is Milton, not the Confuter, who appears to hold most tenaciously to the belief that the character of an individual man—as revealed in his writing—tells the observers everything they need to know about the cause he champions; these are the very grounds for his vitriol against both Joseph Hall and the Confuter.

Given his belief in the strong correlation between a man's character and his literary ability—"how he should be truly eloquent who is not withall a good man, I see not" (*YP* 1:874)—Milton spends the next several pages alternately defending his earlier work and disparaging the *Modest Confutation* by focusing upon the method and style of both. He devotes a full page to considering his opponent's title page, ridiculing nearly every word for its inappropriateness (*YP* 1:876). But although he subjects this and other parts of the Confuter's work to what we might consider an extremely close close reading, the Confuter's comments on Milton himself are what really preoccupy Milton.

The Confuter's attacks are an apparent combination of conjecture and falsehood based upon a few scattered and unilluminating passages in *Animadversions* (typical is the accusation that, because Milton uses a few theatrical metaphors, he must haunt playhouses), but, nasty and haphazard as these attacks are, they amount to only a few charges, most of them recognizable as speculation rather than promoted as documented fact. At first Milton jumps on this weakness, noting that the Confuter "confesses, he has *no furder notice of mee then his owne conjecture*," adding snidely, "it had been honest to have inquir'd, before he utter'd such infamous words" (*YP* 1:882). A moment later, however, Milton reverses himself, saying, "I am credibly inform'd he did inquire, but finding small comfort from the intelligence which he receav'd, whereon to ground the falsities which he had provided, thought it his likeliest course under a pretended ignorance to let drive at randome" (*YP* 1:882). The Confuter may or may not have known Milton's identity or made inquiries into his history and habits, but even if he had—and even if Milton somehow knew as much—it is curious that Milton should announce this fact.[22] If Milton's aim were only to vindicate himself of his opponent's charges, the easiest way would surely be to point to the Confuter's statement that he knows nothing of Milton apart from his writing, and thereby dismiss his attacks as groundless.

There seem to be two likely reasons that Milton emphasizes the Confuter's inquiries: first, to assert that he *has* some kind of public reputation, and that it is a positive one; otherwise the Confuter's statement that he "has no notice" of Milton might be taken as evidence of Milton's obscurity, which is one of the things that Milton's autobiographies seem meant to dispel. Second, if Milton were to argue too vehemently that the portrait the Confuter has assembled from reading Milton's text is flawed, Milton would have to revise his own notions about the relationship between authors and their works. So Milton harps on the supposed duplicitousness of the Confuter, with the perhaps inadvertent consequence that his antagonist appears fiendishly clever. Where some writers might be content with slandering their enemy with whatever weapons came to hand, the Confuter, in Milton's analysis, "burden[s] me with those vices, whereof, among whom my conversation hath been, I have been ever least suspected; perhaps not without some suttlety to cast me into envie, by bringing on me a necessity to enter into mine owne praises" (*YP* 1:883). That is, the Confuter has purposely made the picture so bad that he *intends* for Milton to embarrass himself by making an immodest self-defense. But Milton is not about to fall into his trap:

> I know every wise man is more unwillingly drawne to speak [of himself], then the most repining eare can be averse to heare. Nevertheless since I dare not wish to passe this life unpersecuted of slanderous tongues, for God hath told us that to be generally prais'd is wofull, I shall relye on his promise to free the innocent from causelesse aspersions: whereof nothing sooner can assure me, then if I shall feele him now assisting me in the just vindication of my selfe, which yet I could deferre . . . but that I feare it would but harme the truth, for me to reason in her behalfe, so long as I should suffer my honest estimation to lye unpurg'd from these insolent suspicions. (*YP* 1:883)

Milton's conclusion in the second part of this passage—that God wishes him to defend himself—does not seem to follow from the preceding statements that (a) wise men are reluctant to speak of themselves, and (b) being slandered is not uncommon, and being praised by all men would be worse. If Milton is alluding to the passage in the Sermon on the Mount in which Jesus says, "Blessed are ye, when men shall revile you and persecute you, and shall say all manner of evil against you falsely for my sake," he ought certainly to remember that the passage concludes, "Rejoice, and be exceeding glad, for great is your reward in heaven" (Matt. 5:11–12). Milton, however, seems unwilling to wait for vindication in the next world—he seems, in fact, to be challenging God to prove that he aids the innocent by doing so, *right now,* by helping Milton to vindicate himself. But as in *Church-Government,* Milton again hesitates: even with God's promise, he could still put off this self-defense and get to the important matter of reforming church government—except that no one would heed what he had to say if they thought the Confuter's portrait of him were true.

As he has done earlier, Milton registers anxiety about being unknown, as well as an almost equal anxiety about not being able to control *how* he is known or how his works are read. In *An Apology,* his excuse for his otherwise outrageous self-focus seems to be that who he *is* is more important than what he has done—or even what he has written. According to what he writes elsewhere in the tract, most notably in his statement that "he who would not be frustrate of his hope to write well hereafter in laudable things, ought him selfe to bee a true Poem, that is, a composition, and patterne of the best and honourablest things" (*YP* 1:890), Milton claims that writer and work should correspond perfectly, but his compulsive, overly explanatory autobiographies suggest that the Confuter's attacks on Milton's manner and method of writing have struck deeply at these beliefs.

Taking the Confuter's taunts as a starting point, Milton now enters into his confession of faith proper. He summarizes his university career and the esteem in which he was held in order to counter the claim that he was "vomited out thence" (*YP* 1:884),[23] and, to his antagonist's depiction of Milton's present life—"Where his morning haunts are I wist not; but he that would find him after dinner, must search the *Play-Houses,* or the *Bordelli,* for there I have traced him"[24]—Milton responds with an account of the early hours of his typical day:

> Those morning haunts are where they should be, at home, not sleeping, or concocting the surfets of an irregular feast, but up, and stirring, in winter often ere the sound of any bell awake men to labour, or to devotion; in Summer as oft with the Bird that first rouses, or not much tardier, to reade good Authors, or cause them to be read, till the attention bee weary, or memory have his full fraught. Then with usefull and generous labours preserving the bodies health, and

hardinesse; to render lightsome, cleare, and not lumpish obedience to the minde, to the cause of religion, and our Countries liberty, when it shall require firme hearts in sound bodies to stand and cover their stations. (*YP* 1:885–86)

As Hugh Richmond notes, Milton's detailed description of his morning may be indebted to a similar passage from Pierre de Ronsard's long poem *Reply to the insults and calumnies of various unrecognizable preachers and ministers of Geneva* (1563).[25] If Milton is indeed alluding to a great poet of the French Renaissance, one who was also engaged in public polemical warfare, it is surely to emphasize his own literary aspirations—and to remind his audience (and himself) that poetry is not necessarily incompatible with political and religious engagement.

Whether or not Milton's description of his morning is precisely accurate or precisely original, it is nevertheless nearly the only part of his autobiography that he places in the potentially verifiable present. The Confuter's charge that Milton haunts playhouses provokes a discussion of Milton's reluctant theatergoing at Cambridge, but Milton neither denies the accusation nor admits to it; he simply talks about something else. And when the Confuter charges that Milton frequents bordellos, Milton leaves the realm of facts entirely behind. Since, he writes, the Confuter "would seem privily to point me out to his Readers, as one whose custome of life were not honest, but licentious; I shall intreat to be born with though I digresse: & in a way not often trod acquaint ye with the summe of my thoughts in this matter through the course of my yeares and studies. Although I am not ignorant how hazardous it will be to do this under the nose of the envious . . . and instead of outward actions to bring inmost thoughts into front" (*YP* 1:888). Where most men might deny their opponent's accusations or provide testimonials to their abstemious behavior, Milton declines to do so. Instead, he declares that he will let the reader into his *thoughts* on the subject of sexual morality, and their development over the years. He continues:

With me it fares now, as with him whose outward garment hath bin injur'd and ill bedighted; for having no other shift, what helpe but to turn the inside outwards, especially if the lining be of the same, or, as it is sometimes, much better. So if my name and outward demeanour be not evident anough to defend me, I must make tryall, if the discovery of my inmost thoughts can. Wherein of two purposes both honest, and both sincere, the one perhaps I shall not misse; although I fail to gaine beliefe with others of being such as my perpetuall thoughts shall heere disclose me, I may yet not faile of successe in perswading some, to be such really themselves, as they cannot believe me to be more then what I fain. (*YP* 1:888–89)

Milton continues to be preoccupied with what is internal and unseen. Indeed, beyond simply asserting the value of the internal, his language hints at some actual dissatisfaction with his "outer garment," whose lining is so "much better." This, coupled with the strange negative construction in the last part of the passage, where Milton appears to be presuming failure from the start—no one will believe him, and his only hope is *not* to fail in persuading some of his readers to be what they cannot believe that he is—makes him sound like a man with something to hide.

Even when Milton goes out of his way to show how aboveboard he is being with his audience, he still comes across as protesting too much. At the end of his digression on chastity he gives a new reason for having expanded on the subject at such length: "Thus large I have purposely bin, that if I have bin justly taxt with this crime, it may come upon me after all this my confession, with a tenne-fold shame. But if I have hitherto deserv'd no such opprobrious word, or suspicion, I may hereby ingage my selfe now openly to the faithfull observation of what I have profest. I go on to shew you the unbridl'd impudence of this loose rayler . . . who from the single notice of the animadversions, as he protests, will undertake to tell ye the very cloaths I weare" (*YP* 1:893). After again denying that the "single notice" of his previous text is sufficient to show the character of its author, Milton invites a public investigation of his prepared statements on matters of virtue, as well as public scrutiny of his actions—from this time forward. (An "observation," anyway, that can hardly be made by those who do not know the anonymous author's identity.) Milton seems to be asking for a second chance, saying, in effect, "Judge me not on *that* work but on my others; not on what you *think* my words say about my morals but on what I *tell* you about my morals." As in *Church-Government,* here he offers his audience a deal, and the contractual language in both passages is notable for its combination of boldness and unease: "Neither do I think it shame to covnant with any knowing reader"; "it may come upon me with a tenne-fold shame"; "I may hereby ingage my selfe now openly."

Just as in the previous passage we examined, Milton is acting quite as though he has a guilty conscience. There is no reason to think that this is the case when it comes to Milton's sexual morality, although at the time of writing this tract he does appear to have been contemplating marriage and may have worried about how this ambition reflected upon his youthful devotion to chastity.[26]

More likely, it is his literary career that is concerning Milton. We know from his confession of faith in *Church-Government* how uneasy Milton felt about offering his work to the public before he believed himself ready to do so, and in a mode that he considered second-best. He does not explicitly voice this concern in his *Apology,* but it seems to lie not far below the surface, provoked by the Confuter's criticism of the *Animadversions.* There is no evidence that Milton regrets or is ashamed of the earlier tract, but he does seem vexed that his opponent should have loaded it with so much significance that he proposed deducing Milton's character from it. If Milton hardly felt ready to go public as a writer in *Church-Government*—despite controlling every aspect of his self-presentation—he may have felt that, in the earlier *Animadversions,* the Confuter had caught him entirely unprepared. Whatever satisfaction Milton may have derived from his antiprelatical tracts, he appears not to have taken them quite seriously as literature; for the Confuter to deride one of these immature efforts, then, is to strike too close to Milton's own feelings of literary uncertainty.

Milton's touchiness is not merely the thin skin of a would-be literary luminary. His intellect and his facility with language are, he believes, gifts from God that demand some return—and, so far, he seems not quite sure that he has made one. Moreover, as he repeatedly insists in *An Apology,* an author's poetic and prosaic styles are direct reflections on his moral character (and, it may be, his salvational status). His fierce defenses of himself and his writing and his equally fierce attacks upon his opponents appear to be impelled by a fundamental insecurity about how well he is measuring up in God's eyes. The Confuter's specific claims about Milton's loose morals may be ridiculous, but his sneering dismissal of Milton's writing and his assertion that Milton has done an injustice to the gravity of his subject seem harder for Milton to reject. If Milton were an inept or merely mediocre writer, how could he possibly be an upright person? According to his own arguments, he could not be. His early confessions of faith thus show Milton struggling to reconcile his belief in his literary-spiritual promise with the fact that this conviction has yet to manifest itself in a work with which he himself is satisfied—much less his Creator.

The *Defences*, 1651–1655

There is a gap of some twelve years between Milton's antiprelatical tracts and his next prose autobiographies, which appear in *Pro Populo Anglicano Defensio Secunda* (*A Second Defence of the English People*) and *Pro Se Defensio* (*A Defence of Himself*). In the intervening years the English Church had been disestablished, the Civil War fought and won, and King Charles executed. By 1654 Milton was famous (or in some quarters infamous) for his defenses of the republican cause and his attacks on tyranny in general and Charles in particular. This fame was a long time coming: although he produced numerous prose works during the Civil War, it was not until 1649, after Charles's execution, that he took up the subject of divine right, and not until the 1651 publication of *Pro Populo Anglicano Defensio* (the first *Defence of the English People*) that he truly achieved a name for himself. With the exception of his four divorce tracts, which brought plenty of attention of exactly the wrong sort, none of his early polemics appears to have received much notice, and the publication of a volume of his verse went equally unremarked.[27] In virtually every one of these works Milton expends considerable effort on his self-presentation, and scholarly analyses of these efforts have greatly assisted biographical readings of him.[28] Nevertheless, not one of these publications contains anything like the autobiographical passages to be found in *Reason of Church-Government* or *An Apology Against a Pamphlet*, and this is true even when, as in the responses to the *Doctrine and Discipline of Divorce,* he was personally attacked for his views.[29]

Although his prose works from the 1640s may not have made Milton a household name, apparently they attracted the notice of a sufficient number of leading Parliamentarians to get him appointed as the Commonwealth's Latin secretary. Upon satisfactory service in this position, and probably because of his earlier spirited defenses of the revolutionaries in *Tenure of Kings and Magistrates* and *Eikonoklastes,* Milton appears to have been asked to vindicate the regicides against some of the recently published accusations and expressions of horror from abroad. He obliged with the *Defence of the English People,* which follows the format of the work he is most immediately

refuting: *Defensio Regia pro Carole I* (1649), by the famous French Protestant
Salmasius. Among its many other features and techniques, the *First Defence*
employs the same sort of personal attack familiar from Milton's earlier controversial works, and it seems in part to have been these ad hominem attacks that
inspired a new champion to enter the fray (Salmasius himself having died before he could compose a response). The anonymous *Regii Sanguinis Clamor ad
Coelum adversus Parricidas Anglicanos* (1652), which Milton mistakenly attributed to Alexander More, vigorously defended Salmasius while denouncing
Milton; this work, in turn, provoked Milton's *Second Defence* (1654).

Although the immediate circumstances surrounding Milton's confession
of faith in the *Second Defence* seem similar to those attending *An Apology*—
Milton has been personally attacked and his party has been implicated in
that attack—some differences are readily apparent. In the later work Milton
focuses much more upon the past than the future, and there are virtually
none of the invitations to his innermost thoughts (on a poetic career, on chastity) that periodically punctuate the antiprelatical tracts. Another striking difference is the placement of Milton's confession of faith. In *Church-Government*
and *An Apology* his autobiographical passages form a discrete unit, while in
the *Second Defence* such material is scattered throughout. However, while
many of these passages may seem individually to be confident and controlled,
when taken together the picture changes. Milton will end one passage abruptly
only to resume in an autobiographical vein several pages later, and the portraits
he paints of himself in different places are often remarkably dissimilar. Thus,
despite some superficial differences between Milton's later confessions of
faith and his earlier ones, their effect—and, I believe, their impetus—is quite
similar. As in the antiprelatical tracts, Milton again appears to be wrestling
with feelings of extreme doubt, trying to convince himself that he has made
the right vocational decisions and that God and the world will remember
him with satisfaction. The difference is that here the blind Milton is anxious
not about the future but about the past; fearing that his career may be over,
he seems desperate for a sign that what he has done has been worthwhile, and
that it has been enough.

Milton begins his tract by proclaiming the favors that God has shown
him. He celebrates the threefold blessing of having been alive "when [En-
gland's] citizens, with pre-eminent virtue and a nobility and steadfastness
surpassing all the glory of their ancestors . . . accomplish[ed] the most heroic
and exemplary achievements since the foundation of the world"; of his having been selected "spontaneously with universal consent [for] the task of

publicly defending . . . the cause of the English people"; and, finally, of having done so in a way that "satisf[ied] a host of foreigners . . . [and] so routed my audacious foe that he fled, broken in spirit and reputation" (*YP* 4:548–49).[30] But only a few pages later Milton loses this confident tone and grows defensive: "Although I claim for myself no share in [England's] glory, yet it is easy to defend myself from the charge of timidity or cowardice, should such a charge be leveled. For I did not avoid the toils and dangers of military service without rendering to my fellow citizens another kind of service that was much more useful and no less perilous" (*YP* 4:552). Not only has Milton spent the opening pages of the tract doing just what he here disavows—claiming his right to a share in England's glory—there is no evidence that anyone has accused him of cowardice. No such accusation appears in the *Clamor*, and, as Milton was a middle-aged man with failing eyesight for much of the Civil War, it is unlikely that anyone would have looked at him askance for not having fought. On the other hand, his claim that his pamphleteering was as dangerous as battlefield service might well have resulted in some raised eyebrows: not only did all of his pamphlets prior to the *First Defence* have relatively low circulation, by the time the more inflammatory of these were published Charles had already been executed.[31]

Nevertheless, despite the perilousness that Milton claims for his service, he assures his reader,

In time of trial I was neither cast down in spirit nor unduly fearful of envy or death itself. Having from early youth been especially devoted to the liberal arts, with greater strength of mind than of body, I exchanged the toils of war, in which any stout trooper might outdo me, for those labors which I better understood, that with such wisdom as I owned I might add as much weight as possible to the counsels of my country. . . . And so I concluded that if God wished those men to achieve such noble deeds, He also wished that there be other men by whom these deeds, once done, might be worthily praised and extolled, and that truth defended by arms be also defended by reason—the only defence truly appropriate to man. Hence it is that while I admire the heroes victorious in battle, I nevertheless do not complain about my own role. Indeed I congratulate myself and once again offer most fervent thanks to the heavenly bestower of gifts that such a lot has befallen me—a lot that seems much more a source of envy to others than of regret to myself. (*YP* 4:552–53)

Milton's description of the service he *has* rendered his country provides at least one hint as to why he might be so touchy about his lack of military participation: his contribution to the war effort was praising "those deeds, once done."[32] As he acknowledges through his choice of tense, Milton was not publishing works championing the Parliamentarians or challenging divine right while the Civil War was actually raging; indeed, in 1646–1648 he published nothing at all. Just as he did with the antiprelatical faction, he publicly sided with the regicides only belatedly. He may well believe that he has since made up for his initial inaction, but surely part of his grandiose claims for himself and his penchant for military metaphors—of his dispute with Salmasius he says, "I met him in single combat and . . . I bore off the spoils of honor" (*YP* 4:556)—could be attributed to an uneasy awareness that he has no good answer to the question, "What did you do in the war, daddy?"

Milton's next autobiographical passage is provoked by the description of him given in the *Clamor*'s dedicatory epistle, which is addressed to the exiled Charles II. Toward the end of this letter the author expands on Virgil's characterization of Polyphemus: "'A monster horrible, deformed, huge, and sightless.' Though, to be sure, [Milton] is not huge; nothing is more weak, more bloodless, more shrivelled than little animals such as he, who the harder they fight, the less harmful they are."[33] Although Milton has already paid back the author of those lines with his own nasty and frequently hilarious biographical account of Alexander More's escapades, he seems unable to overlook this passing insult, and replies,

> Although it ill befits a man to speak of his own appearance, yet speak I shall . . . lest anyone think me to be perhaps a dog-headed ape or a rhinoceros, as the rabble in Spain, too credulous of their priests, believe to be true of heretics, as they call them. Ugly I have never been thought by anyone, to my knowledge, who has laid eyes on me. Whether I am handsome or not, I am less concerned. I admit that I am not tall, but my stature is closer to the medium than to the small. . . . But neither am I especially feeble, having indeed such spirit and such strength that when my age and manner of life required it, I was not ignorant of how to handle or unsheathe a sword, nor unpractised in using it each day. Girded with my sword, as I generally was, I thought myself equal to anyone, though he was far more sturdy, and I was fearless of any injury that one man could inflict on another. (*YP* 4:582–83)

Milton does not precisely contradict the earlier explanation he has given for avoiding military service—that his physical condition makes him less useful on the field than in the study—but the two self-portraits certainly differ. Whereas here Milton describes himself as having been a fearless swordsman in his youth, and claims that he is still spirited and strong, in his earlier passage excusing his absence on the field of battle he protests that "any stout trooper might outdo [him]," since, "from early youth," he has had "greater strength of mind than of body" (*YP* 4:553). These previous lines imply a physical delicacy that is repudiated by the passage above, in which Milton asserts that he is neither small nor feeble; indeed, in the very next line he adds, "Today I possess the same spirit, the same strength, but not the same eyes" (*YP* 4:583). Of course, the context of Milton's self-description has changed—he is no longer defending himself against (possibly imaginary) charges of avoiding military service but rather attempting to ensure that his audience does not dismiss him as a useless, frail, blind old man. All the same, his concern with his physical appearance has struck many as curious. Some of it may be simple vanity on his part, but, as his aside about the supposed deformities of heretics suggests, Milton regards calling someone a monstrosity as more than a hyperbolic way of saying that he is ugly. To Milton, for whom outsides and insides have such a fraught relationship, we may well suppose physical defects strongly imply moral ones.

Milton's eyes soon become the locus for his anxieties about both kinds of defects. Milton maintains that his eyes "have as much the appearance of being uninjured . . . as the eyes of men who see most keenly," and this feature appears to have great significance for him (*YP* 4:583).[34] In the context of the ensuing discussion of his blindness and God's role in that affliction, Milton may be suggesting that his unclouded eyes are a sign that he is not hateful to God. The *Clamor* has not raised the possibility that God has blinded him for defending regicide, but Milton seems deeply afraid that *something* he has done might have precipitated his blindness.[35] To preempt such an argument from anyone else, he calls God himself as a witness: "For my part, I call upon Thee, my God, who knowest my inmost mind and all my thoughts, to witness that (although I have repeatedly examined myself on this point as earnestly as I could, and have searched all the corners of my life) I am conscious of nothing, or of no deed, either recent or remote, whose wickedness could justly occasion or invite upon me this supreme misfortune" (*YP* 4:587). In fact, God appears not so much to be a character witness as Milton's most important audience, and in Milton's direct addressing of the deity there is a note of apprehension: "this is so—isn't it?" These are the lines that Alexander More will describe as "really too anxious," and, although Milton does not permit his reader very far inside his head (he does not, for example, reproduce the voices that he hears, as he does in *Church-Government*), his obsessive return to the subject of his blindness, his appearance, and his service to the state strongly supports More's reading—and suggests, moreover, the precise sources of that anxiety: Milton's fear that he has, somehow, failed in his obligations toward God.

Some pages go by before Milton abandons the subject of his blindness. Far from being blinded as a punishment, he maintains, he *chose* blindness rather than reject God's demands:

> As for what I have at any time written (since the royalists think that I am now undergoing this suffering as a penance, and they accordingly rejoice), I likewise call God to witness that I have written nothing of such kind that I was not then and am not now convinced that it was right and true and pleasing to God. . . . Hence, when the business of replying to the royal defense had been officially assigned to me, and at that same time I was afflicted at once by ill health and the virtual loss of my remaining eye, and the doctors were making learned predictions that if I should undertake this task, I would shortly lose both eyes, I was not in the least deterred by the warning. I seemed to hear, not the voice of the doctor . . . but the sound of a certain more divine monitor within. And I thought that two lots had now been set before me by a certain command of fate: the one, blindness, the other, duty. Either I must necessarily endure the loss of my eyes, or I must abandon my most solemn duty. (*YP* 4:587–88)

In this version of events, God has designed the writing of the *First Defence* as a test of Milton's obedience—but Milton, unlike Abraham with Isaac, actually loses what he has agreed to sacrifice. Although he has switched from directly addressing God to talking about him in the third person, this account of his actions and motives reads as much like a petition as the previous lines. Milton seems to be seeking reassurance from God as well as trying to convince himself that this version of events is accurate.

God may have allowed Milton to go blind, but Milton insists that God has not deserted him and never will: "Then let those who slander the judgments of God cease to speak evil and invent empty tales about me. Let them be sure that I feel neither regret nor shame for my lot, that I stand unmoved and steady in my resolution, that I neither discern nor endure the anger of God, that in fact I know and recognize in the most momentous affairs his fatherly mercy and kindness towards me" (*YP* 4:589). Over the course of these lines Milton moves from a more tentative to a more confident position, from *feeling* and *discerning* to *knowing* and *recognizing* God's will, as if taking strength from his own continued strength, in the belief that if God were punishing him, he would not be bearing up as well as he is. He concludes, "So long as I find in God and man such consolation for my blindness, let no one mourn for my eyes, which were lost in the cause of honor. Far be it from me either to mourn. Far be it from me to have so little spirit that I cannot easily despise the revilers of my blindness, or so little charity that I cannot even more easily pardon them" (*YP* 4:591). Even more than the earlier parts of this passage on Milton's blindness, these last lines read like a prayer; Milton appears to be talking to himself—and to God—more than to his readers. As far as we know, he did not keep a diary, and the account of his blindness that occupies these many pages could represent the first time that he has verbalized his thoughts about the darkness that befell him a few years earlier.[36] As we have seen, the confession of faith tends to serve for its authors as a forensic exploration of questions of religious identity or assurance, and in this tract Milton appears to be working through and attempting to lay to rest some of the more distressing fears surrounding his blindness; those fears may not be expressed explicitly, but as with those of James and Donne, their presence is palpable between the lines.

Milton's next autobiographical section is prompted by the biography that his antagonist supplies for him. After filling more than five quarto pages with a refutation of the version of his life given in the *Clamor*, Milton suddenly decides to start over and tell the story of his life from the very beginning—ancestry, boyhood, and all, for a total of thirteen additional pages—as if unwilling to limit his autobiography to the issues raised by his opponent. He describes his decision to enter the field of political polemic in much the same way that he described it in *Church-Government*, but he now makes his antiprelatical tracts and all his subsequent writings out to be part of a single, coherent strategy to address the three kinds of "true and substantial liberty": ecclesiastical, domestic, and civil (*YP* 4:624). Milton then summarizes his arguments in the divorce tracts, *Of Education*, and *Areopagitica*, moves on to the regicide treatises, and brings himself up to the present with the *Defences*. He excuses the great length of this autobiographical account on the grounds that, as he tells More, he had "to stop your mouth . . . and refute your lies, chiefly for the sake of those good men who otherwise would know me not" (*YP* 4:629). This is a familiar argument, a version of which appeared long before in *Church-Government*. However, while Milton is now sufficiently well known for some readers actually to care about the details of his life, the person with the most to gain from such a narrative is now, as it always has been, Milton himself. These smooth, teleological life narratives seem to appear whenever he is facing his most serious crises of faith and self-confidence, as if his ability to project such a shape upon his life meant that his life actually *had* a coherent design—and that its design is of God's making.

After concluding this longest autobiographical section, Milton devotes considerable ink to the biographies of various Parliamentarian heroes. He does so, most immediately, to counter the aspersions cast upon these figures by his opponent, but in doing so he focuses not only on his subjects' external lives but also on the presumed events of their *inner* lives. These speculations seem, in a sense, to be a continuation of Milton's autobiography, for they reveal more about him than they do about their ostensible subjects. As Milton describes Cromwell,

> he soon surpassed well-nigh the greatest generals both in the magnitude of his accomplishments and in the speed with which he achieved them. Nor was this remarkable, for he was a soldier well-versed in self-knowledge, and whatever enemy lay within—vain hopes, fears, desires—he had either previously destroyed within himself or had long since reduced to subjection. Commander first over himself, victor over himself, he had learned to achieve over himself the most effective triumph, and so, on the very first day that he took service against an external foe, he entered camp a veteran and past-master in all that concerned the soldier's life. (*YP* 4:667–68)

Milton does not go so far as to speculate on the details of this self-mastery— what Cromwell's specific fears and desires may have been and how and when he overcame them—but he takes it for granted that this would have been as much a part of the narrative of Cromwell's life as it is of his own. In *Church-Government* he struggles against his desire for delay and development, and in the *Second Defence* he struggles against the fear that God has blinded him out of displeasure. In his account of Cromwell's victory over his "enemy within," one may read both the story of Milton's own life, as he would like it to be told, and its hoped-for outcome: true self-mastery.

Later, in apostrophizing Cromwell, Milton pauses to gives him advice that likewise emphasizes the importance of inner strength for effective leadership: "You have taken upon yourself by far the heaviest burden, one that will put to the test your inmost capacities, that will search you out wholly and intimately, and reveal what spirit, what strength, what authority are in you, whether there truly live in you that piety, faith, justice, and moderation of soul which convince us that you have been raised by the power of God beyond all other men to this most exalted rank. . . . These trials will buffet you and shake you; they require a man supported by divine help, advised and instructed by all-but-divine inspiration" (*YP* 4:673–74). Milton's advice to Cromwell has come under fire by critics from Alexander More onward for its presumptuous tone, and more than one reader has found veiled criticisms of Cromwell's policies in these lines and those that follow.[37] What seems not to have been noticed is the striking applicability of this advice to Milton's own circumstances, or the similarity of the description of Cromwell and his deeds to Milton's own self-descriptions; compare, for example, the above passage with the opening paragraphs of both the *Second Defence* and the *Defence of Himself.* Milton surely has both advice and criticism for Cromwell, but at the same time he seems to be thinking of his own situation and hoping that his writings have indeed "reveal[ed] what spirit, what strength, what authority are in" him.

After Cromwell, Milton administers advice to his fellow citizens, but he seems to have, at best, only a passing interest in them. "If the most recent deeds of my fellow countrymen should not correspond sufficiently to their earliest," he writes, "let them look to it themselves" (*YP* 4:685). For his part, "I have borne witness, I might almost say I have erected a monument that will not soon pass away, to those deeds that were illustrious, that were glorious, that were almost beyond any praise, and if I have done nothing else, I have surely redeemed my pledge. Moreover, just as the epic poet, if he is scrupulous and disinclined to break the rules, undertakes to extol, not the whole life of the hero whom he proposes to celebrate in his verse, but usually one event of his life . . . so let it suffice me too, as my duty or my excuse, to have celebrated at least one heroic achievement of my countrymen" (*YP* 4:685). The pledge that Milton speaks of having redeemed appears to be the obligation he has long felt to use his literary and intellectual talents in the service of God and England. Moreover, the fact that he compares his polemical tracts

to the epic poems of Homer and Virgil strongly suggests that he is remembering, specifically, the pledge he made in *Church-Government* to produce a
poem "so written to aftertimes, as they should not willingly let it die" (*YP*
1:810). There is sadness, however, in the comparison: Milton's literary monument is not the work of epic or lyric or tragic verse that he once envisioned
but a succession of prose pamphlets on events already receding into the past:
deeds that *were* illustrious, that *were* glorious, that *were* almost beyond any
praise.[38] As good a face as Milton puts on his achievements, he seems himself
to believe that he has "done nothing else"—where that "else" represents whatever other ambitions he once held. Perhaps as vexing as the sense of things
left undone is Milton's awareness that the success of his current work depends, in part, on the success of others in maintaining their new society. He
concludes the work by addressing his fellow citizens:

> If after such brave deeds you ignobly fail, if you do aught unworthy
> of yourselves, be sure that posterity will speak out and pass judg-
> ment: the foundations were soundly laid, the beginnings, in fact
> more than the beginnings, were splendid, but posterity will look in
> vain, not without a certain distress, for those who were to complete
> the work. . . . It will seem to posterity that a mighty harvest of glory
> was at hand, together with the opportunity for doing the greatest
> deeds, but that to this opportunity men were wanting. Yet there was
> not wanting one who could rightly counsel, encourage, and inspire,
> who could honor both the noble deeds and those who had done
> them, and make both deeds and doers illustrious with praises that
> will never die. (*YP* 4:685–86)

Although Milton is still projecting his narratives into the future, the future
he imagines here is one in which he plays no active role; it is up to others to
carry on the work begun by the revolutionaries, and he can only hope that
they will. These sound like the words of a man who sees his life as largely
over, and whose seemingly arrogant assessments of his own past importance
only barely disguise a deep sense of loss.

*   *   *

Milton's final lines in the *Second Defence* read like a valedictory to this particular debate—if not to his entire career as a public writer—but Alexander

More's 1654 response, *Fides Publica,* provoked yet another pamphlet, Milton's *Pro Se Defensio (Defence of Himself)*. Despite its title, the *Defence of Himself* is the least overtly autobiographical of the four tracts considered in this chapter, being devoted primarily to defending and justifying Milton's identification of Alexander More as the author of the *Clamor*. Since More had not, in fact, written that work (although he does appear to have written its dedicatory epistle and to have conveyed the work to the printer), he responded with indignation to Milton's ad hominem attacks. In the *Fides* More both returns Milton's personal attacks, making particular fun of his adversary's autobiographical excesses in the *Second Defence,* and attempts to defend his own honor with a great show of piety and false humility. By way of response, Milton provides an angry mishmash of a work, one that first refuses to admit that he could have been wrong about More's authorship, and then finally declares that More's delivering the work to its printer constitutes authorship every bit as much as actually writing it. He provides yet more evidence of More's unsavory life, attacks More's self-defense, and—to a surprisingly limited degree—defends himself against More's accusations. Milton rebuts More's specific charges one by one, but he rarely elaborates and includes no extended autobiographical passages of the sort that we have grown accustomed to or that we might call a confession of faith.

The abrupt change in both the quality of Milton's writing and the nature of his self-presentation has been noted by several critics, who identify Alexander More as the reason for this shift. Annabel Patterson has suggested that when Milton finally faced his error in assigning More the authorship of the *Clamor,* he began to lose faith in his own moral uprightness, and thus his voice of unswerving self-confidence; more recently Stephen Fallon has argued that it was More's expert reading of Milton's *Second Defence,* and the skilled way his tract skewered Milton for his self-importance, that provoked the incoherent and contradictory claims that Milton makes for himself in this final *Defence*.[39] As we have seen, anxiety, contradiction, and even incoherence are not new features of Milton's autobiographies, but Patterson and Fallon are correct in noting that something in Milton's self-presentation has changed, and they are surely also right that a sense of shame is at the root of it. I would point out, however, that the most notable feature of the *Fides* is not its attacks on Milton but rather its own extraordinary passages of autobiography.

More's detailed accounts of his life and habits, which are interspersed with letters from others testifying to his virtue, represent the first time that one of Milton's opponents has attempted an autobiographical defense similar to Milton's own.[40] Milton repeatedly takes issue with More's testimonial letters, accusing him of hiding behind the words of others and not giving the full story, but he seems to have a more difficult time criticizing More's actual passages of autobiography. Rather than denounce the personal account as inherently untrustworthy, Milton generally prefers to give his *own* account of More's inner state, as though he had unlimited access to More's thoughts. About the publication of the *Second Defence*, Milton writes, "As soon as [More] learned . . . that I had published a reply to his *Cry of the Royal Blood,* the man's guilty conscience began to rage and his mind to thrash about in every direction" (*YP* 4:719). More's supposedly guilty conscience makes several more appearances in Milton's pamphlet, with Milton often *telling* More just what he is feeling: "Your dissention with yourself has long been most grave. Nothing is more offensive to you than to live with yourself, to be in your own company; no one do you avoid more willingly than yourself" (*YP* 4:776). Later, of More's laudatory letters, Milton asks, "Why do you foist upon us these matters which are utterly irrelevant—nay, why have you collected for yourself this huge heap of letters and testimonies at all? Was it that you were not sufficiently approved of in the sight of your own conscience? Or was it that you dared believe about yourself neither your own words nor the spontaneous remarks of mankind, unless a multitude of collected testimonies confirmed and attested to you that which you had never otherwise believed: that you could appear to anyone a good man or a tolerable one?" (*YP* 4:816). As he has in *Church-Government* and *An Apology,* Milton again tries to focus on the internal and unseen, but when the inner life in question is someone else's, this is clearly a losing game. He has always appeared to value autobiography because of a belief that it gives a reader access to the "real" inner self of a writer—but in this case, More's mendacity means that Milton has to step in and let the reader know the content of More's heart himself. This is a potentially damning comment on the reliability of autobiography, and Milton seems to know it; one of the reasons that he limits the autobiographical portion of the *Defence of Himself* is surely that he could hardly challenge the veracity of self-revelation in More (most notably in the confessional prayer that concludes the *Fides*) while insisting on it so strongly in himself.[41] As he has in his biographical description of Cromwell, however, in the above passage Milton again seems to be projecting himself upon his subject, imagining how he would feel if he were More and perhaps even admitting obliquely to one motive behind his own confessions of faith: the lack of approval he felt from his own conscience.

More than the other authors considered in this book, Milton seems to have a conscious interest in both the rhetorical uses of autobiography and its forensic possibilities. Like James, at times Milton seems to idealize autobiography as a transparent means of self-explanation and self-revelation, eagerly supplying his reader not only with apparently factual details about his life but also with what he claims are his true beliefs, thoughts, and motivations. Even in his early confessions of faith, however, there are signs that Milton is protesting too much and is far less confident about his own rectitude and vocation than he claims. By the time of the *Defence of Himself* he appears to have soured on the idea that autobiography is a vehicle for pure self-revelation. Nevertheless, as the invocations to books I, III, VII, and IX of *Paradise Lost* demonstrate, Milton does not give up on autobiography entirely—he simply moves away from the confession of faith and into the more stylized mode of verse.

CHAPTER 4

Thomas Browne's Uneasy Confession
of Faith

Thomas Browne's *Religio Medici* initially seems very different from the fragmentary confessions of faith published by James I, Donne, and Milton. Unlike those works, the *Religio* was not published until years after its first composition; its entire subject is explicitly autobiographical; and it does not at first appear to be political or polemical. In the letter to the reader that prefaces the *Religio*'s 1643 publication, Browne insists upon both the work's private nature and the tentativeness of its religious conclusions. Lamenting the unauthorized 1642 publication of his work, which forced him to oversee this corrected one, Browne repeatedly mentions how many years have passed since the work's composition, and he suggests (although he never quite says) that his opinions have changed since then. Browne characterizes his statements on matters of faith as a private record or "memoriall unto me"; they were, he writes, "the sense of my conceptions at that time, not an immutable law unto my advancing judgement"—and now that his private thoughts have inadvertently been made public, he places them "in submission" to the "maturer discernments" of his readers.[1]

There is reason, however, to be skeptical of Browne's insistence upon the private character of the *Religio*, and there is even greater reason to read the work in a context of contemporary religious controversy. Authorial professions of reluctance to publish are, of course, conventional in early modern print culture, and hesitance and anxiety surround all of the confessions of faith that we have examined so far. Even if Browne did not seek to have his work printed (and some readers, dating back at least to Samuel Johnson, have suspected that he did),[2] it circulated widely in manuscript[3] and may be regarded as being what Harold Love calls a "scribal publication" long before it was a typeset one.[4] But although numerous scholars have remarked on the disingenuous aspects of Browne's prefatory letter and some have argued that the work, in its depiction of a "doctor's religion," is staking out distinctly political territory, they have rarely identified that territory correctly. The reason for this is twofold. First, most scholars have read the *Religio* within the political and religious climate of the early years of the English Civil War, the period when the work was first published, rather than within the mid-1630s, when it was originally composed. Second, few readers have looked at the early manuscript copies of the *Religio*, and thus have an imperfect understanding both of Browne's original text and of how he revised it over time.[5] In fact, the *Religio* exists in three distinct versions, which may be tentatively dated to 1635, 1638–1640, and 1643.[6] Most modern editions of the *Religio* rely primarily upon the text of the 1643 printing, operating under the assumption that this final revision best represents Browne's intentions for his work. But while this version may in some ways be the "fullest"—it is indeed the longest—it is also, by definition, the furthest from Browne's original version and the circumstances that produced it. Although the *Religio* certainly did speak to the England of the Civil War period, its earlier versions spoke equally powerfully to the England of first the mid-1630s and then the late 1630s.[7]

Returning to the earliest text of the *Religio* and to the circumstances under which it was written produces a more complex portrait of both the doctor and his religion. Although critics have repeatedly commented on the difficulty of penetrating Browne's authorial persona, at the same time they have repeatedly characterized him as a man of genial tolerance, often adducing the work's style and form as their evidence. The *Religio*'s leisurely expansiveness, its dilations, qualifications, and delight in paradoxes, have convinced many readers that its writer must be a man of great flexibility and generosity of spirit: someone who can be depended upon to see both sides of an issue.[8] In recent decades, critics have linked these presumptions about Browne's temperament to his membership in the Church of England. Over and over Browne tells his audience how he loves to ponder the imponderable and how unconcerned he is that the mysteries of Christianity so often appear contrary to reason. He confesses to past doctrinal errors with seeming ease and assures his readers that any mistakes he may stumble into are redeemed by his good intentions. Thus, the Browne of the *Religio* has often been read as performing or modeling the best qualities of the English Church: liberal, intellectual, and accommodating.[9] Even the *Religio*'s most notable modern detractor, Stanley

Fish, has not significantly challenged this reading of the work. Fish too focuses on Browne's style and sees his mind and personality revealed in his impulse toward amplification—but while most readers of the *Religio* cele-brate this aspect of the work, to Fish it is evidence of intellectual laziness: Browne likes to hear himself talk, but has nothing useful to say.[10]

A reading of the *Religio* that emphasizes both Browne's playfulness and his allegiance to the English Church is plausible if the text is that of the 1643 edition; Browne does appear to have been sympathetic to the Royalists, and his distaste for religious extremism of the Puritan sort is clear, although always understated. Nevertheless, even in the 1643 text, Browne's religious identity is less assured than it is often assumed to be. For all their focus on Browne's style, neither the *Religio*'s many admirers nor detractors such as Stanley Fish have explored the possibility that Browne's slippery and protean persona might be a response to real religious uncertainty.[11] Despite Browne's frequently confident statements on matters of faith, a significant degree of doctrinal anxiety underlies the work. A careful reading of the work's earliest version—especially in light of some of Browne's later revisions—will soon reveal the degree of his theological uneasiness. In a work that is ostensibly about his religion, Browne makes few positive declarations of faith, frets con-tinually over those he attempts, and only barely conceals a number of sympa-thies that are unorthodox or downright heretical. Like the other confessions of faith we have examined, the *Religio* appears to have been motivated less by the cheery good humor and tolerationist spirit that many ascribe to Browne than by doubts about his own orthodoxy. Browne's autobiography focuses on its author's idiosyncratic beliefs and personality in a way most reminiscent of Milton's confessions of faith, but, like James and Donne, its author is a man who seems to feel a reluctant compulsion toward orthodoxy. The conflict be-tween Browne's restless skepticism and his desire to remain within the institu-tional church produces the complexities and convolutions of the *Religio Medici*.

Religio Medici, Circa 1635

Unlike Milton and Donne, who experimented with autobiography in more than one text and at more than one time, Browne's only overtly autobio-graphical work would be the *Religio Medici*; both his next publication, *Pseu-dodoxia Epidemica* (1646), and his major works of the 1650s, *Hydriotaphia* and *The Garden of Cyrus* (both 1658), are shorn of almost all personal references.

One possible reason for Browne's turn to autobiography in the *Religio* emerges in the work's first line, that abrupt opening sentence that reads like a response to a question: "For my religion, though there bee severall circumstances that might perswade the world I have none at all . . . yet in despite hereof I dare without usurpation assume the honourable style of a Christian" (I.1). In other words, the *Religio* begins as if Browne were professing a creed or taking part in a catechetical dialogue. If we think of the work as an exposition of faith rather than as an autobiography, it can be understood as part of a larger literary trend: as Ian Green has shown, in the 1630s England saw the publication of an astonishing number of catechisms and other works of religious didacticism.[12] While fewer new catechisms were produced in the 1630s than in many other decades of the seventeenth century, the *total* number of catechisms published (a figure that includes new works, reprints, new editions, and translations) was higher in the 1630s than during any other decade from the English Reformation to the 1740s; in 1633 alone the English Short Title Catalogue shows nearly twenty different titles.[13]

The question of what it was necessary for a Christian to know or believe was hardly new, but the flood of doctrinal and instructional materials during the 1630s can probably be attributed to the push for greater centralization and conformity then taking place in the English Church under Charles I and Archbishop Laud. From 1628 to 1634 the Thirty-Nine Articles were republished every single year (rather than approximately once every five years, as had been the case since the late sixteenth century), and in 1633 Charles decreed that the Canons of 1604—which had never been systematically implemented—would from then on be rigorously enforced.[14] That year the Canons went through five separate editions: as many as in the preceding twenty-eight years combined.[15] In this climate, it is not surprising to find that such a large number of catechetical works were on the market. Although not all of these works toed the Laudian line and some seem distinctly Puritan, the push for orthodoxy under Laud and Charles appears to have inspired English men and women of all confessions to get their spiritual houses in order with books that purported to provide what the title of one popular catechism promised: "The Summe of Christian Religion."[16]

If examining and declaring one's religious beliefs had a special urgency for many English men and women during this period, it may have had even more urgency for Browne. In 1634 Browne was freshly returned to England from the Continent, where he had spent three or four years studying medicine, first at Montpellier and Padua and then at Leiden, from which he received his medical degree in December 1633.[17] As his biographers have pointed out, Browne availed himself of the best medical education of his day while at the same time conducting a sort of tour of the religious life of the Continent. Although the universities that Browne studied at were in places as different as war-torn France, Catholic Italy, and Reformed Protestant Holland, all three institutions were strikingly independent of their local civil and ecclesiastical authorities, and at least two of the three were associated with notable heresies and heterodoxies, some of which would later make an appearance in the *Religio*.[18] The medical school at Padua, which had long been a center for humanist studies, was also home to considerable skepticism about the nature of the Trinity and the immortality of the soul.[19] According to Jean-Jacques Denonain, the students at Padua "professed hostility to the Pope and Jesuits, and complete tolerance for all customs and opinions . . . the general atmosphere was one either of open skepticism and impiety, or of a cautious dualism."[20]

Leiden too was a town of remarkable religious freedom. Although Holland's official religion was the Dutch Reformed Church, a wide range of denominations were permitted to hold public services in Leiden; even Catholics, whose church was officially illegal, were allowed to worship with a minimum of harassment.[21] The university was more tolerant still.[22] Nevertheless, both the city and the university were at the epicenter of the controversy over Arminianism that eventually led to the Synod of Dort's 1618 condemnation of Arminianism as a heresy. The conflict centered around theology professor Jacobus Arminius's assertion that those whom God predestined for salvation were those whom he had already *foreseen* would be godly. To the Arminians, this rescued God from charges of arbitrariness or injustice and saved Christians from despair. To orthodox Calvinists, on the other hand, this position was a scandalous abridgment of God's omnipotence. Although Arminius had taught at the University of Leiden from 1603 until his death in 1609 and had many local supporters, the synod's official statement condemning Arminianism was formulated by four other Leiden professors of theology and was published in 1625, less than a decade before Browne arrived in the city.[23]

Although, as we shall see, many of the ideas and controversies current at the universities Browne attended appear to have influenced him to a greater or lesser degree, more important for the composition of the *Religio* may be the simple contrast between the England Browne returned to in 1634 and the vigorous, skeptical, and largely tolerant academic environments that he had left behind.[24] As we have seen with James, Donne, and Milton, a culture of religious controversy seems to inspire self-definition and self-declaration even as it limits the nature of those declarations. The *Religio* appears to have been influenced by the orderly and comprehensive approach to the essentials of belief taken by the catechisms and doctrinal digests so popular in England in the 1630s, but as a declaration of faith it is a distinctly cautious and uncertain one.

Nowhere is this more apparent than in the *Religio*'s opening sections. I have noted that Browne begins the work with a profession of belief that sounds rather like an answer to a question, and in fact the entire first section of the *Religio* (which in later versions would be divided into two sections, I.1 and I.2) might be profitably compared with the opening of one of England's most popular catechisms, of which Browne owned a copy.[25] Only a few lines into Alexander Nowell's *Catechisme, or First Instruction and Learning of Christian Religion,* the Maister addresses the Scholar: "Goe to therefore, and tell me what Religion it is that thou professest." The Scholar replies, "The Religion that I professe . . . is the same wherof the Lord Christ is the author and teacher, and which is therefore properly and truely called the Christian Religion."[26] Browne's own statement of faith opens like an amplified version of the Scholar's, adapted for his own particular interests and concerns. After explaining the "severall circumstances" that "might perswade the world" that he had no religion at all—his medical profession, his scientific and philosophical studies, and his unwillingness to engage in polemical attacks—Browne concludes, "Yet in despite hereof I dare without usurpation assume the honourable style of a Christian" (I.1). Although there is a strange edge of defensiveness to Browne's declaration, he begins, like Nowell's Scholar, with the general: he is a Christian. The Scholar, however, lays claim to this title only to deny it to those who worship differently from himself: "As there is one onely true God, so there be but one godly worshyppyng & pure Religion of one onely God. Otherwise we should daily forge our selves new fayned Religions, and every nation, every citie, & every man, would have his owne severall Religion."[27] Browne, on the other hand, uses similar language to make a different point:

> But because the name of Christian is become too generall to expresse our faith, there being a geography of Religion as well as of Land, & everie climate distinguished not only by their lawes & limits, but circumscribed by their doctrines & rules of faith: to be particular, I am of the beliefe our Saviour taught, the Apostles disseminated,

the fathers authoriz'd, the Martyrs confirm'd, but by the sinister ends of Princes, the ambition, & avarice of Prelates, & the fatall corruption of time decay'd, impair'd, and fallen from it's native beautie, that it justly needed the carefull, and charitable hand of these times to restore it to it's primitive integrity.[28] (I.2)

Both Browne and the Scholar discuss the possibility of a "geography of religion," but, unlike the Scholar, Browne apparently accepts that every nation (and perhaps even every man) *does* have its own religion.

Equally significant, for many long lines Browne leaves it unclear just which of these different versions of Christianity he subscribes to. Even in the revised versions of the *Religio* it takes Browne numerous sentences before he describes himself as being "of that reformed new-cast Religion, wherein I mislike nothing but the name," but in the first version of the work that line is entirely absent, and Browne's eventual references to a religion that needs "restor[ing] to it's primitive integrity" occurs only after much winding about, and itself is not unambiguous. Although a Protestant reader would naturally be inclined to read those lines as a description of Protestantism, Browne defers confirmation of this fact for some twenty more sentences, during which time he makes statements at least passingly sympathetic to Roman Catholics (saying, "Wee have reformed from, not against them," and admitting that he himself is "naturally enclin'd to that which misguided zeale calls superstition" [I.3]). Browne's unwillingness to define precisely which group he belongs to is reminiscent of both James and Donne, and like them Browne wishes his reader to know that he owes his beliefs not merely to "my education, or clime wherein I was borne" but to having, "in my riper yeares, & confirmed judgement seene & examined all" (I.1).

Eventually, however, Browne does announce his allegiance: "There is noe church wherein everie thing soe squares to my conscience, whose Articles, constitutions, & customes seeme soe consonant, to reason & as it were fram'd to my particular devotion as this whereof I hold my beliefe[,] the Church of England, to whose faith I am a sworne subject, & have a double obligation to subscribe to her articles, & endeavour to observe her constitutions" (I.5). As a loyal English subject, Browne naturally owes allegiance to the state church, but he also claims a second, purer allegiance: of all the denominations (which Browne implies he has made a thorough study of), *this* is the one most worthy of belief. This should be a ringing endorsement of the English Church, but then, in lines that Browne would omit in the *Religio*'s

1643 version, he immediately adds, "Noe man shall wreath my faith to an-other article, or command my obedience to a cannon more[;] whatsoever is beyond as points indifferent I observe according to the rule of my private reason, or the humour, and fashion of my devotion . . . I disallow not all things in the Councell of Trent, nor believe all in the Synod of Dort. In briefe where the scripture is silent, the church is my text . . . where there is a joint silence of both I borrow not the rules of my religion from Rome, or Geneva, but the dictates of mine owne reason" (I.5). There is an uneasy ten-sion between Browne's initial, seemingly absolutist statement of allegiance to the English Church (there is *no* church wherein *every*thing so squares to his conscience), and this defiant addendum in which Browne sounds almost hostile, as if he felt that he had already been pushed to the furthest verge of what he could accept. He makes a similar point a little later in the work, where he claims that, although he would willingly embrace a necessary mar-tyrdom, "from the morall duty I owe to the commands of God; & the natu-rall respect I tender unto the conservation of my essence & being; I would not perish upon a ceremonie, politique point, or indifferency" (I.26). In both these passages, Browne seems all too able to envision a day when more obe-dience than he would be willing to give might be demanded of him, and in imagining a man or men who would have him "wreath [his] faith to another article, or command [his] obedience to a [canon] more," he shows precious little trust in the leaders of what only a moment before seemed to be his ideal church.

A suspicion that the English Church was requiring obedience to new articles and canons was widely shared in the mid-1630s, when the state's ef-forts to implement the long-neglected Canons of 1604 led many to worry that not only old but also new strictures were being enforced.[29] While the Thirty-Nine Articles of 1562, which primarily concerned basics of Christian and Protestant belief, were worded vaguely enough that they had always been acceptable to most members of the English Church, including those with Puri-tan leanings, the Canons were largely concerned with comportment, ritual, and forms of worship: the very "ceremonies" that until recently had been consid-ered points of indifference. If this prospect awakened the anxieties of Puritans, those of a more Laudian (and Arminian) stripe were equally anxious that the Synod of Dort's 1625 statements on predestination might be adopted by the En-glish Church.[30]

Browne seems troubled by both possibilities, and indeed he cultivates an attitude of tolerant independence. As he writes in the next section, "I could never divide my selfe from anie man upon the difference of an opinion, or be angry with his Judgement in not agreeing with mee in that, from which perhaps within a few daies I should dissent my selfe" (I.6). This is one of the *Religio*'s most frequently quoted lines, and it is usually cited as evidence of Browne's great tolerance. However, just as Browne's statement of complete allegiance to the Church of England shrivels upon inspection into a much more conditional fidelity, so here Browne's declaration of cheerful sectarian disengagement is almost immediately called into question. Browne does not say that he believes representatives of opposing factions are all Christians of good will, or that he can see merit in more than one side; instead, as he continues, it appears that he does not entirely trust himself to know truth from falsehood: "I have noe genius to disputes in Religion, & have thought it wisdome to decline them especially upon a disadvantage, or when the cause of truth might suffer in the weakenes of my reason. [W]here wee desire to bee informed t'is good to confer with men above our selves, but to confirme our opinions t'is best to argue with judgments below our owne, that the frequent spoiles & victories over their reasons, maie settle in us an esteeme, & confirm'd opinion of our owne" (I.6). Although this passage contains sensible statements to the effect that not every believer can argue persuasively on behalf of his belief, and that even a right-thinking Christian might find himself outreasoned by a sophist, Browne does not rest with such unobjectionable remarks. Instead, he seems to urge believers to engage only in those intellectual battles that they can win; it is all very well to *confer* with those above oneself in intellect, but *arguing* with them is risky business. If Browne believes that disputing with those beneath us in brainpower inevitably confirms us in our opinions, the unavoidable implication is that arguing with those who are brighter makes us intellectually vulnerable.

For someone who has elsewhere championed reason and its role in religion, this is a curious argument. Browne has declared that his membership in the Church of England is the result of an active choice, and that he made this choice in large part because the church's "Articles, constitutions, & customes seeme soe consonant to reason"; moreover, when the church and the Bible are both silent on a matter of faith, he has professed always to follow "the dictates of mine owne reason" (I.5). In the section we have just been examining, however, Browne first declares that he will not dispute anyone who can outthink him (suggesting that it is dangerous to do so), and then a few lines later seems to shrug off this worry on the grounds that, as he writes, "if there arise anie doubts in my waie, I can forget them, or at least deferre them till my better setled Judgement, and more manly reason bee able to resolve them" (I.6). With this turn Browne appears to be struggling to redeem the role of reason: although he first claims that he is ready to forget his doubts, he then qualifies that statement, as if aware that his intellect should play *some* role in his search for religious truth. However, this leads him to make a confusing distinction between a younger judgment (which is weak) and a maturer judgment (which is always victorious), without explaining the nature of this distinction. Instead of clarifying the point, Browne concludes the section with another apparent reversal: in order to keep himself free from heresy, he says, he always "follow[s] the great wheele of the church . . . not reserveing anie proper poles, or motion from the epicycles of my owne braine" (I.6).

Negotiating the relationship between faith and reason was certainly not an easy task for anyone in the seventeenth century, but Browne's rhetorical gymnastics hint not just at confusion but at deep anxiety over the role played by each. While no early modern theologian would have considered reason sufficient to bring a person to religious knowledge, most nevertheless regarded it an indispensable component. In her essay on the relationship between *Religio Medici* and liberal theological discourse, Victoria Silver argues that Browne shares—and in the *Religio* is modeling—the views of divines such as William Chillingworth and Jeremy Taylor, who believed that reason, when assisted by grace, was perfectly capable and indeed necessary for distinguishing between religious truth and religious error.[31] In one illustrative footnote, Silver quotes Taylor as saying, "Faith and reason are several [i.e., separate] things . . . but it is reason that carries me to objects of faith, and faith is my reason so disposed, so used, so instructed."[32] Despite Silver's claims, this is not Browne's position—or at least not one that he takes consistently; instead, he alternates between making bold claims for reason and discounting its operation entirely. Whereas Taylor presents reason and faith as operating in tandem, the one essential to the other, Browne seems to believe that the two belong to radically different spheres. As he will write a short while later, "As the propositions of faith seeme absurd unto reason, so the Theoremes of reason unto passion; & both unto faith; yet a moderate & peaceable discourse maie soe order & state the matter, that they may all be as Kings, & yet make but one Monarchy; everie one exerciseing his soveraignety, & prerogative in due time & place according to the restraint & limits of circumstance" (I.19). Browne's version of the harmonious coexistence of faith and reason is not a marriage but a divorce settlement: each faculty gets custody of the issues proper to it, and so long as each stays out of the other's way, all is well.

Although Browne does not come out and say so, his distrust of reason when it comes to matters of faith seems the result of unfortunate personal experience. In following the great wheel of his church, Browne tells his reader, "I leave noe gapp to heresies, scismes, or errors, of which at this present I shall not injure truth to say, I have noe taint, or tincture." But, he adds, "I must confesse my greener studies have beene polluted with 2 or 3, not anie begot in these later Centuries, but old, & obsolete, such as could never have infected anie, but such an extravagant head as mine" (I.6). Browne's tone seems offhand, as if he were both dismissing and taking a kind of casual pride in his youthful heresies: who *else* would ever have thought *that*? As Browne begins to enumerate these errors, however, it becomes clear that he is more apprehensive about his lapses than he seems—and that he is hardly telling his readers the full story.

His first heresy, Browne says, "was that errour of the Arabians, that the soules of men perished with their bodies, but should both bee raised againe at the Last Day" (I.7). He is correct that this was an old heresy, but it was far from obsolete. In fact, during the Reformation both psychosomnolence—the belief that the soul sleeps until the resurrection—and thnetopsychism— the belief that the body and soul both die and then both rise again—were quite common; Martin Luther himself appears to have subscribed to a form of psychosomnolence.[33] The northern Italian humanists, including those centered in the University of Padua, were also notably skeptical about the immortality of the soul, and it was their vocal doubts that led to the fifth Lateran Council's condemnation of psychosomnolence as a heresy in 1515–1517.[34] Although the council met more than a century before Browne reached Padua, the heresy was still very much alive there, and the *Religio* indicates that Browne is familiar with the works of at least one of the Paduan skeptics, Pietro Pomponazzi. In *De Immortalitate Animae* (1516), Pomponazzi contended that, contra Aquinas, all the evidence pointed toward the mortality of the soul. Nevertheless, Pomponazzi maintained his allegiance to the church by declaring that since the immortality of the soul could not be proved by philosophy, it must be accepted on ecclesiastical authority.[35] This sentiment is echoed in Browne not only in a general way (as in his remarks about submitting his reason to the great wheel of his church) but in quite a specific one: as he discusses this first heresy, Browne describes mortalism, in a parenthetical aside, as something "which faith not philosophy can throughly disprove" (I.7).

Browne goes on to describe the specifics of his mortalist error—he did not believe in the complete mortality of the soul, only in its temporary somnolence—and then gives an explanation: "T'is but the merits of our un-worthy nature if wee sleepe in darkenes till the last alarme[;] a serious reflex upon mine owne demerits did somewhat make mee backward from challeng-ing this prerogative of my soule. [S]oe I might enjoie my Saviour at last, I could with patience be nothing allmost unto eternity" (I.7). While it is cer-tainly possible that Browne came to his heresy for the reasons and in the manner he specifies, I think we do well to be suspicious. Browne has already substantially shaded the truth in implying that psychosomnolence was an obsolete heresy, and, given the currency of this heresy in at least one of the universities at which he studied, it seems unlikely that he fell under its spell simply as a result of his private and independent reflections upon the nature of his soul. More likely, he encountered the belief in the course of his studies or through his fellow students, and its appeal probably had less to do with his sense of his spiritual state than with his consideration of the scientific and philosophical evidence for the soul's immortality.

Browne's second and third heresies, which are equally concerned with what happens after bodily death, should raise similar red flags. He describes his second error as "that of the [O]riginists or Chiliasts; That God would not allwaies persist in his vengance, but after a definite terme of his wrath hee would release the damned soules from torture" (I.7). Where or how Browne came upon this heresy is not certain, although Origen was popular with many Renaissance humanists, in part because of his own early immersion in the phi-losophy of Plato and the Stoics.[36] In fact, in stating Origen's views on the re-demption this generally, what Browne omits is the element that most humanists found most appealing, which is that Origen argued for the possibility of the salvation of virtuous pagans. As we shall see, the fate of classical writers is also a preoccupation of Browne's, and probably has a certain amount to do with the appeal of Origen's eschatology.

This is how Browne explains his second heresy: "[This] errour I fell into upon a serious contemplation of that great Attribute of God[,] his Mercie . . . because I found therein noe malice, & a readie waight to weigh from that other extreame of despaire whereunto Contemplative & melancholy natures are too readily dispos'd" (I.7). This is the second time that Browne has im-plied that despair is at the root of his heresies. Given his emphasis here on God's mercy, it is possible that he is obliquely expressing concern about the kind of God who could condemn those whom Browne will later call the "honest worthies" who simply had the misfortune to be born before Christ; it is also possible that he is hinting at sympathy for an Arminian position on salvation. Such doubts about God's justice, if Browne indeed had them, would have amounted to a much more serious heresy than the one on which he here puts such a relatively innocuous spin. He does something similar with his final heresy, a belief in the efficacy of prayers for the dead. He prefaces his announcement of this error with an elaborate qualification: *this* heresy he never actually believed but just wished might be true (I.7). Given that this "heresy" refers to a common practice in the Catholic Church, however, it is even further from being obsolete than the other two.

Browne spends a fair amount of time describing and excusing all three heresies on the grounds that his motives were always good—for instance, in thinking that the damned might eventually be saved he was simply carried away with a love of God's mercy—but in the end he undoes all these excuses by declaring that his errors were not really heresies to begin with: "These opinions I never maintained with pertenacity, or endeavoured to inveigh anie mans beliefe to mine; not soe much as ever revealed, or disputed them with my dearest friend, by which meanes I never propagated them in others, nor confirm'd them in my selfe; but suffring them to flame upon their owne substance without addition of new fewell they went out allmost of themselves. Therefore these opinions though condemned by law, were not heresies in mee but bare errours, & single lapses of my understanding without a joint depravity of my will" (I.7). Despite his earlier claim that he outgrew his heresies, and despite the good impulses that supposedly undergirded them, Browne now denies that they even *were* heresies to begin with; instead, they amounted only to private errors of reason made by one who nevertheless always regarded himself as a conforming Christian. Like Milton in his own confessions of faith, Browne seems to be protesting too much. Both men supply a surprising amount of autobiographical material, as if laying bare their beliefs, but a careful look at the content and the texture of their autobiographical passages shows how nervous, defensive, or downright contradictory their narratives are.

For however confident Browne may say he is that these lapses did not amount to heresies, his many different explanations for their innocuousness— and especially the alterations that Browne would make to this portion of the *Religio* in the work's later two versions—suggest that he himself is not as convinced as he would have his readers be. Whereas in the first version of the *Religio* Browne's announcement that he always follows the great wheel of his church in order to keep himself free from heresies is immediately followed by a discussion of those errors that "polluted" his "greener studies," which is then followed by his denial that these even *were* heresies to begin with, in the

Religio's second and third versions Browne makes a number of changes. After his remark about following the wheel of his church, Browne inserts a long, leisurely, very general discussion of heresies and their tendency to disappear in one place only to pop up again in another. *Then* he discusses his own heresies, and after *that* he inserts a reflection about the villainy of Lucifer and all subsequent schismatics, as well as another very general meditation on the fact that we have Christ's word that heresies will always arise, but no guarantee that they will disappear. Finally, he gets to the disclaimer for his own heresies. These changes more than double the amount of text in which he discusses heresy, but at the same time they significantly dilute the autobiographical content of the subject. As rewritten, in the 1643 version of the *Religio* that most readers know, Browne's own heresies are easily overlooked; they seem like mere illustrations of a larger point about the nature of heresy—when in the original version, Browne's heresies *were* the point.

If Browne's nervousness about these three heresies causes him to leave out some of their important details, there is another heresy that he never even mentions, but whose fingerprints are all over the *Religio*: antitrinitarianism. This was a particularly resilient heresy throughout the Renaissance and Reformation, perhaps because the scriptural evidence for a tripartite God is rather scanty, and the evidence for a coequal, coeternal tripartite God almost nonexistent; as more people began to read the Bible for themselves, the nature of the godhead inevitably came in for questioning.[37] One can imagine that Browne—who wrestles so mightily with such biblical brainteasers as how Noah could have fitted all those animals in the ark, along with enough food to sustain them (I.22)—would have tried to reconcile the church's notion of the Trinity with the scriptural evidence for it.[38] Antitrinitarianism also frequently went hand in hand with mortalism, and Browne's discussion of his one Origenist heresy may hint at a second: Origen was frequently accused of a form of antitrinarianism much like Arianism.[39]

The evidence, however, is more than merely circumstantial. Although Browne's statements on the Trinity throughout the *Religio* maintain a superficial orthodoxy, there are signs of great strain. In the Pembroke manuscript, the section immediately following the one in which Browne discusses his heresies is a consideration of "those wingie misteries of Divinity, & aerie subtilties of Religion, which have unhing'd the braines of better heads" (I.9).[40] Despite this danger, Browne assures his readers that his own brains are in no danger: "I love to loose my selfe in a misterie . . . t'is my solitary recreation to pose my apprehension with those envolv'd Enigma's & riddles of the Trinity,

Incarnation, and resurrection, I can answer all the objections of Satan, & my
rebellious reason with that odd resolution I learn'd of Tertullian, Certum est
quia impossibile est [it is certain because it is impossible]" (I.9). Once again
Browne presents himself as someone who is cheerfully following the wheel
of his church, undisturbed by what he cannot fully understand. Only a few
sections later, however, the Trinity appears to give him considerably more
trouble. "There is noe attribute," Browne reflects—meaning, attribute of
God—"adds more difficulty then the misterie of the trinity; where though in
a relative way of father, & son, wee must denie a priority. I wonder how Aristotle should conceive the world eternall, or how hee could make good 2
eternities" (I.12).[41]

As Browne attempts to understand a Christian mystery such as the Trinity, it is striking that he has recourse (as he does so frequently) to a pagan
philosopher. In fact, he will eventually have recourse to three, moving from
Aristotle to Pythagoras to Hermes Trismegistus as he searches for the right
metaphor and skitters away from a direct investigation of the paradox of the
Trinity. I shall quote the entire remainder of the section to illustrate the uneasy progress of Browne's argument:

> [Aristotle's] similitude of a triangle comprehended in a square doth
> somewhat illustrate the Trinitie of our soules, & that the triple uni-
> tie of [G]od, for there is in us not 3 but a Trinity of soules; because
> there is within us, if not 3 distinct soules, yet different faculties that
> doe and can subsist apart in different subjects, yet in us are so united
> as to make but one soule & substance[;] if one soule were soe perfect
> as to informe 3 distinct bodies that were a pretty Trinity; conceive
> the distinct number of 3 not divided or separated by the intellect,
> but actually comprehended in it's unity; & that is a perfect Trinity; I
> have often admired the Mysticall way of Pythagoras, & the secret
> Magicke of Numbers. [B]eware of philosophie, t'is a precept not to
> bee received in a narrow sense; for in the masse of nature there is a
> sett of things which carrie in their front, though not in capitall letters;
> yet in Stenography, & short character, something of Divinity; which
> to wiser reasons seeme as Luminaries in the A.B.C. of knowledge, &
> to judicious beliefe, as scales & roundats to mount the pinacles,
> & highest peeces of Divinity; the severe schooles shall not laugh mee
> out of the phylosophie of [Hermes]; that this visible world is but a
> picture of the invisible, wherein as in a portraite things are not truly

but in Aequivocall shapes, & as their counterfaites some more reall substance in that invisible fabricke. (I.12)

As Browne's first critic, Sir Kenelm Digby, writes, when Browne "goeth about to illustrate this admirable mystery . . . [he falls into a mistake] by a wild discourse of a *Trinity* in our *Soules*."[42] Digby sympathetically notes that the Trinity is impossible to understand and has no parallels in the natural world, but in describing Browne's attempts as a "wild discourse" Digby identifies a feature of his prose that few modern readers have been willing to comment on: sometimes Browne's endless metaphors and amplifications seem not so much fanciful as compulsive, their sheer volume suggesting a writer who may not completely trust himself. Even Stanley Fish, who has owned to finding Browne's dilations exasperating, assumes that they reflect a masturbatory rather than an anxious or irresolute mind.[43]

The passage that I have just quoted at such length tells quite a different story, however. Browne begins by declaring that there is no aspect of the Trinity more difficult than the coequality and coeternality of its three persons. He then turns to Aristotle, implying that the Greek would be baffled by the idea of three eternities—but immediately concludes that, actually, Aristotle's metaphor of a triangle inscribed in a square, which indicates the tripartite nature of the soul, works as a metaphor for the divine Trinity as well. But Browne does not rest here, instead veering off into a discussion of the three faculties of the soul—which he admits is not really the same thing as three distinct souls—and so in effect he starts over: what if, he says, there were instead not three souls in one body but only *one* soul that animated three different bodies? That, Browne claims, would be "a pretty Trinity." Perhaps, but from the standpoint of the church it would also be a heresy: Sabellianism.[44] Whereas Arians believed that there were three distinct persons in the godhead who were not perfectly coequal (the Father existing before and willing into being the other two persons), Sabellians took the reverse position, envisioning a single divine person who assumed three different (but coequal) forms. In his attempt to describe the Trinity Browne begins by wrestling with what seems an essentially Arian notion of the godhead—but ends by having talked himself away from that and into the opposite, Sabellian extreme.

Browne may or may not realize the heretical nature of his example, but he certainly does not seem satisfied with it as a description. Instead, he makes one last attempt to understand the Trinity, by trying to "conceive the distinct number of 3 not divided or separated by the intellect, but actually comprehended in its unity"; this, of course, is not so much a description of the Trinity as it is a definition. At this point, Browne abandons his effort to understand the nature of the Trinity. He begins to speak loftily but rather irrelevantly of "Pythagoras, & the secret Magicke of Numbers" and then of "the phylosophie of [Hermes]; that this visible world is but a picture of the invisible"—never mind that Browne has not actually provided an example of something in the visible world that could serve as a picture of the Trinity. By the end of the section he has completely failed to come to terms with the nature of the Trinity, but by changing the subject to something about which he *can* take a definite stand ("the severe schooles shall not laugh me out of the phylosophie" of Hermes), he seems to be trying to distract his audience from this failure, and perhaps also himself.

Other indications of Browne's possible antitrinitarian sympathies emerge with similar indirection, either in what he fails to say or in passages whose very orthodoxy seems for some reason suspect. He immediately discounts the only scriptural passage that he produces as possible evidence for the Trinity (I.22), and in the entire *Religio* he mentions the Holy Ghost only once, in passing (I.20).[45] As both Leonard Nathanson and Debora Shuger note, Browne also seems generally uninterested in the second person of the Trinity, although he does routinely use the epithet "my Saviour" and on one occasion goes out of his way to say of him, "I believe hee was dead[,] buried & rose againe" (I.9).[46] But while this statement of belief should be thoroughly unremarkable—it is practically a line from the Apostles' Creed—it comes in a work that is otherwise starved for such statements.

A similarly forceful and similarly suspect statement of belief appears in a meditation midway through the *Religio*. Browne has again been worrying about whether the soul is organic or inorganic; when and how it gets infused into the body; and what happens to it after bodily death (I.36–37). At the end of these speculations, Browne suddenly launches into an impromptu creed: "I beleeve that the whole composition or frame of a beast doth perish after his death; and is left in the same estate after death as before; It was materiall unto life[;] that the soules of men know neither contrary nor corruption that they subsist beyond the body, & outlive death by the priviledge of their proper nature, & without a miracle, that the soules of the faithfull as they leave earth take possession of heaven, that those apparitions and ghosts of departed persons are not the wandreing soules of men; but the unquiet walkes of Devills" (I.37). Syntactically, this passage is more direct and affirmative than almost any of the others we have examined: there are almost none of the tangled negative constructions, ambiguous pronouns, or anxiously qualifying conjunctions so characteristic of Browne; for once, his meaning is absolutely clear. However, since we know that at one point in his life Browne held views quite the opposite of these, this passage, like those on the Trinity, should alert us to his continuing nervousness about his ostensibly repudiated heresies. It is impossible to know whether he makes these statements in good faith, and his precise beliefs at the moment of writing are beside the point. What seems certain is that he is anxious about his orthodoxy when it comes to the Trinity—as he is when it comes to the immortality of the soul—and when he has failed either to describe or to reason himself through that mystery, he resorts to a blunt declaration of faith otherwise wholly out of character for the work. Just as James's creedal statements appear in places where narrative autobiography seems to have failed him, so Browne's creedal declarations signal a move away from the personal. Like James, Browne appears to take solace in the recitation of central, communal beliefs when the specifics of his personal beliefs are too complicated to discuss.

For although catechetical works seem to have provided some initial inspiration for the *Religio,* the declarative mode with which Browne opened his work proves to be one to which he is largely unable to return. If he indeed began the *Religio* because he was concerned about how well his beliefs, after years abroad in relatively free-thinking circles, squared with the increasingly rigid positions of the Church of England, it has to be said that he seems not to have resolved these anxieties with total success. Although he opens virtually every section of the work by contemplating a more or less theological issue, as the work progresses, his explorations of these issues are significantly diluted by his autobiographical investigations into his own temperament and intellectual processes; he may still begin sentences with the phrase, "I confess," but what he actually confesses is, increasingly, a habit, opinion, or personality trait rather than an article of faith. He continues to make nervous gestures in the direction of orthodoxy—especially when he seems to think that he has strayed too far from it—but we wind up learning surprisingly little about his position on most essential matters of Christian belief.

Of course, it is possible that Browne simply does not *have* any position on—or any real interest in—many of the expected articles of faith; it is striking, for example, how little he says about sacramental issues such as infant baptism or the nature of the Eucharist.[47] For Browne, science, philosophy, and religion bleed into each other to an extraordinary degree, and it is likely that his heresies and heterodoxies owe less to the influence of radical Christian thinkers or any particular religious sect than to what he calls, in the work's opening sentence, "the naturall [i.e., the scientific and philosophical] course of [his] studies" (I.1). As I noted in his discussions of the Trinity, when he deals with things of a spiritual nature he refers surprisingly often to the works of the ancient pagans, especially the Epicureans and the Stoics, and from the *Religio*'s very first line he seems preoccupied with warding off whatever suspicion of atheism might attach to this fondness; at one point he goes so far as to declare that the Epicureans and the Stoics themselves were not actually atheists (I.20).

Browne's attraction to these philosophers appears to have been both intellectual and temperamental. Whatever some Christian interpreters might be inclined to think, the Stoics believed in the soul's mortality—indeed, they denied that there was anything at all after death—and they regarded human life as a generally cold and irrational affair.[48] As we have seen, each of Browne's heresies is concerned, to a greater or lesser degree, with what happens after death, and Browne's uneasiness about the soul echoes throughout the *Religio*. Moreover, by his own description, Browne appears to have suffered from fits of melancholy, and he may well have been in the grips of one as he wrote the *Religio*. In addition to his apparent worries about his orthodoxy, he seems preoccupied by his approaching thirtieth birthday, which he never mentions without seeming to heave a deep sigh; he refers to suicide three times; discusses marriage and children with a lack of interest bordering on contempt; and indicates that he feels the entire world to be in a state of decline.

Browne first alludes to a sense of his own decline at the approximate midpoint of his text, when he cites a commonplace of biblical scholarship: "Some Divines count Adam 30 yeares old, when hee was made; because they suppose him created in the perfect age & stature of man" (I.39). Although Browne does not seem interested in disputing Adam's age, he does dispute the "perfection," or at any rate the significance, of thirty—pointing out, first, that we can never know our own age precisely, as we begin life at some mysterious point in our mother's womb, and then that perfection is unattainable on earth, no matter what our age (I.39). A short while later he again mentions the age of thirty, this time alluding to his own approaching birthday—and again he winds up focusing not on the age's perfections but instead on its unsatisfactory aspects: how very many years thirty is to have lived, and how much worse things get afterward: "As yet I have not seene one revolution of Saturne, nor hath my pulse beate 30 yeares, & yet . . . mee thinkes I have outliv'd my selfe, & begin to bee wearie of the sun" (I.41).[49] Although Browne has not yet married and has only just begun his career, he speaks as though feeling himself a much older man, exhausted by life and uninterested in what more it might have to offer.[50]

Turning thirty may only remind Browne of his inevitable end, but it is an end he appears prepared to accept with equanimity. "In expectation of a better, I can with patience embrace this life," he writes, "yet in my best meditations doe often desire death. . . . [I] thinke noe man ever desired life as I have sometimes death" (I.38). This somewhat alarming statement is essentially Stoical, yet what Browne describes is not endurance in the face of death but rather an active desire for it. A few sections later he will criticize such a sentiment as cowardly, but his criticism does not appear entirely wholehearted. Describing himself as having been "much taken with two verses of Lucan," ever since he could understand them, he quotes the lines, translates them, and then comments upon them:

> *Victurosque Dei celant (ut vivere durent)*
> *Felix esse mori* ———— ————
>
> *W'are all deluded vainly searching waies*
> *to make us happie by the length of daies;*
> *for cunningly to make's protract this breath*
> *the gods conceale the happines of death.*

There bee manie excellent straines in that Poet wherewith his Stoicall Genius hath supplied him . . . yet herein [the Stoics] are in an extreame that can allow a man to bee his owne Assassine, & soe highly extoll the end of Cato, this is indeed not to feare Death, but to bee afraid of life; T'is a brave act to valour to contemne death, but where life is more terrible then death, t'is then the truest valour to dare to live. (I.44)

This is certainly a properly Christian take on the matter, but Browne seems struggling to believe the words he writes. His translation reveals the morbid track of his mind: from a simple Latin statement about the gods' concealing the happiness of death from those who must keep living, Browne derives a meditation on the futility of life and the cruel machinations of the gods—one that has no basis in either the lines themselves or their original context in book IV of Lucan's *Pharsalia*.[51] Although Browne condemns the Stoics' eagerness for death, the way in which he translates Lucan's lines and his admitted attraction to them suggest that, here again, he may be talking himself back into orthodoxy.

Browne makes the same movement in his next reference to suicide. Toward the end of the *Religio,* after giving thanks that none of his sins is "singular," Browne adds, however, "Even those common & quotidian infirmities that so necessarily attend mee . . . so breake the estimation which I hold otherwise of my selfe that I repute my selfe the abject'st peece of mortalitie; I detest my owne nature, and in my retir'd meditations, cannot withold my hands from violence on my selfe" (II.7). Browne will swiftly draw back from this worrying statement with the rather lame explanation, "tis noe breach of charitie to our selves to bee at variance with our vices, or to detest that part which is an enemie to the grand object of charitie" (II.7), but this does not succeed in moderating his references to self-violence; it only indicates that he is aware of and concerned about his self-portrait, and that he will correct it when he feels it necessary. In his 1643 revision of the *Religio* he will go still further, deleting both this reference to suicide and the one in I.38—leaving only the passage from Lucan, which concludes with Browne's stern rejection of suicide.

If Browne is discontented with his own life, he appears equally discontented with the state of affairs in the world around him, perhaps especially in England. The only events in his country's recent history that he cites as evidence of God's favor are the discovery of the Gunpowder Plot and the defeat of the Spanish Armada—both of which were, in 1635, distinctly historical events. After mentioning these former acts of divine Providence, Browne concludes, "All cannot bee happie at once, for . . . the glorie of one state depends upon the ruines of another [and] there is a revolution & vicissitude of their greatnes, which must obey the swinge of [Fortune's] wheele" (I.17). Whatever states Browne might imagine to be the favorites of Fortune in 1635, England appears not to be among them.

The *Religio*'s depiction of the impermanence and corruption of life on earth extends to its treatment of all natural bonds. Browne's dismissive remarks on marriage and the sex act are well known ("I could wish we might procreate like trees, without conjunction" [II.9]), but a similar sense of alienation permeates passages dealing with other potential claims on one's affections: Browne characterizes "the love of our parents, the affections of our wives & children" as no more than "dumbe showes without reality, truth, or constancy" (II.14), and while he *does* celebrate same-sex friendship—the work originally seems to have been written with one special friend in mind—the sense he gives the reader is that his one adored, intimate friend is the exception to all other people and indeed all other friends.[52]

Browne's melancholy temperament may have made the writings of the Stoics congenial to him, and their philosophy may also have provided him with a certain degree of solace in his more depressive moments. At one point Browne reveals that he has actually gone so far as to attempt to live his life according to their moral philosophy—practicing, he says, "that honest Artifice of Seneca" and imagining the presence of his worthiest friends as a way to refrain from sin (I.47). Although he apparently had great success with this experiment and was able to "be honest without a thought either of heaven or hell," he insists that he found his resolution weak and doubts whether he could have persevered in that course for very long (I.47). This account may well be the truth, but the way that he seems once again to be pulling himself up short is striking; the impression his words give is that he was either unwilling to pursue his Senecan inclinations any further or is reluctant now to tell his audience the full story of what happened when he did. Accordingly, he abruptly swerves away from this autobiographical narrative. He concludes, "The life therefore & spirit of all our actions, is the resurrection, & stable apprehension, that our actions shall enjoy the fruits of our pious endeavours, without this all religion is a fallacie, & those impieties of Lucian, Euripides, & Julian are noe blasphemies, but subtile verities, & Atheists have been the only Philosophers" (I.47). However appealing moral philosophy may have been to Browne, it appears to have one crucial shortcoming. What religion offers him in this account is not so much a way to live a good life as the hope for something *beyond* life. Christianity may not have proven itself essential for a moral existence, and the *Religio* has certainly shown that it contains doctrines that Browne finds vexing, but I think it is not too much to say that it offers him a refuge from despair that classical philosophy does not: a religion or moral system that does not offer the hope of life after death deserves to have its gods mocked as Lucian and Euripides mocked theirs, or to be disestablished as the emperor Julian disestablished Christianity.

The afterlife is the aspect of Christianity that most engages Browne and that most seems to assure him of his orthodoxy. As we have seen, each of Browne's heresies is concerned, to a greater or lesser degree, with what happens after death, and a huge portion of the *Religio*, right in the middle of the work, is dedicated to a Christian exploration of the subject (see sections I.38–59); moreover, nearly every one of Browne's references to suicide or the decline of the world is also followed by a discussion of the resurrection. As Browne pursues these speculations, his tone also becomes increasingly confident.

In the end, Browne's statement of faith is an awfully attenuated one. On the evidence of this work, Browne cannot be said fully to have conquered either the religious doubts or the deeper sense of melancholy that inform the *Religio*, although in the Resurrection he seems to have found a possible cure for both. In holding fast to this one article of faith, he is able to enact some form of English Church orthodoxy. Like Donne in the *Devotions,* he seems to be hoping that his beliefs outweigh any doubts—and that his *desire* to conform is more important than whether he actually does in every particular.

The Revised *Religio Medici*, Circa 1638 and 1643

The first version of the *Religio* is the confession of faith of a man whose Christianity is quite sincere—if uneasy and not entirely orthodox—and who very much wants to find comfort in the arms of the Church of England. This desire and this nervousness are underscored by many of the changes that Browne makes to the later versions of the *Religio*. His first revision, reflected in six of the eight extant manuscript copies as well as the 1642 unauthorized printing, includes a great number of additions (Denonain counts sixty-nine new "major passages"),[53] but in reworking the *Religio* Browne also omitted a number of lines and altered hundred of passages and individual readings. Taken together, these suggest that he was deliberately recasting the *Religio* for a different audience and a different political climate. If the first version of the *Religio* begins as an exposition of faith that often devolves into a more ad hoc series of autobiographical explorations, the second version tries harder to keep the work on the subject of religion, and to keep that discussion on a more orthodox footing. Whereas the first version is divided into sections but not parts, the second version has no section divisions but arranges itself into two parts ostensibly corresponding to the double law of charity: love for God in the first part and love for neighbor in the second. Divisions of this sort were common for seventeenth-century devotional and theological works, from Jeremy Taylor's *Holy Living* to Milton's *De Doctrina Christiana* to numerous catechisms.[54] Although the original version of the *Religio* does indeed declare, approximately two-thirds through the work, that Browne is now turning to "that other Vertue of Charity," the remaining portion of the work is in fact only occasionally interested in charity as a theological virtue; instead, Browne uses "charity" as an excuse to contemplate his own nature, the value of friendship, and other subjects in what ultimately seems more a statement of Epicurean philosophy than of Christian. In the second version of the *Religio* Browne's actual treatment of charity changes only slightly, but by arranging the work according to this familiar division, he signals to his audience that the *Religio* should be understood as a product of a recognizable devotional tradition.

Browne's views also come to seem less heterodox through dozens of more local changes, several of which I have already noted. As a rule, these changes work to temper or even obscure Browne's statements on religious matters, as in the case of Browne's discussion of his heresies. Browne also continually moderates or qualifies formerly absolute statements, as when he replaces such remarks as "I believe" with "I *could* believe" and "it is" with "*I think* it is." At other times, he does not so much disguise as simply delete material that he may have felt verged on the overly revelatory—as in his omission of two of his original three allusions to suicide (I.38 and II.7). All of these changes amount to a moderation of the beliefs and ideas expressed in the *Religio*'s first version, and they suggest that when Browne revised his work he did so with an eye toward an audience. It may be that the first version had already circulated in manuscript beyond a community of his intimates, or it may only be that he saw the potential of the new version to do so, but either way he seems to be anticipating a readership that does not know him intimately and before whom he wishes to be more circumspect.

But if the second version of the work seems primarily concerned with smoothing out Browne's persona and smoothing over many of his singularities, it nevertheless also reflects some new tensions. Whereas the original version suggests that Browne has reservations about the English Church under Laud, in the revised version his unease is directed more toward the Puritans than the Laudians. Although he retains his defiant remark about not subscribing to a single canon or article more, he also inserts disparaging references to "Insolent zeales" who "decry good workes and rely upon faith" (I.60), and later he observes that "charity growes cold . . . [especially] in those which most doe manifest the fires and flames of zeale" (II.4). In referring thus critically to those he perceives as overzealous, he aligns himself more clearly with a ceremonial church and against nonconformist Calvinists than he did in the *Religio*'s first version.

The most explicit of Browne's references to the would-be reformers within the English Church helps both to date the revision and to give a more specific sense of Browne's political concerns. In a passage that we have already examined, Browne originally described his religion as that taught by Christ and disseminated by the apostles, "but by the sinister ends of Princes, the ambition, & avarice of Prelates, & the fatall corruption of time [is now] decay'd, impair'd, and fallen from its native beautie" (I.2). In the second version, however, he replaces the word "Prelates" with "Presbyters." Although in the primitive church the two terms were virtually interchangeable, in the late 1630s and 1640s the words represented opposed notions about the proper form of church government. Calls for the reform of the English Church along presbyterian lines (which advocates felt was less arbitrary and more democratic than the episcopacy) became increasingly vocal during the two Bishops' Wars from 1638 to 1640. The wars, which had their origins in Charles's attempts to impose the English Prayer Book on the Scottish Kirk, were extremely unpopular in England, and the Presbyterian cause was taken up by many Puritans who saw themselves as being in much the same position as the oppressed members of the Kirk.[55] Although Browne's substitution of *presbyter* for *prelate* does not necessarily tell us anything about his support for the war, in implying that presbyters are actually responsible for the very corruptions that the supporters of a presbyterian-style overhaul of the church argued would root out, Browne registers greater antipathy for the reformers than for the Laudians.

These allusions suggest that Browne's first revision of the *Religio* probably took place sometime between 1638 and 1640; much beyond this date, in the thick of the first Civil War, his references to presbyters would likely have felt too charged—indeed, in the 1643 version Browne changes the word back to "prelates." It may even be that his concerns about the political situation of the late 1630s and his distaste for those whom he characterizes as intolerant and overzealous are actually responsible for some of the changes that he makes to his autobiographical persona. In revising the *Religio,* he appears no longer to have seen the work as an opportunity to explore his religious beliefs, for the second version addresses no new issues and at most disguises rather than truly alters the opinions expressed in the original. Instead, in revising the work he may have intended his smoother and more carefully controlled autobiographical self to serve as a model to his age: an example of someone whose free-thinking ways never led him into serious error, and whose charitable disposition always inclined him to think well of his fellow Christians.

The third-stage version of the *Religio* continues much the same process that Browne began with the second. In this case, however, there is no dispute about the date of the revision, for in 1642 a manuscript from the second stage made its way to the printer Andrew Crooke and was published under the name *Religio Medici*.[56] Very soon thereafter, presumably upon learning of the unauthorized printing, Browne began revising his work to publish his own version, which in turn appeared in 1643.[57] Despite Browne's claims that he was only providing a "full and intended copy of that Peece which was most imperfectly and surreptitiously published before" ("To the Reader"), the authorized edition does more than merely correct the corruptions of the unauthorized one. In fact, Browne did not actually base his new edition upon an earlier manuscript version but instead took the 1642 publication as his copy text, thereby retaining many errors unique to the 1642 edition.[58] Browne does correct some errors, of course, but he also makes hundreds of small changes and adds approximately twelve major passages, including four wholly new sections and the lengthy letter "To the Reader."[59]

These changes (and the lack of other changes) indicate that Browne's concerns about the unauthorized version may have had less to do with textual corruptions than with textual *accuracies*: that is, elements of the work that originated with Browne but that for one reason or another he came to feel were inappropriate. Most of his changes in the third version are essentially the same in kind as those in the second, further moderating his autobiographical persona into that of a man whose eccentricities never lead him beyond the embrace of the English Church. Browne interjects yet more qualifying words and phrases into former statements of certitude while making lengthier additions that distract attention from nearby discussions of sensitive topics.[60]

More than in the second version, however, in the third Browne seems intent on demonstrating his submission to the Church of England. He deletes his formerly striking declaration that he would not accept another canon or article from his church (I.5); declares right in his prefatory letter that all his statements are subject to "maturer discernments" and "the best and learned judgements"; and makes a few adjustments that seem intended to forestall charges of crypto-Catholicism.[61] Browne's confession of faith might thus be said to undergo a subtle shift in emphasis in this last version. If the second version foregrounded Browne's singularity, suggesting that his willingness to try every idea on for size actually made him a good and charitable Christian, the third version foregrounds Browne's allegiance to the Church of England: he still demonstrates great speculative freedom, but by insisting more strongly that he always submits himself to his church, Browne neutralizes most of the remaining evidence of his heterodoxy—and he winds up yoking his tolerant, skeptical version of Christianity to the English Church itself.

This may or may not be intentional. As we have seen, the *Religio* is concerned about the appearance of unorthodoxy, and with the potential of a printed version to reach a much larger audience—not to mention the recent imprisonment of Laud and the abolition of bishops—Browne may well have felt either that he could not afford to or that now was not the time to seem to be questioning his church. On the other hand, it may be that the embattled state of the Church of England genuinely increased Browne's affection for and allegiance to that institution, and that in his revision he is taking a deliberate political position on the side of his church and his king.

*   *   *

What a careful reading of *Religio Medici* in all the stages of its composition reveals is that the work is as complex a confession of faith as those of James, Donne, and Milton, and as involved as theirs in a climate of religious controversy. The pressures of the mid-1630s through the mid-1640s seem to have motivated Browne to take stock of himself and his beliefs, and to assert that he is still orthodox *enough*. However, the anxiety that prompts this self-scrutiny— his evident nervousness about that orthodoxy—causes him to project an idealized and perhaps somewhat fictitious self. Browne's may well have been a whimsical and extravagant personality, but such scholarship as regards his dilations and expansions as *merely* playful misses their compulsive and circular nature, as well as the escape they seem to provide him from the dangerous temptations of reason. As Browne writes, "T'is not an easie point of art to [u]ntangle our selves from this riddle & web of sin . . . wee naturally know what is good, yet naturally pursue what is evill; the Rhetoricke wherewith I perswade another, I cannot persuade my selfe" (I.54). We probably cannot know whether Browne ever did persuade himself of his orthodoxy, but the *Religio*'s confession of faith stands as a complex record of that attempt.

PART III

Loyal Dissents?

CHAPTER 5

John Bunyan's Double Autobiography

At the end of *Grace Abounding to the Chief of Sinners,* John Bunyan describes his arrest six years earlier for preaching before an illegal assembly. He portrays himself as a man of unshakable resolve, one who submitted to the civil authorities without ever doubting the justice of his cause or the truth of his convictions: "I was made to see," he writes, "that if ever I would suffer rightly, I must . . . reckon my Self, my Wife, my Children, my health, my enjoyments, and all, as dead to me, and my self as dead to them" (*GA* §325).[1] This stoicism does not last long, however, and within a few lines he will give a very different account of his state of mind: "Notwithstanding these helps, I found myself a man, and compassed with infirmities; the parting with my Wife and poor Children hath oft been to me in this place as the pulling the flesh from my bones . . . I should have often brought to my mind the many hardships, miseries, and wants that my poor family was like to meet with, should I be taken from them, especially my poor blind Child, who lay nearer my heart than all I had besides; O the thoughts of the hardship I thought my blind one might go under, would break my heart to pieces" (*GA* §327). In recounting these emotions, Bunyan seems to be inadvertently blurring the chronology of his arrest and imprisonment: ostensibly he is describing his feelings in the weeks *before* his arrest (but after he had received word that the authorities would be coming for him). However, in the passage's second sentence he jumps ahead to the present: "The parting with my Wife and poor Children *hath oft been to me in this place*"—that is, prison—"as the pulling the flesh from my bones." Midway through the next sentence, after noting that he is (presumably still) too fond of his loved ones, he jumps back into the past to describe the fears he once had for the fate of his family, *"should I* be taken from them."

While Bunyan's verbs may have returned to the past tense, his anxiety for his family appears ongoing. Having mentioned his heartbreak over his blind daughter once, Bunyan does not immediately move on, erupting into a yet more emotional account of his fears for his young girl: "Poor Child! thought I, what sorrow art thou like to have for thy portion in this world? Thou must be beaten, must beg, suffer hunger, cold, nakedness, and a thousand calamities, though I cannot now endure the wind should blow upon thee. . . . O I saw in this condition I was as a man who was pulling down his house upon the head of his Wife and Children" (*GA* §328). The torn and despairing Bunyan of these lines is quite unlike the Bunyan who appears in the first lines I quoted, and he is equally unlike the Bunyan of popular fame: that fierce nonconformist so committed to his principles that he would spend an eventual twelve years in prison and face the possibility of execution rather than abandon the ministry that he believed to be his calling.[2] But while Bunyan himself works hard to promote this image, depicting whatever fears he may once have had as firmly in the past, as these passages show, even his own declarations of self-assurance can rapidly dissolve into anxiety and uncertainty.

Like the confessions of faith of the other authors examined in this book, *Grace Abounding* is a response to an immediate political and personal emergency. In this case, it is the Restoration, which brought about Bunyan's arrest and imprisonment, and the interruption—seemingly the termination—of his preaching ministry. Although readers have long noted the compulsive and despairing elements of *Grace Abounding*'s central narrative, which is the story of Bunyan's conversion,[3] the work as a whole is typically read as a confident retrospective spiritual autobiography, narrated from the distance of many years by an author now secure in his sense of salvation. The above passages suggest a more complicated reading. Not only do they indicate that Bunyan suffered from at least occasional bouts of despair while in prison, but they highlight his tendency to blur chronology, overlaying episodes from the present onto the past and reading older experiences in light of more recent ones. As with the autobiographies of James I, Donne, Milton, and Browne, *Grace Abounding* must therefore be read in the context of its composition. It is not "Bunyan's spiritual autobiography," if by that we mean a relatively fixed account of the events in Bunyan's early religious life, the narrative of which would have taken essentially the same form no matter when it got written down. Rather, *Grace Abounding* is the autobiography that Bunyan produced in 1666, in specific response to his arrest and imprisonment and the ongoing struggles of the Bedford congregation in his absence.

So although *Grace Abounding* has long been regarded as a paradigmatic spiritual autobiography (and as such an important ancestor to the modern secular autobiography), the pressures that its text manifests and the complexities of its narrative suggest that it is equally a confession of faith. Certainly, Bunyan's text participates in the seventeenth-century spiritual autobiographical tradition that found its inspirations in the life of Paul and the *Confessions* of Augustine; the work's titular assertion that Bunyan is "the chief of sinners" is only the first of many proofs.[4] However, *Grace Abounding* is in many ways an atypical spiritual autobiography.[5] Most spiritual autobiographies were not published, and many more were either not written down or not preserved; by far the most common spiritual autobiographies were those that were composed as a condition of joining a nonconformist congregation. Others were penned as private memorials or as testimonials for their authors' children and posterity. The average spiritual autobiography was also much shorter than *Grace Abounding* and had a more straightforward narrative:[6] one of the enduring oddities of Bunyan's work is the way it comes to focus on Bunyan's psychological and emotional states, almost completely untethered from whatever events may have provoked these internal reactions.[7]

This oddity, and many others, can be explained by reading *Grace Abounding* in the context of Bunyan's imprisonment. Because stories only acquire meaning in light of their endings—a phenomenon explored by Frank Kermode and Peter Brooks, among others—the events of Bunyan's conversion would have looked different to him and to his readers depending on whether the "end" of the story were understood to be Bunyan's emergence as a popular and charismatic preacher or his arrest and removal from that ministry.[8] At the time of *Grace Abounding*'s composition, Bunyan's public ministry appeared to be over, and although the termination of that phase of his life could not change the facts of his earlier experiences, it could not help but color their interpretation. Perhaps his arrest was a divine test: a trial that Bunyan could overcome as he had overcome the trials and temptations he encountered during his conversion. But it was equally possible to read it, instead, as a punishment from God—whether for falsifying his vocation or for having had the presumption to believe he was saved in the first place.

As the passages with which I opened this chapter indicate, the text of *Grace Abounding* continually evokes the experience of Bunyan's incarceration. Although the work's primary focus is Bunyan's conversion some ten years earlier, the temptations the narrative lingers over and the language it

employs reveal anxieties much nearer at hand. The work's final section, entitled
"A brief Account of the Authors Imprisonment," deals with Bunyan's imprisonment explicitly: Bunyan describes not only his fears for his family but also
his fears for himself. He recounts the despair into which he was plunged during his early years of confinement and his sense of abandonment by God, and
he even hints that he considered renouncing his ministry in order to regain
his freedom. However, much of the main body of the work, though ostensibly focused on his conversion, is equally suffused with this post-incarcerational
despair. When the account of Bunyan's imprisonment at the end of the work
is set alongside the lengthy central portion of *Grace Abounding*, which concerns the temptations he apparently endured during his conversion years
earlier, striking parallels emerge. The longest-lasting and most extreme of the
temptations that Bunyan claims his younger self underwent was a compulsion to "sell Christ for the things of this world." This is a temptation that he
does not mention in the autobiographical accounts he gives in the works that
predate *Grace Abounding*, and "selling Christ" is a temptation with an obvious potential relevance to his imprisonment, for he could have left jail at any
time if he had promised not to preach again.[9] In telling the story of his conversion, then, he appears to be looking back on his life and trying to reassure
himself that he really was saved—and that his imprisonment is thus not a
punishment but a test.

Establishing the truth of his salvation is not a purely personal matter for
Bunyan. The prefatory letter to *Grace Abounding* is addressed explicitly to the
members of his congregation, and implicitly to an even wider audience, quite
possibly including his judges, jailers, and political opponents; unlike the letters that he wrote to his congregation in the early 1660s recounting the details of his arrest and trial, *Grace Abounding* was intended for publication.[10]
As N. H. Keeble has noted, vindicating Bunyan as genuinely saved and genuinely called to the ministry is, in the context of the Restoration's violent
repression of nonconformity, an unmistakably public and political act.[11]
However, as Keeble and Sharon Achinstein have also commented, Bunyan
was a canny assessor of how overtly oppositional his works could be without
courting censorship or other punishment, and at this distance *Grace Abounding*'s political significance is easily overlooked.[12] Like the other confessions of
faith we have examined, Bunyan's emerges out of a context of religious controversy, but compared with the autobiographies of James, Donne, Milton,
and Browne, *Grace Abounding* seems relatively uninterested in the institutional church—even though its author is, like Milton, in conflict with it.

Bunyan clearly disagrees with the Church of England's theology, ecclesiology, and forms of worship, but in *Grace Abounding* he rarely even mentions those disagreements, and he tends not to define his own religiosity according to or in opposition to it.[13] The pressures that inform and help to shape Bunyan's autobiographies are always political, but they do not involve a negotiation between his private beliefs or personal history, on the one hand, and the demands of the institutional church, on the other. We shall see something similar with James II. Although both Bunyan and James II are cast as threats by the Church of England, neither one presents conformity as especially important, and neither one professes any desire to overturn the state church. In part, this is surely because the Church of England no longer had an exclusive claim on Britons' attention: during the Interregnum the institutional church was organized along Presbyterian lines, and the rise of sects such as the Ranters and the Quakers meant the fight over the nature of true belief had to be waged on more than one front. In such a climate, Bunyan's and James II's works manage the surprising feat of presenting their authors as loyal dissenters. What each man *really* believed may be another matter, but in his autobiographical self-presentations neither one aligns himself with or overtly opposes himself to the institutional church. In this respect, their works differ from the confessions of faith we have previously examined.

Early Autobiographies

Bunyan may well have composed an autobiographical narrative upon joining the Bedford congregation in the mid-1650s, but if so it is now lost. However, a number of his early works draw directly from Bunyan's personal religious experience; even his first publication, an anti-Quaker treatise entitled *Some Gospel Truths Opened,* contains an account (albeit in the second person) of the typical Christian's spiritual development, which seems to parallel much of Bunyan's own.[14] I shall look briefly at several of Bunyan's early works, both to note the ways and places in which Bunyan turns to autobiography and to compare the shifting emphases that he gives in different works to some of the same life events. The fact that Bunyan wrote multiple life narratives, at different points and for different purposes, allows us to track the ways his self-representation evolves under pressure.

Bunyan's fourth published work, *The Doctrine of the Law and Grace Unfolded*, is the first of Bunyan's works to use passages of explicit autobiography.

A response to the Quakers and the Ranters that runs to more than four hundred pages in the original quarto edition, the work seems to be using his autobiography in an exemplary fashion: to show his readers how Bunyan, too, was cast down by the severity of Mosaic law but finally came to believe in God's saving grace. These first autobiographical excursions, however, are as unexpected as they are brief. Just past the work's halfway mark, Bunyan interrupts a more general discussion of Christ's righteousness with the sudden declaration, "Sometimes I blesse the Lord my soul hath had the life that now I am speaking of"; goes on to describe a time "when I was under many condemnings of heart, and feared because of my sins my soul would misse of eternall glory"; and explains that he overcame this fear through God's grace by clinging to the sentence, *thy righteousness is in heaven*" (*MW* 2:147). This episode, which Bunyan also describes in *Grace Abounding*, may be intended as an instructional example, but he does not frame it in that way; rather, he seems to enter into this autobiographical moment almost by accident, his discussion of grace in the abstract triggering a reflection upon his own experiences.[15]

Several pages later, Bunyan again turns to autobiography, and this time he is more explicit about his reasons for doing so. In the midst of a description of the way a sinner is justified through grace, and the various effects that this has on his soul, Bunyan abruptly declares, "Now before I go any further, I must needs speak a word from my own experience of the things of Christ" (*MW* 2:156). The mistaken notions of the Ranters and the Quakers, he says, might dissuade people of the truth of the Gospels, but his own life illustrates that truth: "Therefore, for the further conviction of the *Reader*, I shall tell him (with *David*) something of what the Lord hath done for my soul" (*MW* 2:156). Bunyan's primary explanation for sharing his autobiography is that his personal experience will confirm the truth of his theological arguments. However, in insisting twice upon the rhetorical necessity of telling his story—and then adding that in doing so he is following the example of King David, who was believed to have poured out his heart in the psalms—Bunyan hedges his autobiography with more justifications than seem strictly necessary.

Although Bunyan tells his reader that it would be "too tedious" for him to recount the full story of his conversion, the account he gives is nevertheless substantial, amounting to several long paragraphs of text. "Reader," he begins,

> when it pleased the Lord to begin to instruct my soul, he found me one of the black sinners of the world; he found me making a sport of

oaths, and also of lies, and many a soul-poysoning meal did I make out of divers lusts, as drinking, dancing, playing, pleasure with the wicked ones of the world. The Lord finding of me in this condition, did open the glass of his Law unto me, wherein he shewed me so clearly my sins, both the greatnesse of them, and also how abominable they were in his sight, that I thought the very clouds were charged with the wrath of God, and ready to let fall the very fire of his jealousie upon me: yet for all this I was so wedded to my sins, that thought I with my self, I will have them, though I lose my soul. (*MW* 2:156–57)

Although this passage more or less parallels §§8–24 of *Grace Abounding*, the terms in which Bunyan describes both his early sinfulness and his first encounter with God are more general than the narrative he will supply in *Grace Abounding*.[16] This generalization may be the point: to provide a narrative that is more exemplary than personal, and that might simultaneously illustrate the truth of the rest of his work and resonate with the life experiences of many of his readers. Interestingly, Bunyan *does* provide some specifics about just how the Lord "open[ed] the glass of his Law" unto him—but he relegates these specifics to a side note. In the margin beside the text I have just quoted, he adds this rather lengthy explanation: "This conviction seized on my soul, one Sabbath day when I was at play . . . which when it came, though it scared me with its terrour, yet through the temptation of the devil immediately striking in therewith, I did rub it off again, and became as vile for some time as I was before; like a wretch that I was" (*MW* 2:157). In both the text and the margin Bunyan makes essentially the same point: he recognized his sinfulness but was unable or unwilling to change his ways. However, the account that he gives in the marginal note is more detailed than the account he gives in the text; we learn that this episode occurred on a Sunday and while he was "at play" (although we will have to wait until *Grace Abounding* to learn what kind of game he was playing). It is not clear why he divides the narrative like this, or why he repeats some of the same substance. However, by excluding autobiographical particulars from the main narrative, but providing them as a kind of marginal gloss, Bunyan's text creates the impression of a story that is larger than its context will permit it to be.

After this marginal note, Bunyan's autobiography continues in generalities: despite the blackness of his sins, God did not cast Bunyan away but gradually "won upon my heart, by giving of me some understanding . . . that there might be hopes of mercy . . . and thus the Lord won over my heart to some desire after the means" (*MW* 2:157). God gives him *some* understanding and *some* desire to learn about divine mercy, but Bunyan does not specify how or in what form these gifts occur; he is only slightly more specific about his temptations. These followed him very hard, he says, "especially such temptations as did tend to the making of me question the very way of salvation, *viz.* whether Jesus Christ was the Saviour or no" (*MW* 2:157).[17] These temptations lasted more than a year, during which time Bunyan says he had no certainty about his salvation until, at long last, "the Lord . . . did set me down so blessedly in the truth of the Doctrine of Jesus Christ, that it made me marvail, to see first, how Jesus Christ was Born of a Virgin, walked in the world a while with his Disciples, afterwards hanged on the Cross, spilt his Blood, was Buried, Rose again, Ascended above the Clouds and Heavens, there lives to make intercession; and that he also will come again at the last day to judge the World, and take his Saints unto himself" (*MW* 2:157–58). The creedal formulation of the things Bunyan "sees" might be intended for the instruction of his readers—as a way of reminding them of the core tenets of their faith and distinguishing it from that of the Quakers or the Ranters—but he expresses these impersonal articles of faith in strikingly immediate, personal terms, even to the point of implying that he "saw" Christ on earth. As we have seen in the works of James I and Browne, creedal statements frequently accompany autobiography as a way of tethering the particular religious experience of an individual to a larger, shared faith. Bunyan, however, is the only writer to render the historical element of his belief into the present tense, collapsing the distance between himself and the events of the Bible. (This is, of course, something he does more famously in *Grace Abounding,* in describing his engagement with biblical texts over the course of his conversion.)

Bunyan spends several more lines expanding on what exactly God showed him and then remarks, "Much of this, and such like dealings of [God's], could I tell thee of; but my business at this time is not so to do, but onely to tell what operation the blood of Christ hath had over, and upon my conscience" (*MW* 2:158). For all his insistence that what he is doing is intended only for the conviction of his reader, Bunyan continues for several more paragraphs to give vague examples of the "several times" and "several frames of spirit" in which Christ's sacrifice has soothed his soul, and he mentions in passing that several temptations have sometimes burdened his spirit—but, in an irritable aside that might remind us of James I's refusal to enumerate the "particular poynts" of his religion, Bunyan inserts a marginal note that reads, "I cannot stand here to tell thee of particular temptations" (*MW* 2:158–59).[18] One again, the text seems caught between competing impulses: to provide a more general, exemplary version of Bunyan's autobiography, and to tell a more personal and detailed one.

Law and Grace is the only one of Bunyan's religious tracts to contain such explicit and sustained passages of autobiography, but it remains cagey about specifics. While there are many possible reasons both for Bunyan's turn to autobiography in this particular work and for his reluctance to go into details, the part of his autobiography that is most notably absent from a work that attempts to refute the teachings of the Ranters is the fact that Bunyan himself was once deeply attracted to them.[19] Christopher Hill has suggested that Bunyan's vehement antagonism toward the Ranters in his pamphlets is the result of his having "so nearly been convinced by them."[20] While this overstates the tone of *Law and Grace* (which rarely even mentions the Ranters by name), Hill is right, I think, to point to Bunyan's own experiences with the Ranters as the unacknowledged motive behind his animosity toward their beliefs— and perhaps also the unacknowledged motive behind his strangely urgent but strangely nonspecific autobiography in *Law and Grace*. Bunyan is moved to share and to celebrate his own escape from those erroneous beliefs but reluctant to admit to their appeal by going into too many details.

The year after Bunyan published *Law and Grace*, England restored its monarchy. In 1660 Bunyan had been preaching for approximately four years and had already gained some significant regional fame, but with the return of the king came the reestablishment of the English Church and the reinstitution of the Book of Common Prayer. Regular attendance at Church of England services became compulsory, and nonconformity subject to legal punishment. As a preacher outside this system, Bunyan was regarded as operating without a license—and, not incidentally, as having abandoned his proper station and true calling as a tinker. In November 1660 he was arrested under an Elizabethan law prohibiting unlawful assemblies, and asked to desist under pain of banishment or even execution.[21] Although neither of these threats was ever carried out, they hung over Bunyan's head for years. Nevertheless, even when Bunyan feared that his life was in the balance, he refused to promise that, if freed, he would give up his ministry. As a result, he remained in prison for almost twelve straight years.[22]

Bunyan's only detailed account of his arrest and trial comes in the posthumously published *A Relation of the Imprisonment of Mr. John Bunyan*, which appears originally to have been a series of letters written to his congregation from prison.[23] Although the work was not published until the late eighteenth century, its five separate letters seem to have been written shortly after the events they depict (which range from late 1660 until early 1662), and they were clearly intended for a public audience—albeit a limited one. The Bunyan this work presents is a man unjustly persecuted, entirely unafraid, and much cleverer than his opponents. He repeatedly notes the opportunities that he had to evade arrest but that he declined to take, conscious that he had to be "[as] strong in deed, as I was in word" (*Relation* 106). He never falls into any of the traps laid by his persecutors, always gets the better of them when they come to trade Bible verses, and insists that he felt confident of God's approval at every stage of the process.

On a few occasions in these letters Bunyan does suggest some potentially persuasive reasons for a man in his position to submit to the authorities, but he raises those reasons only to reject them. In the third letter, which depicts events some twelve weeks into his imprisonment, he is visited by Mr. Cobb, Clerk of the Peace. Mr. Cobb appears to have been an acquaintance of Bunyan's, and the work casts him as a well-intentioned man with genuine sympathy for Bunyan's predicament. Addressing him as "Neighbour *Bunyan*," Cobb urges him to comply with the authorities and give over his preaching ministry, pointing out that Bunyan would still be able to "exhort [a] neighbour in private," and thus "do much good to the church of Christ" even without convening an assembly (*Relation* 120). Bunyan need not give up his faith, or even his evangelizing, Cobb implies, if he would just proselytize a bit more discreetly. But Bunyan is not swayed. If he may be permitted to exhort one neighbor, he says, why not two? And then why not four or eight? Cobb shakes his head but persists, finally voicing the consequences if Bunyan continues to resist: "You may do much good if you continue still in the land," Cobb says. "But alas, what benefit will it be to your friends, or what good can you do to them, if you should be sent away beyond the seas" (*Relation* 124)? Although Bunyan presents himself as standing firm even in the face of exile, the reasonableness of Cobb's claim that Bunyan could do more for God's church as a free man—even if not as a preacher—is never fully refuted.

An equally persuasive reason for submitting to the authorities is made, albeit more implicitly, in Bunyan's fourth letter, which describes how his young wife, at his request, repeatedly petitioned his judges to rehear his case.[24] His wife receives worse treatment than anything Bunyan claims to have received himself; she is roundly mocked and dismissed even when she mentions that she went into premature labor upon hearing of his "sentence of banishment or hanging" and lost the baby—and that in his absence she and her four stepchildren have been forced to rely on charity (*Relation* 125).[25] His descriptions of his family's plight are filled with pathos, and although he portrays his wife as brave and determined, she is also a pathetic and abused figure. Through her, he implies his own victimization as he will never do directly. Toward the end of the letter he quotes his wife as saying to his judges, "Because [Bunyan] is a Tinker, and a poor man[,] therefore he is despised, and cannot have justice" (*Relation* 128). Bunyan himself never suggests that he is treated badly, only unjustly. He does not refer to his physical comfort or discomfort, or any emotional difficulties, and though he paints his judges as condescending, he shows himself continually turning the tables on them and emerging victorious from every verbal battle. Only the argument made by Mr. Cobb and the pitiable plight of Bunyan's young wife and family even hint that a man in Bunyan's position *could* have had doubts, or worries, or any reason to act otherwise than Bunyan does.

Despite his self-portrait in *A Relation*, however, it is clear that Bunyan's first years in prison were often bleak. The passages from *Grace Abounding* with which I began this chapter indicate that Bunyan was distraught at the plight of his family and felt personally responsible for it; a few sections later in that work he speaks of having been in "a very sad and low condition" when he was "but a young Prisoner" (*GA* §333). He says that this depressive state lasted only "many weeks," but the evidence suggests otherwise; his most recent biographer, Richard Greaves, suggests that it lasted for nearly a year, and that depressive episodes probably recurred subsequently.[26] Usually a prolific writer, Bunyan published only one work during his first four years in prison—and all the works he published from prison in the years prior to *Grace Abounding* contain hints of a spiritual crisis. The earliest of these works, *I Will Pray with the Spirit*, was published in 1662, the same year as the Act of Uniformity that mandated the use of the Book of Common Prayer.[27] The work makes an impassioned case in favor of extemporaneous prayer, but near the end of the treatise there are two short autobiographical passages in which Bunyan discusses the difficulty of prayer and admits to experiencing long periods in which he found prayer nearly impossible and wondered whether God had abandoned him (*MW* 2:256–57).

After three years in which he published nothing at all, in 1665 Bunyan published three works, all containing passages that suggest a fixation on death and eternal judgment. *Christian Behaviour* concludes with a stern warning to his audience about the terrors of hell that await those who backslide, as well as three references to his own death, which he implies is imminent (*MW* 3:62). In *The Holy City* Bunyan depicts the Second Coming through an exposition of Revelation 21–22 ("And I saw a new heaven, and a new earth"), and he continues his focus on the end times in *The Resurrection of the Dead*.[28] Of the issues that the latter work covers, Bunyan gives particular attention to the Last Judgment. Among the damned, he says, the worst off will be those who were converted to the things of God and yet fell away, for their "own Vows and Promises shall be a Witness against [them]" (*MW* 3:282). All three works, then, have a significant focus on death and the judgment that awaits after death. Although the vagueness of the law under which Bunyan was sentenced originally led him to fear that he might be executed if he did not renounce his ministry, the threat of capital punishment seems to have disappeared long before 1665. His interest in the end times surely reflects the apocalyptic fervor of many nonconformists, who often sublimated their political opposition (and fears of their political powerlessness) in visions of God's coming vengeance.[29] However, it seems equally plausible that Bunyan's terrifying depictions of the punishments for backsliding in both *Christian Morals* and *Resurrection* are related to the depression and sense of divine rejection that he experienced in prison and seems to have blamed on his own spiritual failings.

Grace Abounding

Although Bunyan's first years in prison may have been stressful and full of doubt, the opening pages of *Grace Abounding* have the confident tone of Bunyan's letters to his congregation in *A Relation*. The work's prefatory letter addresses the members of that congregation explicitly and emphasizes Bunyan's pastoral role: since he has been "taken from [them] in presence," Bunyan, like Paul, must minister to them by epistle (Preface 1).[30] Toward that end, he is sending them his autobiography, which he describes as "a drop of that honey, that I have taken out of the Carcase of a *Lyon*" (Preface 1). This allusion to Judges 14 places him in the role of Samson—the savior of his people, who brought death and destruction down upon his opponents.[31] Bunyan does not linger on this particular comparison but proceeds to others that place him in equally exalted company while also helping to frame his decision to write and publish his autobiography. Like the Israelites, whom Moses commanded to remember their forty years in the wilderness; like David, who sang of the Lord's goodness and of his own transgressions; like Paul, who told even his judges and jailors about "the manner of his Conversion," so Bunyan remembers his own spiritual tribulations and magnifies the God who tested him and comforted him (Preface 2).

His autobiography should also, Bunyan says, serve as an aid to remind his readers of God's actions in their own lives. He urges his readers to "call to mind the former days, the years of ancient times; remember also your songs in the night, and commune with your own heart. . . . Remember also your tears and prayers to *God*; yea, how you sighed under every hedge for mercy. . . . Have you forgot the Close, the Milk-house, the Stable, the Barn, and the like, where *God* did visit your Soul? . . . If you are down in despair, if you think *God* fights against you, or if heaven is hid from your eyes; remember 'twas thus with your father, *but out of them all the Lord delivered me*" (Preface 3). As he did in *Law and Grace*, Bunyan is presenting his spiritual autobiography as exemplary, but this time its exemplarity has a larger political and religious significance. His autobiography is not simply an encouraging story, nor just a model for his readers to follow. Rather, as his comparisons with the Israelites, King David, and St. Paul suggest, Bunyan's autobiography and his readers' autobiographies should be understood as analogous to and subsumed by the story of the true church, which has erred and suffered and been persecuted from the beginning. In reading about Bunyan's past struggles and past deliverances, then, his congregants are encouraged to see his and their current personal and political struggles as part of a larger pattern—and one that ends, eventually, in victory.

Although Bunyan foregrounds the fact of his imprisonment in the letter to his readers, he spends no time on the story behind that imprisonment, which will get told only briefly in the separate section I have already quoted from.[32] As Keeble observes, this permits Bunyan to keep the focus on his conversion, and to "imply [the] inconsequentiality" of his trial and imprisonment, "their total inability to jeopardize or call in question the saving experience of grace."[33] But while I agree with Keeble that this is Bunyan's intention, I would argue that the division Bunyan attempts to impose between the two narratives is not wholly successful, and that the self-assured tone of *Grace Abounding*'s preface does not survive even a third of the way into the work proper.

In *Grace Abounding*'s early pages, however, the narrator of Bunyan's autobiography seems identical with the confident Bunyan of the work's preface. In these opening sections, the narrator seems to be an older man looking back on his younger years from a position of greater wisdom, and his autobiography casts a fond eye on his earlier life.[34] Unlike *Law and Grace*, which tended toward generalities, *Grace Abounding* seems to revel in the particular details of Bunyan's life experience. After a quick review of his parentage and a brief summary of his early years, Bunyan gives a greatly expanded description of the Sabbath-day game of "tipcat" during which he felt God's displeasure—a story that he told in more abbreviated fashion in *Law and Grace*.[35] In this version, just as Bunyan is about to strike the "cat," "a voice did suddenly dart from Heaven into my Soul, which said, *Wilt thou leave thy sins, and go to Heaven? or have thy sins, and go to Hell?* At this I was put to an exceeding maze; wherefore, leaving my Cat upon the ground, I looked up to Heaven, and was as if I had . . . seen the Lord Jesus looking down upon me, as being very hotly displeased with me" (*GA* §22). This voice and Bunyan's impression that he sees Jesus looking down from the clouds are not present in the version of the story that Bunyan gives in *Law and Grace*, which provides a far less vivid and immediate account of the episode.

There are many other such moments in the first fifty or sixty sections of *Grace Abounding*: arresting episodes or images, such as Bunyan's encounter with the loose and ungodly woman who shames Bunyan by describing him as *"the ungodliest Fellow for swearing that ever she heard in all her life,"* or his fear that the church steeple will topple upon him if he takes pleasure in bell-ringing, or his temptation to work a miracle by commanding the puddles in the road to become dry and the dry places to become the puddles (*GA* §§26, 34, 51). Such moments have often been regarded as merely charming local color, but Bunyan's own words in his prefatory letter suggest that he is asserting the significance of the homely particulars of his and his readers' lives— particulars in which the truth of God's word is illustrated and given meaning. These specific, almost tactile details with which Bunyan illustrates his spiritual development give the lie to such scholarship as claims that he is too preoccupied with his internal states to linger over the external details of his life;[36] clearly, such details are crucial to his narrative method and his desire for his story to produce an affective response in others.

And yet, shortly after the temptation of the puddles, *Grace Abounding* starts to change. As the work continues Bunyan will gradually leave behind both the confident persona of the prefatory letter and the richly detailed narrative of the work's opening sections. As he relates the temptations that he experienced in his search for assurances about his faith, the work slows down and starts to lose a clear sense of direction. Bunyan's descriptions of these temptations grow messily expansive, filled with vague details and following a

confusing chronology. As I suggested in the introduction to this chapter, I believe that as Bunyan begins to recount the temptations that he experienced in
his earlier life, he starts to relive and to overlay his more recent temptations—
those of his prison years—upon those of his youth. Just as the passages with
which I opened this chapter show him conflating his feelings in prison with
his feelings prior to his arrest, so in the middle section of *Grace Abounding*
Bunyan seems at times to be telling the story of his imprisonment rather than
that of his conversion.

Among the many early temptations that Bunyan briefly mentions—his
fear that the day of grace might already have passed; or that he was not one of
those called to salvation; or that the religion of the Jews or Muslims might be
as true as that of the Christians—were also, he tells his reader in a parenthetical aside, "many other which at this time I may not, nor dare not utter,
neither by word nor pen" (*GA* §§66, 72, 97, 99). This parenthetical revelation
that Bunyan is not sharing the full extent of his fears is reminiscent of the
similar statement that he makes in *Law and Grace,* where he announces in a
marginal note that he "cannot stand here to tell thee of particular temptations" (*MW* 2:159). However, unlike in his earlier work, where he quickly
changed the subject, in *Grace Abounding* he does not abandon the topic of his
temptations but instead continually circles back to them, dwelling on the
emotions they inspired—even while strangely omitting almost all sense of
the context of these temptations.

In Bunyan's telling, his temptations multiplied almost of themselves.
Their force and persistence were such that "I concluded that God had in very
wrath to my Soul given me up unto them," and while in their grip "I should
often find my mind suddenly put upon it, to curse and swear, or to speak
some grievous thing of *God,* or *Christ* his *Son,* and of the *Scriptures*" (*GA*
§§99, 100). The fact that Bunyan is tempted at all causes him to doubt God's
love for him, which in turn tempts him to blaspheme God, and *this* temptation then casts Bunyan into despair: "So that whether I did think that God
was, or again did think there were no such thing; no love, nor peace, nor
gracious disposition could I feel within me" (*GA* §101). Bunyan's phrasing,
here as elsewhere, seems deliberately roundabout, but what he seems to be
saying is that despair over his temptations eventually led him to doubt God's
very existence. Bunyan does not specify just which temptations provoked
such a vicious cycle—they may be those he described earlier or they may be
the ones he claims he cannot name—and neither does he indicate whether
he is describing a single episode or a pattern of events that accompanied

numerous different temptations. As he continues his account, however, correspondences emerge between this portion of *Grace Abounding*, which ostensibly describes the temptations that beset him in the early years of his conversion, and the final section of *Grace Abounding* in which he discusses the despair he endured when first imprisoned.

A fuller summary of this final portion of the work may be useful. After the main narrative of *Grace Abounding*, which ends with Bunyan's apparent victory over his many temptations, there are two separate sections, the first devoted to his calling to the ministry (which I discuss later in this chapter) and the second devoted to his arrest and imprisonment. Bunyan begins the latter with a very quick summary of his arrest and indictment, followed by several lengthy expressions of thanksgiving to God for the great blessings Bunyan received while in prison: "I never had in all my life so great an inlet into the Word of God as now"; "I never knew what it was for God to stand by me at all times . . . as I have found him since I came thither"; "I have been able to laugh at destruction" (*GA* §§321, 323, 322). Bunyan then says that even before he was arrested, he "saw what was a coming" and was perfectly well prepared for what he had to do (*GA* §§324–26). However, a moment after establishing this stoicism, he bursts forth with the deeply emotional description of his agony at parting from his wife and children and his ongoing fears for their well-being that I quoted earlier.

What helped Bunyan through this agony was the fear that, if he were to forsake God out of concern for himself or his family, he would "falsifie [his] profession" (*GA* §§329–30). He adds that the passage of the Bible "where Christ prays against *Judas*" for "sell[ing] his Master" further strengthened his resolve, as did envisioning "the torments of Hell, which I was sure they must partake of, that for fear of the Cross do shrink from their profession of Christ" (*GA* §§330–31).[37] Once again, Bunyan's confident tone does not last long, and a moment later he abruptly begins to recount another period of woe: the "sad and low condition" that afflicted him when he was "but a young Prisoner" and Satan beset him with the fear that, if he were to die, he would not reach heaven (*GA* §333). Bunyan says that he tried to pray, but he received no answer from God. Finally, although God was still hiding his face from him, Bunyan decided that while the deity "might chuse whether he would give me comfort now, or at the hour of death . . . I might not therefore chuse whether I would hold my profession or no: I was bound, but he was free: yea, it was my dutie to stand to his Word, whether he would ever look upon me or no, or save me at the last" (*GA* §337). Upon making this resolution, Bunyan says, he was immediately filled with comfort and the conviction that God was with him—and upon this note, he ends *Grace Abounding*.

With this final section of the work in mind, let us return to the account that Bunyan gives of the temptations that occurred during his conversion. He has told his readers that his (unspecified) temptations caused him to doubt God's presence, and he adds that he also believed "that such things [i.e., such temptations] could not possibly be found amongst them that loved God. I often, when these temptations have been with force upon me, did compare my self in the case of such a Child, whom some Gypsie hath by force took up under her apron, and is carrying from Friend and Country. . . . I thought also of *Saul,* and of the evil spirit that did possess him; and did greatly fear that my condition was the same with that of his, 1 Sam. 16.14" (*GA* §102). Although many scholars have focused on the first part of this passage, noting the way that Bunyan distances himself from his doubts by externalizing his temptations—like a gypsy, they seize him unwilling and almost unaware—Bunyan's reference to Saul is more revealing. The verse from 1 Samuel that Bunyan cites describes the spirit of the Lord leaving Saul, who is then immediately afflicted with a "distressing spirit." This distressing spirit, which visits Saul several times in the course of 1 Samuel, was long understood by readers of the Bible as a description of depressive mental illness, but Saul would have represented more to Bunyan than simply a fellow melancholic.[38] Saul was the first king of the Israelites, and a leader chosen by the people themselves; although he was crowned by the prophet Samuel with God's apparent approval, after a few years he unexpectedly loses God's favor.[39] Despite Saul's attempts at propitiation, God withdraws, hiding himself from Saul and remaining silent before his prayers. From then on Saul is adrift, and while God speaks to others—even going so far as to secretly appoint David as Saul's successor—he never again shows his face to Saul.

Although this is the only time that Bunyan mentions Saul by name, the account he gives of his period of despair after his arrest uses terms that seem very near to Saul's experience. "At that time," Bunyan writes in the final part of *Grace Abounding*, "all the things of God were hid from my soul" (*GA* §333). Three sentences later, he says, "I prayed to God that he would comfort me, and give me strength to do and suffer what he should call me to; yet no comfort appeared, but all continued hid" (*GA* §335). And in the following section, he says again, "But yet all the things of God were kept out of my sight" (*GA* §336). Reading these episodes side by side illuminates both: the echo of Saul's rejection in Bunyan's own feelings of abandonment after his indictment suggests that Bunyan—who, like Saul, was a leader who had been chosen by the people—may well have feared that his arrest was a sign from God that he was unsuitable for a position within the Bedford church, and that, perhaps, he had never been saved to begin with. Likewise, placing the conclusion of *Grace Abounding* alongside Bunyan's extraordinarily vague descriptions of the temptations he experienced in his youth illustrates their shared elements: in both cases, Bunyan's fear that he is abandoned by God is succeeded by a temptation to blaspheme, which is succeeded by a fear that he might not be among the saved. While it is possible that Bunyan, all his life, experienced temptation in a more or less identical fashion, it is at least as likely that, as he writes from prison about his conversion, his more recent experience is coloring that earlier one.

Such a reading grows more probable as Bunyan introduces *Grace Abounding*'s central temptation, which he does immediately after comparing himself to Saul. This temptation, to commit the sin against the Holy Ghost, will eventually come to occupy more than a third of Bunyan's entire work. Although the sin is named but not described in the three Synoptic Gospels, Bunyan and his contemporaries understood it to be the willful rejection of Christ after having first accepted the truth of Christianity.[40] According to *Grace Abounding*, from the moment Bunyan first heard about this sin, he was intrigued. In fact, he says, every time someone referred to it, "the Tempter [would] so provoke me to desire to sin that sin, that I was as if I could not, must not, neither should be quiet until I had committed that. . . . If it were to be committed by speaking of such a word, then I have been as if my mouth would have spoken that word whether I would or no" (*GA* §103). In its first incarnation, this temptation seems born of simple perversity, for as far as a reader can tell, Bunyan's obsessive fascination appears to have less to do with this sin's particular content than with the simple fact that it is forbidden.

In this form, the temptation afflicted Bunyan for approximately a year, during which time he hints that he may even have been suicidal (*GA* §111). Although the temptation lifts eventually, Bunyan does not explain exactly how or when. He mentions the occasional reassurances he received from God and the comfort he found in the guidance of John Gifford, the pastor of the Bedford congregation, but none of these descriptions is particularly detailed or concrete, until Bunyan suddenly announces, "Now had I an evidence, as I thought, of my salvation from Heaven, with many golden Seals thereon" (*GA* §128). He does not tell his reader when this happened, or where, or what events immediately provoked it, and neither does his reassurance last for very long. While many commentators have regarded this episode as the moment at which Bunyan became assured of his election (a moment analogous to the point in *Pilgrim's Progress* when Christian's burden falls from his back and he receives a "roll with a seal upon it"),[41] only one sentence after God gave Bunyan this assurance of his salvation, the Tempter returns "with a more grievous and dreadful temptation then before"—that of selling Christ "for the things of this life" (*GA* §132–33).

Although Bunyan implies that this is a new temptation, he will soon describe it, too, as that of committing the sin against the Holy Ghost. Once again his temptation lasted, he says, for a year, and once again he is frustratingly vague in his descriptions of the nature of that temptation: "I could neither eat my food, stoop for a pin, chop a stick, or cast mine eye to look on this or that, but still the temptation would come, *Sell Christ for this, or sell Christ for that; sell him, sell him*" (*GA* §135). While the frantic and obsessive quality of his temptation is quite clear, it is less clear what prompts this compulsion—or what selling Christ for a pin would actually have entailed for Bunyan.[42] Finally, one morning as he lay in bed, Bunyan was again assailed by this temptation, hearing in his mind the repeated phrase "sell him, sell him," until "at last, after much striving, even until I was almost out of breath, I felt this thought pass through my heart, *Let him go if he will!* And I thought also that I felt my heart freely consent" (*GA* §139). With this, Bunyan became convinced that he had sold Christ, and he soon came to fear that doing so was the sin against the Holy Ghost.[43] The next seventy or so sections, which he claims cover an additional two years, show the younger Bunyan attempting to find reassurance that he had not, in fact, committed the unpardonable sin—but more often than not being left in despair.

Interestingly, although Bunyan refers to the sin against the Holy Ghost in *Law and Grace* and other early tracts, he never formulates this sin as "selling Christ" until *Grace Abounding*. This language of selling one's savior *is* present, however, in the final section of *Grace Abounding*, where, as I have noted, the imprisoned Bunyan frets about the consequences of "falsifying" his profession and "den[ying] the way of God," and imagines in vivid colors the torments of hell that await those who, like Judas, "do shrink from their profession of Christ" (*GA* §330, 331).[44] In recounting the temptation that he experienced as a young man, Bunyan likewise compares his deed to Judas's selling Christ for thirty pieces of silver, as well as to Esau's selling his birthright for a mess of pottage (*GA* §§154, 141). After much agonizing the younger Bunyan concluded that his sin was not quite as bad as Judas's—for while

"*Judas* did his intentionally . . . mine was against my prayer and strivings" (*GA* §158)—but the figure of Esau is not so quickly banished, and will continue to haunt Bunyan until nearly the conclusion of his work.[45]

In the depths of his despair over having (as he thinks) sold Christ, the young Bunyan found it hard to pray, believing that "Prayer was not for any in my case, [and] neither could it do me good." The Tempter encouraged him in this belief, whispering in his ear, "God . . . hath been weary of you for these several years already, because you are none of his; your bauling in his ears hath been no pleasant voice to him; and therefore he let you sin this sin, that you might be quite cut off" (*GA* §§176–77). Bunyan seems to be afraid that, if he is not another Judas, then perhaps he is another Saul. This episode, likewise, seems to correspond with the passage at the end of *Grace Abounding* where Bunyan describes God's silence in the face of the imprisoned Bunyan's prayers and Satan's taunts about his uncertain salvationary status (*GA* §§333–36).

A further suggestion that Bunyan may actually be fretting about much more recent sins as he purports to describe those of his youth comes in the very next section. Explaining why he was tempted to believe Satan's tauntings, Bunyan says, "As 'tis said in another place, *Exod.* 21.14, *The man that sins presumptuously, shall be taken from Gods Altar, that he may die*: even as *Joab* was by King *Solomon,* when he thought to find shelter there, 1 Kings 2.28, &c." (*GA* §178).[46] Coming from a man who has, in fact, been dragged away from God's altar, this passage is almost impossible to read without reference to Bunyan's arrest and imprisonment. If so, the question is just what sin the elder Bunyan thinks he has done to have brought about his misfortune. His reference to "the man that sins presumptuously" being taken from God's altar might suggest that Bunyan fears that something he did *prior* to his arrest angered God, and his imprisonment (and consequent removal from the ministry) is his punishment for it. At the same time, Bunyan's lengthy treatment of his fear that he "sold" Christ might instead suggest that he is afraid either that he will in the future falsify his profession or somehow has already falsified it, thus failing a test that God set for him.

We know that Bunyan did not in fact renounce his calling as a preacher, and his eventual twelve years in prison are a powerful testimony to his fidelity to his beliefs. It is possible, however, that something akin to the scene Bunyan describes his younger self enduring instead occurred (or occurred again) during his arrest or imprisonment: he may have had a passing moment of doubt in which he said to himself, about his service to God, something equivalent to "Let him go if he will," which he later feared amounted to selling

Christ as surely as if he had actively worked to secure his release from prison. For Bunyan, even *contemplating* striking a bargain with the authorities might have been enough to convince him that he was among the reprobate. Alternately, he may simply have feared that he might not be strong enough to endure whatever might come to pass after his arrest, and so in recalling an episode from his more distant past he freights it with many of the anxieties and doubts of his recent past.

Although the passages from Exodus and 1 Kings about removing the wicked from God's altars apparently tormented Bunyan, "yet," he says, "my case being desperate, I thought with myself, I can but die; and if it must be so, it shall once be said, That such a one died at the foot of Christ in Prayer" (*GA* §178). This decision of Bunyan's is almost identical to the one he makes at the end of *Grace Abounding*. There, Bunyan says that, despite his doubts as to whether he was saved or not, or whether God would ever speak to him again, he would "ventur[e] my eternal state with Christ, whether I have comfort here or no . . . I will leap off the Ladder even blindfold into Eternitie, sink or swim, come heaven, come hell; Lord Jesus, if thou wilt catch me, do; if not, I will venture for thy Name" (*GA* §337). In both situations Bunyan resolves, in a kind of Pascal's wager, to die for Christ even if he is not completely sure that God exists or that he has chosen Bunyan for salvation.

The version of the story that Bunyan tells at the end of *Grace Abounding* concludes with the imprisoned Bunyan immediately receiving assurances from God upon his declaration that he would "venture for [Christ's] name." However, in the version that comes in the middle of the work, even after his decision to stick with Christ the younger Bunyan remained sunk in despair and virtually unable to pray. And while he says that he "desire[d] the Prayers of the people of God for me . . . I feared that God would give them no heart to do it; yea I trembled in my Soul to think that some or other of them shortly would tell me, that God had said those words to them . . . . *pray not for him, for I have rejected him*: Yea, I thought that he had whispered this to some of them already, onely they durst not tell me so, neither durst I ask them of it, for fear [that] it should be so" (*GA* §179). Once again, a reader might wonder whether Bunyan is describing events ten years in the past or whether these words could not equally well describe his situation following his arrest. Given that he does not admit to any feelings of despair in the letters to his congregation that make up the *Relation*, and that he limits and circumscribes such admissions in *Grace Abounding*, it seems reasonable to suppose that he is reluctant to confess to any spiritual dryness, in the period after his arrest, out of concern for what his readers and congregants might think. Even worse than doubting one's own election or vocation would be having those doubts shared by others.

This is not to suggest, of course, that the younger Bunyan did not have the above experience—or any of the others that I have been reading through the lens of his time in prison. Quite simply, we do not know. But the passages I have highlighted from the middle of *Grace Abounding* have strong parallels with his period of despair in prison, as Bunyan recounts that period at the end of the work, and it seems likely that at least some of them were, in their particulars, influenced or shaded by his memories of his more recent period of despair. Moreover, reading the central portion of *Grace Abounding* as at least partly a meditation on his imprisonment (whether Bunyan himself sees it that way or not) provides a more satisfying explanation for the dramatic stylistic and tonal shifts that take place a third of the way through the work, when the controlled narrative voice and detailed, concrete imagery of the opening sections give way to the fevered emotional psychodrama of his temptations.

Still afraid that he has sold Christ, the younger Bunyan continued in a state of near-despair for a long while. Eventually two biblical texts battle it out in his heart: Hebrews 10–12, describing Esau's sin as the sin against the Holy Ghost, and 2 Corinthians 12:9: *"My grace is sufficient for thee"* (*GA* §§204–6). The passage about grace triumphs, and from then on, Bunyan begins frequently to get the better of Satan in their disputes. Finally, he has a vision while passing through a field: he sees Christ at God's right hand and hears the words, *"Thy righteousness is in Heaven,"* and he realizes that Christ alone is his righteousness (*GA* §229). "Now did my chains fall off my Legs indeed, I was loosed from my affliction and irons, my temptations also fled away: so that from that time those dreadful Scriptures of God left off to trouble me" (*GA* §230). This vision may be the same one Bunyan describes more elaborately, almost in the form of a creed, in *Law and Grace*.[47] The metaphorical description of the chains and irons falling off him was not present in that earlier vision, however, and it seems likely that it is indebted in some fashion to his stay in prison—if only to make the point that although he still languishes in jail, his soul is free.

After Bunyan concludes the story of his great temptation, only some thirty sections of the main narrative remain. He describes his rapture at realizing his share in Christ's redemption and the comfort that followed for "about a twelve-month" (*GA* §236), and he asserts that the temptation to sell Christ strengthened his soul, just as he will later say that his imprisonment was as much an occasion for grace as for torment (*GA* §§244–47, 320–23). In both cases, however, he almost immediately goes on to talk about his *other* fears and temptations. Thus, although the main narrative of *Grace Abounding* concludes with his liberation from one of his more minor temptations, it is an open question for just how long this happy state endured.

The last two parts of Bunyan's autobiography, *A brief Account of the Author's Call to the Work of the Ministry* and *A brief Account of the Authors Imprisonment*, are placed under separate headings and can seem like lame addendums to the work's central narrative. However, as I have shown in my discussion of the second of these, they are actually crucial to an interpretation of *Grace Abounding*. These two final narratives, along with the preface to the reader, serve to frame the account of Bunyan's youthful temptations, making clearer the work's context and pressures. *Grace Abounding*'s project may be to show that Bunyan's conversion is genuine, and thus make a case for his particular experience of God and calling to the ministry. However, while in these concluding portions of his text Bunyan resumes the more straightforward narrative style of *Grace Abounding*'s opening sections, they too reveal tensions between what seem to be two conflicting autobiographical impulses.

In the first of these two final parts Bunyan describes his calling, disavows any personal ambition, and casts himself as a surprised and reluctant preacher: it was not Bunyan but "some of the most able among the Saints" who recognized the gift that God had given him and urged him to address the Bedford congregation (*GA* §265). The experience of public speaking "at the first . . . did much dash and abash" his spirit, but others found his preaching moving, and gradually they persuaded him to believe in his gifts. But while Bunyan asserts the authenticity of his calling and insists that he did not seek it for vainglorious reasons, he admits that in his preaching he *has* "been often tempted to pride and liftings up of heart." He immediately qualifies this statement, saying that "for the most part I have had but small joy to give way to such a thing [pride]: for it hath been my every-days portion to be let into the evil of my own heart . . . [which] hath caused hanging down of the head under all my Gifts and Attainments" (*GA* §296). The telling phrase, "for the most part," with which Bunyan amends his assertion that he is not inclined to pride is one he repeats a moment later: the reflection, he says, that without God all his talents left him as nothing more than a sounding brass or a tinkling cymbal "was *for the most part* as a maul on the head of pride and desire of vain-glory" (*GA* §300, emphasis added). His preoccupation with the problem

of pride and the proper attitude toward the gifts that God has given continues through the end of his account of his call to the ministry: "So I concluded, a little Grace, a little Love, a little of the true Fear of God, is better
then all these Gifts [i.e., of preaching]: Yea, and I am fully convinced of it,
that it is possible for a Soul that can scarce give a man an answer, but with
great confusion as to method, I say it is possible for them to have a thousand
times more Grace . . . then some who by vertue of the Gift of Knowledge,
can deliver themselves like Angels" (*GA* §300).[48] Bunyan's reiteration of this
point—"So I concluded"; "yea, and I am fully convinced"; "I say it is possible"—
suggests someone who is not entirely convinced that the things he claims are
true, or that he has avoided pride as much as he ought to have.

If we are reading *Grace Abounding*, as we have read other confessions of
faith, as produced by the tension between the desire to speak the truth of
one's religious experience and the limited ways available to speak it in a given
historical, political, and religious moment, we might say that Bunyan's apparent interest in exploring his own fears, doubts, and temptations—here, as
in the rest of the work—is in conflict with what seems to be *Grace Abounding*'s central purpose: to vindicate Bunyan as a truly saved, truly called, preacher
of the Gospel. Bunyan's own autobiographical desires and impulses appear to
align only imperfectly with the political goals of *Grace Abounding*.

*   *   *

Bunyan wrote no explicit autobiographies after *Grace Abounding*, and although
his works continued to draw upon his life narrative (and especially the story
of his conversion), after 1666 that material is mostly fodder for his fiction.[49]
Bunyan did revise *Grace Abounding* several times, but those changes, unlike
Browne's revisions to *Religio Medici,* do not notably alter the original work.[50]
Many scholars have argued for a close relationship between *Grace Abounding*
and *Pilgrim's Progress*, but while a number of episodes in the latter do indeed
have an identifiable analogue in Bunyan's spiritual autobiography, there are
also significant differences; if anything, *Pilgrim's Progress* seems to offer a corrected version of Bunyan's conversion experience, one that edits out the more
messy and complicating details. For example, when Christian leaves his wife
and children behind, it is because he is compelled to do so: they are unbeliev-
ers, and will not flee the City of Destruction with him. Bunyan still depicts
this decision as a difficult one—Christian runs from his family with his fingers in his ears in order to drown out their cries—but it is not complicated by

their innocence, or by reminders of their helplessness, in the way of Bunyan's decision to submit to his imprisonment. Similarly, once Christian receives his "roll with a seal upon it," neither he nor Bunyan's readers are left in much doubt that he is among the elect, even though he certainly still has moments of weakness and even despair. By contrast, Bunyan's receipt of "evidence . . . from Heaven, with many golden Seals thereon," is far less decisive, arriving abruptly and without explanation and being immediately followed by Bunyan's fiercest and longest-lasting temptation.

Although it is not the project of this book to examine the autobiographical bases or possible inspirations of works of fiction, one might read *Pilgrim's Progress* as being, unlike *Grace Abounding*, a truly retrospective reading of Bunyan's conversion: narrated from a place of confidence and assuming the clear, teleological shape that his actual autobiography so often seems to lack. Perhaps, after 1666, Bunyan had no further need to mine his life story for proof (either for himself or for an audience) of his own election and vocation. In other words, Bunyan went from writing confessions of faith to writing autobiographies.

CHAPTER 6

James II and the End of the Confession
of Faith

Bunyan's age represents a transitional moment for the confession of faith. By the last decades of the seventeenth century the religious, political, and generic pressures that had served to fuse controversial literature with autobiography seem to have abated. Although religious conflict was far from a thing of the past, its political and professional stakes were different; the relationship between an individual Christian and the institutional church had changed dramatically between the accession of James I and the Restoration. As we have seen, the confessions of faith of James and Donne are intent on proving their authors' allegiance to the state church, and the vigorousness of that determination has as much to do with their political moment as with each man's personal or family history; concerns about the stability of the Elizabethan Settlement, especially in the wake of the Hampton Court Conference and the Gunpowder Plot, brought questions of conformity to the fore. A generation or so later, Milton and Browne and their compatriots had a different relationship to the institutional church. In the midst of the Civil War the option of identifying oneself in opposition to the Church of England was greater (if still fraught with its own perils and pressures), but so too was the option of identifying with the church only partially and conditionally, as Browne does. Nevertheless, in the 1640s one's position relative to the institutional church remained a central and defining fact of most English Christians' religious identities.[1]

After the restoration of the monarchy, the English Church, though also restored and initially quite repressive of nonconformity, seems to have had a less complete imaginative hold over English Christians. Bunyan's *Grace*

Abounding does depict Bunyan's religiosity and especially his calling to the ministry in implicit contrast with the Church of England, but the work focuses on a private, personal experience of God, the validity of which is not compromised by the existence or even the institutional dominance of the Church of England. Similarly, the snippets of religious autobiography that appear in James II's political writings also seem strikingly unconcerned about the authority of the institutional church or with what James's worshipping outside it might mean.

Even more than his grandfather, James II foregrounds his religious identity in his speeches and other prose, and he has an even more urgent reason for doing so: James II was a Catholic convert whose conversion was not only public knowledge but the primary objection to his succession during the Exclusion Crisis of 1678; his Catholicism also appears to have been the basis for the limited support that his nephew, the Duke of Monmouth (Charles II's illegitimate son), later received during his attempted rebellion of 1686. But whereas James I seems to have felt great pressure to declare the alignment of his faith with that of his subjects, his grandson apparently felt no such need; James II does not use his autobiographical statements to explain or moderate his Catholicism or to render it less threatening to his subjects (for example, by declaring himself free from superstition or independent of the pope). James II's blithe indifference to the claims made upon him by the state church may be partly due to his sense of monarchal prerogative, but James I was also an absolutist, and he responded quite differently to the contrast between his private history and his public role as head of the English Church. Although the autobiographical passages of the second King James are occasioned by political necessity as much as the autobiographies of the other writers examined in this book, his are written in a different religious and political climate, and they manifest none of the rhetorical signs of conflict or anxiety that we have seen elsewhere in this book. Indeed, James II's autobiographies probably do not deserve to be called confessions of faith at all.

James II's first speech to the Privy Council after his succession addresses fears about his Catholicism and rumors that he is "a Man for Arbitrary Power."[2] This speech, which was published in the official newspaper and read in every town and village throughout the kingdom, assures James's subjects that he will "preserve the Government, both in Church and State, as it is by Law Established" and emphasizes the reciprocal obligations of monarch and subjects: James will support and defend the Church of England because "the Principles of the Church of England are for Monarchy, and . . . the Members

of it hath shewn themselves good and Loyal Subjects" (*Royal Tracts* Br–Bv).
So long as the church and its members acknowledge James's legitimacy, he
will acknowledge *its* legitimacy.

Surprisingly, given the debates surrounding royal succession and religious identity in the sixteenth and earlier seventeenth centuries, James's subjects initially seem to have accepted this compromise. Despite the general
suspicion directed at Catholics in early modern England, most historians today believe that the majority of James's subjects were relieved by his succession and greatly heartened by his speech to the Privy Council and the other
similar declarations he made in the first months of his reign.[3] The smooth
transfer of power and the continuation of the Stuart dynasty surely explain
most of this relief, but James's subjects apparently accepted his argument that
a Catholic monarch could be king of a Protestant nation—so long as he up-
held its institutions and the rule of law. As James's reign continued, more of
his subjects would come to doubt the depth of his support for the Church of
England, and they may have had good reason to do so. All the same, the fact
that James could make the argument that his religious identity was separable
from his public role, and that the majority of his subjects were willing to
accept this argument (at least initially and at least in principle), marks a
dramatic change in the popular conception of religious identity: no longer was
religious affiliation seen as *necessarily* related to loyalty, much less to Englishness
itself.

This is not to say that Britons suddenly came to believe that religion was
a purely private affair, for they did not, and few indeed would have argued
that the Protestant and Catholic Churches made equivalent truth claims or
were equally viable routes to salvation. James's own conversion had been the
result of his persuasion that the Catholic Church was the *only* source of religious authority, and even after his succession he made no secret of his wish
that all his subjects were likewise persuaded. In 1686 he published two papers
allegedly in Charles II's hand proving his brother's deathbed conversion to
Catholicism and expressing Charles's belief that the Church of Rome was the
only true church on earth.[4] And although James expressed his commitment
to freedom of religion through the 1687 Declaration of Indulgence, which
suspended the legal penalties against Protestant dissenters as well as Catholics, he admitted that he "heartily wish[ed] . . . all the People of Our Domin-
ions were Members of the Catholick Church" (*Royal Tracts* C3r). Nevertheless,
while average Britons may still have seen their choice of religion as deciding
their fate for all eternity, there seems to have been an emerging consensus not

only that "an exact Conformity in Religion" among all the island's inhabitants was not possible but also that legal or legislative attempts to produce such conformity were destructive to the nation's social and economic health (*Royal Tracts* C3v).

This change in attitude had implications for the confession of faith. James II is the first writer we have seen who admits to any contradiction between his religious identity and his public role while seeming entirely unfussed by this contradiction. Whereas the other confessions of faith that we have examined are full of qualifications, explanations, or attempts to hedge or finesse inconvenient facts, James's autobiographical moments reveal no such tensions. In his speeches and other public addresses, James freely declares his Catholicism, but he says little about his conversion, his beliefs, or the nature of his religiosity. After his abdication and exile, James produced some fragmentary life narratives that focus on his religious experience, but even these tend to be generic and unrevelatory. James's 1692 collection of devotional meditations are keyed to the major events in his political life, but as prose hymns of sorrow or thanksgiving they use language inspired by the psalms and might have been written by any Christian.[5] The memoirs left unpublished at James's death are more personal and detailed, and do include some account of his conversion—but although they involve plenty of personal and political score settling, they are also relatively unforthcoming about James's religiosity.[6]

Unlike his grandfather, James I, James II apparently did not find autobiography useful as either a rhetorical strategy or a forensic device. The unanxious and undefensive nature of the second King James's religious autobiography cannot be chalked up simply to a difference in personality. It is certainly possible that James was a notably self-confident or unreflective individual—but to argue that these or any other personality traits are responsible for the fact that his published autobiographies are not particularly revealing and do not manifest much religious or political anxiety misses the point. The confession of faith is not the product of a particular temperament, although personality does affect the form and style of each individual confession of faith. Rather, the confession of faith is the result of a particular cultural moment in which religious identity could not easily be walled off from one's public role, and in which both the terms and the literary genres available for exploring that identity were sharply limited.

James II may have misrepresented his support for the Church of England or the role that his own religious identity played in his religious policies; he

may even have intended, as the old Whig interpretation has it, to use the
Declaration of Indulgence as a Trojan horse through which to smuggle in increasingly pro-Catholic policies and eventually return England to the Church
of Rome.[7] But any disingenuousness on James's part is not apparent in his
autobiographical writings, which deal with his religious identity in a strikingly minimal way, especially when compared with the works of James I.
Neither would such disingenuousness change the fact that both James II and
his subjects spoke, at least for a time, as if his religious identity could be di-
vorced from his religious policies and his actions on the public stage. And
although James's particular vision of religious toleration was not to be, the
Revolution of 1688 led to the Toleration Act of 1689—which, by permitting
worship outside the Church of England, officially separated church from
state and ensured that religious policy was no longer a matter of royal prerogative.[8]

The confession of faith as I have defined it throughout this book therefore does not survive the seventeenth century. Bunyan's *Grace Abounding* is
still recognizable as a confession of faith, but it is a step closer to the autobiographies of the eighteenth and nineteenth (and indeed the twentieth and
twenty-first) centuries. Unlike the confessions of faith of James I, Donne,
Milton, and Browne, *Grace Abounding* is a book-length life narrative, and
one that devotes at least as much time to charting its subject's internal development as to recounting the external events of his life. The writing and publication of Bunyan's autobiography are occasioned and shaped by the political
crises of the Restoration and his own arrest and imprisonment, but Bunyan's
interest in exploring and reflecting on the story of his conversion goes beyond
anything we have seen in the works of the other writers considered in this
book. Bunyan's autobiography may at times be as narratively incoherent as
those of James I, Donne, Milton, and Browne, but his autobiography, unlike
theirs, shapes and frames his work's political content, not vice versa. By Bunyan's day, the events of an ordinary man's life were coming to be seen as inherently interesting, and autobiography as its own justification.

But while the confession of faith may be a historically contingent form
and only one of many genres in which autobiography has operated throughout the centuries, it can nevertheless help us to broaden both *what* we consider autobiography and *how* we consider it. In recent decades, autobiography
studies has rejected the idea that "an autobiography" necessarily involves a
coherent, overarching narrative that depicts an autonomous self. An increas-
ing number of scholars—especially those who work on the life-writing of

women and minorities—have argued for the importance of reading individual self-depictions in the context of group identity: as the author's attempt to live up to (or live down) community expectations or stereotypes.[9] The confession of faith, which so clearly shows the tensions between collective identity and individual experience, has much to contribute to such discussions. These works of seventeenth-century religious prose may also prove unexpectedly useful in the age of the Internet, when virtually everyone has a webpage—if not also a blog, a Facebook account, and a Twitter feed—and when hardly a week seems to go by without a piece of opinion journalism weighing in on the performative or downright deceptive nature of identity construction on the Web. The confession of faith helps to highlight the simultaneous control and lack of control that characterize any autobiographical endeavor, reminding us that every self-representation is circumscribed by outside pressures, the author's self-knowledge or lack of self-knowledge, and her ability to manipulate her form. The confession of faith should remind us, too, that none of us can ever live up to all the expectations or reflect well on all the groups of which we are a part—and none of us, ultimately, can determine how we will be read.

NOTES

INTRODUCTION

1. See *Reason of Church-Government* and *An Apology Against a Pamphlet* (both 1642) in *Complete Prose Works of John Milton,* vol. 1, ed. Don M. Wolfe (New Haven: Yale University Press, 1953).

2. Two of Milton's other tracts contain explicit autobiography: *Second Defence of the English People* (1654) and *Defence of Himself* (1655). For a fuller discussion of all four tracts, see Chapter 3.

3. For detailed considerations of the way these two works employ autobiography, see Chapters 2 and 4, respectively.

4. Jesse Lander, *Inventing Polemic: Religion, Print, and Literary Culture in Early Modern England* (Cambridge: Cambridge University Press, 2006). See also the discussion of the literary legacy of religious polemic in Joseph L. Black's introductory essay in Black, ed., *The Martin Marprelate Tracts: A Modernized and Annotated Edition* (Cambridge: Cambridge University Press, 2008), esp. xxv–xxxiv, lxxiv–xciv.

5. See, for example, Irenaeus's preface to Book 1 of *Against Heresies* (text available online through the Gnostic Society Library, www.gnosis.org/library/advh1.htm) or Book 26 of Epiphanius's *Panarion* (Frank Williams, trans., *The* Panarion *of Epiphanius of Salamis* [Leiden: Brill, 2009], esp. 104–9).

6. In his *Confutation of Tyndale's Answer,* for example, More responds at some length to attacks made by Tyndale and his supporters—but More's self-defenses are defenses only of the claims and methods of his previous polemics; even when his use of the first person is witty and ironic, it reveals nothing personal about More himself. See *Complete Works of St. Thomas More,* vol. 8.1, ed. Louis A. Schuster et al. (New Haven: Yale University Press, 1963), 26–40, 177–81. For a few relevant examples from the Marprelate controversy, see Black, *Martin Marprelate,* 115–16, 122, 200–201. Even Martin Luther—to take a Continental example—says virtually nothing that is directly autobiographical in his major controversial works or in his debates with Erasmus, Henry VIII, and More. In *The Bondage of the Will* (1525), Luther actually steps back from autobiography fairly dramatically, saying, "But this is not the place to tell the story of my life or works. . . . The sort of person I am, and the spirit and purpose with which I have been

drawn into this affair, I leave to [God]" *Luther's Works*, vol. 33, ed. Philip S. Watson (Philadelphia: Fortress Press, 1972), 73.

7. As decades of scholarly debate over the theological inclinations of John Donne and George Herbert have illustrated, the compression and syntactic flexibility of lyric permits a poetic speaker to balance between theological and devotional positions, expressing an attitude or a mood rather than announcing a denominational affiliation. The category of self-vindication includes juridical examinations, such as Anne Askew's *Examinacyon* (1546) and John Lilburne's *Work of the Beast* (1638) and *Christian Man's Triall* (1641) (among many other titles by Lilburne), but it also includes retrospective, first-person histories such as *Bishop Hall's Hard Measure*, first published with *The Shaking of the Olive Tree: The Remaining Works of that Incomparable Prelate, Joseph Hall* (1660). What all these works have in common is that they are straightforward historical accounts, interested in factual details more than inner states. For a fuller discussion of the differences between the kinds of autobiography permitted by lyric and polemic, see Chapter 2; for more on spiritual autobiography, see Chapter 5, as well as subsequent discussion in this Introduction.

8. Alexandra Walsham, *Church Papists: Catholicism, Conformity, and Confessional Polemic in Early Modern England* (Woodbridge, Suffolk: Boydell Press, 1993), 3; Christopher Haigh, *English Reformations: Religion, Politics, and Society Under the Tudors* (Oxford: Clarendon Press, 1993), 256–62. See also Patrick Collinson, *Birthpangs of Protestant England: Religious and Cultural Change in the Sixteenth and Seventeenth Centuries* (New York: St. Martin's Press, 1988), ix, 140.

9. For more on contemporary responses to James's succession, see Chapter 1.

10. Francis Bacon is the usual source for this quotation. See Patrick Collinson, "Elizabeth I," *Oxford Dictionary of National Biography* (Oxford: Oxford University Press, 2004; online edition, 2008).

11. For the importance of attending to the texture of language when reading early autobiographical works, see Stephen M. Fallon, *Milton's Peculiar Grace: Self-Representation and Authority* (Ithaca: Cornell University Press, 2007), 12–13; Meredith Anne Skura, *Tudor Autobiography: Listening for Inwardness* (Chicago: University of Chicago Press, 2008), 8–9.

12. The term "disnarrative" is the coinage of the narratologist Gerald Prince, whose essay "The Disnarrative" identifies as meaningful categories both events that *are not* narrated (some of which are apparently "unnarratable" and others of which are simply "unnarrated"), and alternative, hypothetical, or counterfactual narratives. All three categories will be relevant to my analyses in this book. See "The Disnarrated," *Style* 22, no. 1 (1988): 1–8.

13. See, for example, Collinson, *Birthpangs*, esp. 94–120; Brian Cummings, *The Literary Culture of the Reformation: Grammar and Grace* (Oxford: Oxford University Press, 2002); Eamon Duffy, *The Stripping of the Altars: Traditional Religion in England 1400–1580*, 2nd edition (New Haven: Yale University Press, 2005); Christopher Haigh, *English Reformations: The Plain Man's Pathways to Heaven* (Oxford: Oxford University Press, 2007), and Haigh, ed., *The English Reformation Revised* (Cambridge: Cambridge Univer-

sity Press, 1987); Peter Lake, *Anglicans and Puritans? Presbyterianism and English Conformist Thought, Whitgift to Hooker* (New York: HarperCollins, 1988); Alexandra Walsham, *Church Papists* and *Charitable Hatred: Tolerance and Intolerance in England 1500–1700* (Manchester: Manchester University Press, 2006).

14. Walsham, *Charitable Hatred*, 207–12.

15. For a discussion of the frequency of interconfessional conversion, see Michael Questier, *Conversion, Politics and Religion in England 1580–1625* (Cambridge: Cambridge University Press, 1996), and Molly Murray, *The Poetics of Conversion in Early Modern English Literature: Verse and Change from Donne to Dryden* (Cambridge: Cambridge University Press, 2009).

16. Lander, *Inventing Polemic*, 34. My phrasing is a slight alteration of Lander's.

17. One of the best investigations of these questions is Haigh, *Plain Man's*. See, e.g., 6–9.

18. Judith Maltby, *Prayer Book and People in Elizabethan and Early Stuart England* (Cambridge: Cambridge University Press, 2000), 1–2, 5–8; Haigh, *Plain Man's*, 6ff.

19. The term "turn to religion" appeared first in Ken Jackson and Arthur Marotti's essay "The Turn to Religion in Early Modern English Studies" (*Criticism* 46, no. 1 [2004]: 167–90), which then led to several sessions over the next few years at the annual conferences of Renaissance Society of America, the Shakespeare Association of America, and the Modern Language Association; it was later applied to a special issue of the journal *Christianity and Literature* (58, no. 2 [2009]). The phenomenon itself, however, has been gathering momentum since at least the events of September 11, 2001, which many scholars have identified as a catalyzing moment. See, for example, Stanley Fish, "One University Under God?" *Chronicle of Higher Education*, January 7, 2005, http://chronicle.com /article/One-University-Under-God-/45077.

20. Until recently, works on early modern English autobiography were few. The best and most influential of the early studies is Paul Delany, *British Autobiography in the Seventeenth Century* (London: Routledge and Kegan Paul, 1969). Others include Wayne Shumaker, *English Autobiography: Its Emergence, Materials, and Form* (Berkeley: University of California Press, 1954); Margaret Bottrall, *Every Man a Phoenix: Studies in Seventeenth-Century Autobiography* (London: John Murray, 1958); Dean Ebner, *Autobiography in Seventeenth-Century England: Theology and the Self* (The Hague: Mouton, 1971).

21. See Henk Dragstra, Sheila Ottway, and Helen Wilcox, eds., *Betraying Our Selves: Forms of Self-Representation in Early Modern English Texts* (New York: St. Martin's Press, 2000); Ronald Bedford, Lloyd Davis, and Philippa Kelly, eds., *Early Modern Autobiography: Theories, Genres, Practices* (Ann Arbor: University of Michigan Press, 2006); Skura, *Tudor Autobiography*; Adam Smyth, *Autobiography in Early Modern England* (Cambridge: Cambridge University Press, 2010); Sharon Cadman Seelig, *Autobiography and Gender in Early Modern Literature: Reading Women's Lives 1600–1680* (Cambridge: Cambridge University Press, 2006); Patrick Coleman, Jayne Lewis, and Jill Kowalik, eds., *Representations of the Self from the Renaissance to Romanticism* (Cambridge: Cambridge University Press, 2000).

22. The term "autobiography" is technically anachronistic for works written in the sixteenth and seventeenth centuries—the *Oxford English Dictionary* gives 1809 as the first occurrence of the term—but its use to describe self-narratives from all eras is by now long established. For one of the most influential critiques of the idea that autobiography is a genre, see Paul de Man, "Autobiography as De-Facement," *MLN* 94, no. 5 (1979): 919–30.

23. Smyth, *Autobiography*, 10–11. Although few scholars today would accept without significant qualifications Jacob Burckhardt's argument that the autonomous individual self was the product of the European Renaissance, the nature of early modern subjectivity remains a major area of debate and analysis. Patricia Fumerton, for example, insists that early modern England did see the emergence of "a new kind of subjectivity" more analogous to "a modern notion of singularity and disconnection." See *Unsettled: The Culture of Mobility and the Working Poor in Early Modern England* (Chicago: University of Chicago Press, 2006), 49.

24. Jaroslav Pelikan, *Credo: Historical and Theological Guide to Creeds and Confessions in the Christian Tradition* (New Haven: Yale University Press, 2003), 35.

25. Ibid., 35–57, 123–25.

26. Ibid., 189–93.

27. Ibid., 46–47, 64–65. See also Ian Green, *The Christian's ABC: Catechisms and Catechizing in England c. 1530–1740* (Oxford: Clarendon Press, 1996), 93–96.

28. See, for example, William Haller, *The Rise of Puritanism* (New York: Columbia University Press, 1939), 98–99; G. A. Starr, *Defoe and Spiritual Autobiography* (Princeton: Princeton University Press, 1965), 4–13. Delany, in *British Autobiography*, also discusses the influence of the Calvinist focus on the individual's inner life (and inner depravity) on the rise of English autobiography—but he considers it only one influence among many (33–37).

29. Dante's *Vita Nuova*, Petrarch's *Secretum*, the *Life* of Teresa of Avila, and the *Essais* of Montaigne are the most familiar examples.

30. Luther's best-known passage of autobiography comes from the preface to his Latin complete works (1545), where he tells the story of how he was "born again" while reading Paul's epistles (*Luther's Works* 34:327–38). There are other places where Luther engages in brief passages of autobiography, such as his 1530 *Exhortation to All Clergy,* but even those passages, more often than not, are straightforward, chronological narratives of events explicitly intended as a self-defense—*not* stories of spiritual awakening or otherwise introspective reflections (34:14–15). Augustine's *Confessions* was well known in Latin but was not translated into English until 1620, by the Catholic Tobie Matthew, who had it published at Saint-Omer; another English translation, by William Watt (this time published in London), appeared in 1631. The English spiritual autobiography did not develop until at least the mid-seventeenth century, with published spiritual autobiographies lagging still further behind (although spiritual *bio*graphies were popular dating back at least to Foxe's first edition of *Actes and Monuments* in 1563).

31. From the Reformation onward, catechisms were reliable sellers and available in dizzying numbers and varieties. According to Green's figures, however, the number of

different catechisms published in a given year spiked in the 1580s and again in the period 1610–1640. See Green, *Christian's ABC*, 68, 76–77.

32. There is a rich body of work on early modern inwardness and the emergence of the subject, including Patricia Fumerton's *Cultural Aesthetics: Renaissance Literature and the Practice of Social Ornament* (Chicago: University of Chicago Press, 1991); Katharine Eisaman Maus's *Inwardness and Theatre in the English Renaissance* (Chicago: University of Chicago Press, 1995); and Elizabeth Hanson, *Discovering the Subject in Renaissance England* (Cambridge: Cambridge University Press, 1998). This book's interests, however, lie less with the development of inner experience than with literary self-presentation.

33. Joan Webber, *The Eloquent "I": Style and Self in Seventeenth-Century Prose* (Madison: University of Wisconsin Press, 1968), 3–5.

CHAPTER I. JAMES VI AND I AND THE AUTOBIOGRAPHICAL DOUBLE BIND

1. James Craigie, ed., *The Basilicon Doron of King James VI*, 2 vols. (Edinburgh: Scottish Text Society, 1944), 1:30, 1599. All quotations from *Basilikon Doron* are taken from the first volume of this parallel-text edition and are cited in the text as *BD* with the year of publication (either 1599 or 1603), followed by Craigie's page numbers.

2. Of the book-length studies, only Rickard's focuses exclusively on James's writings. See Jonathan Goldberg, *James I and the Politics of Literature: Jonson, Shakespeare, Donne, and Their Contemporaries* (Stanford: Stanford University Press, 1989 [reprint; original, Baltimore: Johns Hopkins University Press, 1983]); Jane Rickard, *Authorship and Authority: The Writings of James VI and I* (Manchester: Manchester University Press, 2007); Linda Levy Peck, ed., *The Mental World of the Jacobean Court* (Cambridge: Cambridge University Press, 1991); Curtis Perry, *The Making of Jacobean Culture: James I and the Renegotiation of Elizabethan Literary Practice* (Cambridge: Cambridge University Press, 1997); Stephen Orgel, "The Royal Theatre and the Role of the King," in *Patronage in the Renaissance*, ed. Guy Fitch Lytle and Stephen Orgel (Princeton: Princeton University Press, 1981), 261–73; Peter C. Herman, "Authorship and the Royal 'I': King James VI/I and the Politics of Monarchic Verse, *Renaissance Quarterly* 54, no. 4 (2001): 1495–1530.

3. The few treatments of James's religious identity as manifested in his prose include Rickard, *Authorship*; Herman, "Authorship and the Royal 'I' "; Su Fang Ng, *Literature and the Politics of the Family in Seventeenth-Century England* (Cambridge: Cambridge University Press, 2007), 21–48. Perhaps the best examination (although it is not a literary one) of James's religious policies and their relationship to his own interests is the historian W. B. Patterson's *King James VI and I and the Reunion of Christendom* (Cambridge: Cambridge University Press, 1997).

4. Goldberg is the most insistent proponent of this position, but he is not the only one. See Goldberg, *James I*, 12–17, 20–21, 113–19. Rickard's book notes the contradictions in James's textual self-presentations more neutrally, in order to observe that he does not

have quite the control over his works and their interpretation that he claims he does. See, for example, 1–13, 60–63, 84–85, 105–6, 112, 202–3.

5. Mary was the great-granddaughter of Henry VII. Her grandmother, Henry VIII's sister, married James IV of Scotland.

6. D. Harris Willson, *King James VI and I* (New York: Henry Holt, 1956), 20–21, 39; Alan Stewart, *The Cradle King: The Life of James VI and I* (New York: St. Martin's, 2003), 42–44.

7. Willson, *King James*, 40.

8. See, for example, G. P. V. Akrigg, ed., *Letters of King James VI and I* (Berkeley: University of California Press, 1984), 46. Additional letters from this volume are cited in the text as *Letters*.

9. Although there is no evidence that Mary was involved in the initial plotting, she was informed of the plan in advance and sent a reply that seemed to approve of the conspirators' proposed actions. Retha M. Warnicke believes that the phrases in the letter that approve Elizabeth's assassination (none of which is in Mary's hand) were forged additions. See *Mary Queen of Scots* (New York: Routledge, 2006), 235–39.

10. OED, "perplexity," definition 2.

11. Rickard, *Authorship*, 85–90.

12. See especially Willson, *King James*, 54–55, 73–78; Goldberg, *James I*, 14–17.

13. The letter is dated January 26, 1586/7, and is in James's own hand.

14. See Akrigg, *Letters*, 81 (headnote); Goldberg chooses to ignore this letter, instead leaping ahead to James's formal and rather awkward forgiveness of Elizabeth after the fact. Janel Mueller more accurately describes the letter as showing James's struggle to remain courteous and calm despite the crisis. See "'To My Very Good Brother the King of Scots': Elizabeth I's Correspondence with James VI and the Question of Succession," *PMLA* 115, no. 5 (2000): 1068–69.

15. Akrigg notes that the edges of this letter have been charred; the words or syllables that appear in brackets have been supplied by him as the most likely representations of the missing parts. *Letters*, 81.

16. For the relevant letter from Elizabeth, see Elizabeth I, *Collected Works*, ed. Leah S. Marcus, Janel Mueller, and Mary Beth Rose (Chicago: University of Chicago Press, 2000), 296–97.

17. Goldberg, *James I*, 12–17. See also Rickard, *Authorship*, 65–66, 88–90.

18. Jenny Wormald, "'Basilikon Doron and 'The Trew Law of Free Monarchies': The Scottish Context and the English Translation," in Peck, *Mental World*, 48–51. Proof that the work reached a wider readership can be found in the criticism that it attracted almost immediately from members of the Scottish Kirk; the *Basilikon Doron* was discussed at the Synod of Fife in September 1599. See James Doelman, "'A King of Thine Own Heart': The English Reception of King James VI and I's *Basilikon Doron*," *Seventeenth Century* 9, no. 1 (1994): 1; Craigie, ed., *Basilikon Doron*, 2:10–16.

19. Also lurking behind this image is the old idea of the child as the mirror image of his parent, as in Shakespeare's Sonnet 3.

20. As Brian Cummings notes, a lack of due respect for God was a common anti-Calvinist charge. *Literary Culture,* 316–17.

21. In the 1603 edition, this passage is revised so that the crime is described as "the false and unreverent writing or speaking of malicious men against your Parents and Predecessors" (*BD* 1603, 1:65)—which makes it seem that James is only concerned with libel, rather than merely irreverent speech.

22. See Anastasii Bibliothecari, *Historia de vitis Romanorum Pontificum.* I am indebted to my colleague Austin Busch for locating this source.

23. OED, "synagogue," definition 2. The term appears to have been used most frequently to refer to Catholics but was also used to refer to Puritans.

24. Given that four of the original seven recipients of the *Basilikon Doron* were noblemen with Catholic associations whose loyalty James appears to have been rewarding, it is possible that this second passage was written with the intent of flattering or complementing them (see Rickard, *Authorship,* 115).

25. As John D. Staines notes, James also seems to have been sensitive about the charges of sexual incontinence that were lodged against Mary for marrying Bothwell shortly after he murdered James's father. In fact, the already married Bothwell seized and probably raped Mary as part of his own grab at power, but many saw Mary as at least willingly seduced, and possibly also complicit in her previous husband's murder. See *The Tragic Histories of Mary Queen of Scots, 1560–1690* (Burlington, VT: Ashgate, 2009), 23–24, 146, 163.

26. Goldberg, *James I,* 113–16.

27. Doelman, "'A King,'" 1; Craigie, ed., *Basilikon Doron,* 2:9–16. The phrase appears to be that of Andrew Melville, a Scottish clergyman who saw the book right before it went to press and presented extracted passages to the Synod of Fife, urging the Kirk to censure James.

28. See Wormald, "Basilikon Doron," 51–52, and Doelman, "A King," 1.

29. As Rickard notes, however, there is evidence that many English readers had heard about *Basilikon Doron* and had a sense of its contents as early as 1599. Rickard, *Authorship,* 113.

30. See note 18.

31. The Jesuit polemicist Robert Persons is the paradigmatic example. While before the succession Persons argued strongly against James's claim to the throne, he quickly changed his tune after the succession, insisting that there was good reason for English Catholics to believe in James's eventual conversion. See R. Doleman [Robert Persons], *A Conference about the Next Succession to the Crowne of Ingland* (1594), esp. 248–49; N.D. [Robert Persons], *A Treatise of Three Conversions of England from Paganisme to Christian Religion* (St. Omer, 1603), *2 1r–*5 2r. Other hopeful Catholic works include *Petition Apologeticall, Presented to the Kinges Most Excellent Majesty, by the Lay Catholikes of England* (Doway, 1604). See also M. C. Questier's discussion of Catholic toleration pamphlets in "Catholic Loyalism in Early Stuart England," *English Historical Review* 123 (October 2008): 1133. James's own wife, Anna of Denmark, had converted to Catholicism

some time after joining the Scottish court; it does not seem that this fact was public knowledge, but Anna did not receive Communion at the service that accompanied her coronation ceremony in London—a clear sign, to those who looked for such things, that England's new queen was not aligned with its church. For a fuller discussion of Anna's Catholicism, see Albert J. Loomie, S. J., "King James I's Catholic Consort," *Huntington Library Quarterly* 34, no. 4 (1971): 303–16; J. Leeds Barroll, *Anna of Denmark, Queen of England: A Cultural Biography* (Philadelphia: University of Pennsylvania Press, 2001), 162–72; and her entry in the *Dictionary of National Biography*.

32. Patterson, *Reunion*, 38–42.

33. See Persons's *A Treatise of Three Conversions*, *4 1r–*5 2r.

34. See G. P. V. Akrigg, *Jacobean Pageant, or, the Court of King James I* (Cambridge, MA: Harvard University Press, 1962), 304. For contemporary works celebrating James's Protestantism, see, for example, [John Hayward] *An Answer to the First Part of a Certain Conference, Concerning Succession* (London, 1603); Robert Pricket, *Unto the Most High and Mightie Prince, his Soveraigne Lord King James* (London, 1603); Anon., *To the Kinges most excellent Majestie: The Humble Petition of two and Twentie Preachers in London* (1605?).

35. See Patterson, *Reunion,* 35–40.

36. Ibid., 48; Cummings, *Literary Culture,* 392–95; Timothy Rosendale, *Liturgy and Literature in the Making of Protestant England* (Cambridge: Cambridge University Press, 2007), 129. For a recent rebuttal of this position, see Alan Cromartie, "King James and the Hampton Court Conference," in *James VI and I: Ideas, Authority, and Government,* ed. Ralph Houlbrooke (Aldershot: Ashgate, 2006), 61–80.

37. This is one of four speeches that James published shortly after their delivery. The only speeches that his predecessor prepared for publication were those involving Mary's execution.

38. James VI and I, *Political Writings,* ed. Johann P. Sommerville (Cambridge: Cambridge University Press, 1994), 138. Unless otherwise noted, quotations from James's speeches are taken from this edition, which are cited in the text as *PW.*

39. This is a common rhetorical move, one that we shall see again in Thomas Browne.

40. James makes a similarly ambiguous confession of faith in a speech given in Star-Chamber on June 20, 1616. He tells his audience: "I have resolved, as Confirmation in Majoritie followeth Baptisme in minoritie; so now after many yeeres, to renew my promise and Oath made at my Coronation concerning Justice, and the promise therein for maintenance of the Law of the Land. And I protest in GODS presence, my care hath ever beene to keepe my conscience cleare in all the points of my Oath, taken at my Coronation, so farre as humane frailtie may permit mee, or my knowledge enforme mee. . . . For Religion, I hope I am reasonably well knowen already" (*PW* 208).

41. Cummings, *Literary Culture,* 282, 287, 390.

42. Like James's speech of March 19, 1603/4, this one was published soon after its delivery.

43. Willson, *King James,* 16; Stewart, *Cradle King,* 9–10.

44. See Questier, *Conversion,* 106–8, 137, and "Loyalty, Religion, and State Power in Early Modern England: English Romanism and the Jacobean Oath of Allegiance," *Historical Journal* 40, no. 2 (1997): 311–29.

45. James had ordered the expulsion of Catholic priests before, but apparently it did not work. See the royal proclamation issued on February 22, 1603/4 (in the wake of the Hampton Court Conference) for what appears to be his first attempt, and the proclamation of June 10, 1606, for the second.

46. *An Act for the better discovering and repressing of Popish recusants* (1606).

47. Patterson, *Reunion,* 78–81. M. C. Questier, on the other hand, argues that the oath was intended as a seriously repressive measure. See "Loyalty," 311–29, and "Catholic Loyalism," 1137–54. Rebecca Lemon also inclines toward Questier's view. See *Treason by Words: Literature, Law, and Rebellion in Shakespeare's England* (Ithaca: Cornell University Press, 2006), 120–21.

48. The first edition of *An Apologie* (1607) contains the text of both of Pope Paul V's breves (October 10, 1606 and September 10, 1607). Bellarmine's letter to George Blackwell (September 28, 1607), Blackwell's response to Bellarmine, and his letter to English Catholics, can all be found in *A Large Examination Taken at Lambeth, according to his Majesties direction, point by point, of M. G. Blakwell* (London, 1607).

49. This quotation comes from the preface to the second edition of 1609. James I and VI, *Triplici nodo, triplex ceneus: Or An Apologie for the Oath of Allegiance* (London: R. Barker, 1609), 4. All further references to *An Apologie* refer to this second edition and are cited in the text as *Apologie.* For a detailed analysis of James's decision to write anonymously and its results, see Marcy L. North, "Anonymity's Subject: James I and the Debate over the Oath of Allegiance, *New Literary History* 33, no. 2 (2002): 215–31.

50. The earliest Catholic responses to *An Apologie* were Cardinal Bellarmine, *Responsio Matthaei Torti,* and Robert Persons, *Judgment of a Catholike English-Man* (both 1608). Persons's authorial persona purports to be extremely indignant on James's behalf about the many errors and impertinencies in *An Apologie* (1–5).

51. These arguments are made most relentlessly by Paul V, Bellarmine and Persons, though they are made more obliquely by others, especially after the second edition of *An Apologie,* when James explicitly denies being a heretic and apostate.

52. The preface, which is frequently identified by the separate title *A Premonition to All Most Mightie Monarches,* is 135 quarto pages long, while the text of the book is 112. Both sections are in the same font and typeface.

53. William Patterson is the only exception I know of; he describes the preface as "the most ambitious literary undertaking of [James's] career" (*Reunion,* 89).

54. Matthew Stewart, Earl of Lennox, James's paternal grandfather, at midlife promised Henry VIII to become a Protestant, but he either did not do so or soon reverted to Catholicism. Shortly before Mary's exile, however, and as a result of falling out of favor with her, he aligned himself with the Scottish Protestant lords and appears to have remained a Protestant for his final half-dozen years. Similarly, Henry, Lord Darnley,

James's father, was raised Catholic, worshipped as a Protestant while living in England before his marriage to Mary, wed her in a Catholic ceremony (although he declined to participate in the Mass), and switched back and forth between Catholicism and Protestantism several more times in the last few years of his life.

55. James's biographer confirms that Elizabeth did indeed send a font for James's baptism. See Willson, *King James*, 17–18.

56. Staines, *Tragic Histories*, esp. 145–77. This narrative of Mary as a staunch Catholic is, to some degree, a posthumous fabrication exploited by both Catholic and Protestant polemicists for their own purposes; Mary's Catholicism appears to have been sincere, but for most of her reign she was extremely cautious about advancing a Catholic political agenda.

57. Ibid., 163–73.

58. And indeed in the 1609 edition of *An Apologie* James declares that he is a "Catholike Christian" (35).

59. Patterson, *Reunion*, 1–3, 35–48, 57, 69–70.

60. Ibid., 127–54. In the later years of his reign James also made overtures to the Greek Orthodox Church.

61. James also uses this metaphor in one speech that does not concern recusancy: in a speech delivered on March 31, 1607 (and published soon thereafter), James discusses the proposed union between Scotland and England, saying, again, "I will discover my thoughts plainly unto you; I study clearenes, not eloquence, And therefore with the olde Philosophers, I would heartily wish my brest were a transparent glasse for you all to see through, that you might looke into my heart, and then would you be satisfied of my meaning" (*PW* 162).

CHAPTER 2. CONVERSION AND CONFESSION IN DONNE'S PROSE

1. The best-known instance is James's "Directions to Preachers," issued in 1622, but that was not the first of the attempts by James (or Elizabeth or their ministers) to limit public discussion of predestination. See Cummings, *Literary Culture*, 282–83, 287–96, 308–19, 390, as well as Jeanne Shami, *John Donne and Conformity in Crisis in the Late Jacobean Pulpit* (Cambridge: D. S. Brewer, 2003), 13–15.

2. The desire to read Donne's verse autobiographically is a strong one. Attempts to find Donne the man in his love poems abound in earlier Donne criticism, while in the 1950s Helen Gardner reordered the *Holy Sonnets* into what she argued was a chronological sequence by grouping them according to their perceived themes or concerns and then matching those groups to the ups and downs of Donne's life during the years before and just after his ordination. See John Donne, *The Divine Poems,* edited and with an introduction by Helen Gardner (Oxford: Clarendon Press, 1952), xxxvii–lv. Although many of these efforts are flawed, an autobiographical approach in and of itself certainly does not preclude sound scholarship. For more recent and more nuanced autobiographical read-

ings of Donne's poems, see for example many of the essays collected in *John Donne's "Desire of More": The Subject of Anne More Donne in His Poetry*, ed. M. Thomas Hester (Newark: University of Delaware Press, 1996).

3. Philip Sidney, *The Oxford Authors: Sir Philip Sidney*, ed. Katherine Duncan-Jones (Oxford: Oxford University Press, 1989), 235.

4. Murray, *Poetics of Conversion*, 82–92.

5. See Walton, *The Lives of John Donne, Sir Henry Wotton, Richard Hooker, George Herbert, and Robert Sanderson* (London: Oxford University Press, 1966), 25–26. Donne's "Satyre III" seems to support the account given in *Pseudo-Martyr* that Donne underwent a lengthy period of comparing the doctrines of the churches of Rome and of England, and suggests that at least part of this process took place in the 1590s. Not everyone agrees with the 1590s dating, however, and Dennis Flynn has suggested that it may have occurred as late as the period just following the discovery of the Gunpowder Plot. See Flynn, "Donne's Politics, 'Desperate Ambition,' and Meeting Paolo Sarpi in Venice," *Journal of English and Germanic Philology* 99, no. 3 (2000): 353, and *John Donne and the Ancient Catholic Nobility* (Bloomington: Indiana University Press, 1995), 173–76.

6. For a more detailed history of Donne's family background and Catholic heritage, including his relationship with his uncles Ellis and Jasper Heywood, see Flynn, *Ancient Catholic*, esp. 1–79. Henry apparently died of the plague, which he contracted while in prison. The priest himself was hanged, drawn, and quartered. See also R. C. Bald, *John Donne: A Life* (Oxford: Oxford University Press, 1970), 58.

7. The most notable proponent of this view is John Carey, although others have taken a version of this same position. See Carey, *John Donne: Life, Mind, and Art* (Oxford: Oxford University Press, 1981), 31–35; Bald, *John Donne*, 160–63, 227; Arthur Marotti makes a similar case in "John Donne's Conflicted Anti-Catholicism," *Journal of English and Germanic Philology* 101, no. 3 (2002): 358–79.

8. See David Norbrook, "The Monarchy of Wit and the Republic of Letters: Donne's Politics," in *Soliciting Interpretation: Literary Theory and Seventeenth-Century English Poetry*, ed. Elizabeth D. Harvey and Katharine Eisaman Maus (Chicago: University of Chicago Press, 1990), 7–8; and by implication Flynn, *Ancient Catholic*, 36–53. For Donne's critique of the post-Tridentine Catholic Church, see Shami, *Conformity*, 27–28, 32–35; Marotti, "Conflicted," 359–60, 365–66.

9. Barlow's work is a direct response to Persons's *Judgment of a Catholike English-Man* (1608), and appears to have been written after James's revised edition of *Triplici Nodo*. See William Barlow, *An Answer to a Catholike English-man* (London, 1609).

10. The letter continues, "The Book is full of falsifications in words, and in sense, and of falsehoods in matter of fact, and of inconsequent and unscholarlike arguings, and of relinquishing the King, in many points of defence, and of contradiction of himself, and of dangerous and suspected Doctrine in Divinitie, and of silly ridiculous triflings, and of extreme flatteries, and of neglecting better and more obvious answers, and of letting slip some enormous advantages which the other [disputant] gave, and he spies not." Probably spring or summer 1609. John Donne, *Letters to Severall Persons of Honor* (London, 1651),

139–41. Facsimile edition, ed. Charles Edmund Merrill Jr. (New York: Sturgis and Walton, 1910).

11. Ibid., 138–39.

12. There is no date on Donne's letter, but Barlow's work was entered in the Stationers' Register on April 14, 1609, while Donne's was entered on December 2, 1609. Bald, *John Donne*, 216, 221.

13. See Carey, *John Donne*, 31–33; Arthur Marotti, *John Donne: Coterie Poet* (Madison: University of Wisconsin Press, 1986), 186–91. See also Cummings, *Literary Culture*, 376–85, and Olga Valbuena, "Casuistry, Martyrdom, and the Allegiance Controversy in Donne's *Pseudo-Martyr*," *Religion and Literature* 32, no. 2 (2000): 56. Although all of these scholars read *Pseudo-Martyr* as a bid for royal favor, there are immense differences in how each reads the pressures on Donne or interprets his motives. There is also critical debate over the role that King James may or may not have played in commissioning or encouraging *Pseudo-Martyr* (Bishop Thomas Morton, whom Donne assisted in other polemical endeavors, almost certainly had a role). However, whether Donne wrote the work by request or entirely of his own initiative, the debate over his loyalty or disloyalty to the faith in which he was raised would remain largely unchanged. See Bald, *John Donne*, 210–21; Carey, *John Donne*, 31–33; and Lander, *Inventing Polemic*, 147–49.

14. See Goldberg, *James I*, 210–19; Debora Shuger, *Habits of Thought in the English Renaissance: Religion, Politics, and the Dominant Culture* (Berkeley: University of California Press, 1990), 159–217; Lemon, *Treason by Words*, 22, 126–34; Douglas Trevor, "*Pseudo-Martyr* and the Oath of Allegiance Controversy," *Reformation* 5 (2001): 106–9; Patterson, "All Donne," in Harvey and Maus, *Soliciting Interpretation*, 49–51, and "John Donne, Kingsman?" in Peck, *Mental World*, 258–62. See also Valbuena, "Casuistry," 49–50; Victor Houliston, "An Apology for Donne's *Pseudo-Martyr*," *Review of English Studies* 57 (2006): 477–81.

15. Lemon, *Treason by Words*, 22, 126–34; Trevor, "*Pseudo-Martyr*," 106–9.

16. John Donne, *Pseudo-Martyr*, revised edition, ed. Anthony Raspa (Montreal: McGill-Queen's University Press, 1993), 4. Subsequent page numbers refer to this edition and appear in parentheses in the text.

17. Jonathan Goldberg also argues that in *An Apologie* "Donne found a voice" that he was able to use in *Pseudo-Martyr* (and elsewhere), but Goldberg is speaking not of the two men's use of autobiography but rather of what Goldberg sees as Donne's whole-hearted embrace of James's absolutist vision of kingship. See *James I*, 213, 214.

18. See Patterson, "Kingsman," 258–59; Cummings, *Literary Culture*, 372–75.

19. Norbrook has suggested that the post-Tridentine Catholic Church's promotion of More as an anti-Protestant hero involved a rewriting of More's life and legacy that may have been particularly vexing to the Donne who appears to have seen great differences between More's Catholic Church and his own. Norbrook, "Monarchy," 7–8. See also Shami, who shows that in his sermons Donne not only presents the pre-Tridentine Catholic Church as a different, truer faith but also at least occasionally suggests that reconciliation between *that* church and the Protestant might be possible. Shami, *Conformity*, 27–28, 32–33.

20. See, for example, Questier, *Conversion*, 29.

21. In *Complete Poetry and Selected Prose of John Donne,* ed. Charles M. Coffin (New York: Modern Library, 1994), 303.

22. Brian Cummings notes that Donne's remarks about wrestling against Catholic "reasons" is almost certainly an allusion to the late Edmund Campion's *Ten Reasons* and the pamphlet warfare debating the merits of the churches of Rome and England that grew out of it and was still lively in the years after the Gunpowder Plot; Cummings sees *Pseudo-Martyr* as a self-conscious part of that debate. Cummings, *Literary Culture,* 378–85.

23. See, for example, Theophilus Higgons, *The Apology of Theophilus Higgons Lately Minister, Now Catholique* (1609); Anon., *The Satisfactorie Epistle of a Late Converted English Protestant, unto Catholyke Religion* (1630). Facsimile edition, ed. D. M. Rogers, *English Recusant Literature 1558–1640,* vol. 153 (Menston: Scolar Press, 1973). See also the later *Copies of Two Papers Written by the Late King Charles II. Together With a Copy of a Paper written by the late Duchess of York* (London, 1686), which James II published as proof of his brother's and first wife's conversion to Catholicism.

24. Donne does refer to the Reformation a few times, approvingly, but he seems to suggest that the reforms that took place are compatible with the Roman Catholic Church rather than necessarily representing a break from it. See, for example, *PM* 20–22.

25. While it is certainly possible to read both of these phrases as substitutes for "Catholic," that is not the first sense either one conveys. That "Roman Catholic" is a contradiction in terms was a Protestant commonplace, but it is more difficult to argue that Catholicism is an upstart religion (although it could, arguably, be described as "some newer name than Christian").

26. Douglas Trevor and Jesse Lander make similar arguments, although both see what Trevor calls Donne's "efforts to present himself as a universalist surrounded on either side by polemical extremists" as part of an explicitly Protestant polemical strategy. See Trevor, *"Pseudo-Martyr,"* 115; Lander, *Inventing Polemic,* 153, 156.

27. These statements are made, most strikingly, in the epistle to the reader in the second edition of *Basilikon Doron* and in the preface to the second edition of *An Apologie.* See my Chapter 1.

28. Bald, *John Donne,* 227, 271.

29. Kate Gartner Frost's chapter on the *Devotions* and spiritual autobiography is the most detailed consideration of what autobiography consisted of in the early modern period and how this tradition relates to the *Devotions.* See *Holy Delight: Typology, Numerology, and Autobiography in Donne's Devotions upon Emergent Occasions* (Princeton: Princeton University Press, 1990), 15–38. Apart from Frost, most references to the *Devotions* as autobiography are merely made in passing. See Starr, *Defoe and Spiritual Autobiography,* 34; Roger B. Rollin, "John Donne's *Holy Sonnets*—The Sequel: *Devotions upon Emergent Occasions,*" *John Donne Journal* 13, nos. 1–2 (1994): 52; Webber, *The Eloquent "I,"* 28–31.

30. In *The Poetry of Meditation* Louis L. Martz argues for the Catholic, specifically Ignatian, influence on Donne's works; although Martz does not discuss the *Devotions,*

his arguments have been extended to that work by Thomas F. Van Laan and Thomas J. Morrissey. See Martz, *The Poetry of Meditation* (New Haven: Yale University Press, 1954), 43–56; Van Laan, "John Donne's *Devotions* and the Jesuit Spiritual Exercises," *Studies in Philology* 60 (1963), 191–202; and Morrissey, "The Self and the Meditative Tradition in Donne's *Devotions*," *Notre Dame English Journal* 13:1 (1980), 29–49. Katherine Narveson, on the other hand, argues that Donne is a "contented conformist" within the Church of England (see Kate Narveson, "Piety and the Genre of Donne's *Devotions*," *John Donne Journal* 17 [1998], 107–36, as well as Katherine Ruth Narveson, "The Soul's Society: Genre, Community, and Identity in Early Stuart Devotional Literature" [Ph.D. diss., University of Chicago, 1996]), while Mary Arshagouni Papazian discusses what she sees as the strong influence of Puritan literature on the *Devotions* in her own unpublished dissertation and several articles. See Mary Arshagouni, "John Donne's *Devotions upon Emergent Occasions*: A Puritan Reading" (Ph.D. diss., UCLA, 1988); Mary Arshagouni Papazian, "Donne, Election, and the *Devotions upon Emergent Occasions*," *Huntington Library Quarterly* 55, no. 4 (1992), 603–19, and "Literary 'Things Indifferent': The Shared Augustinianism of Donne's *Devotions* and Bunyan's *Grace Abounding*," in *John Donne's Religious Imagination*, ed. Raymond-Jean Frontain and Frances M. Malpezzi (Conway, AR: UCA Press, 1995), 324–49.

31. For references to Donne's ordination, see the work's dedicatory epistle and Expostulation 8.

32. John Donne, *Devotions upon Emergent Occasions*, ed. Anthony Raspa (Montreal: McGill-Queen's University Press, 1975), 3. All subsequent citations refer to this edition and its pagination.

33. Jonathan Goldberg, Roger Rollin, Frank Warnke, and Sharon Cadman Seelig are among the many who have argued that Donne's spiritual condition is the focus of the *Devotions*, not his sickness. Warnke sees the theme of the work as "human sinfulness, as symbolized by proneness to physical diseases," and Rollin as "the effects upon a susceptible Christian of what might be called 'spiritual malaise.'" Warnke, *John Donne* (Boston: Twayne, 1987), 101, quoted in Rollin, "*Holy Sonnets*—The Sequel", 51; Goldberg, "The Understanding of Sickness in Donne's *Devotions*," *Renaissance Quarterly* 24, no. 4 (1971), 507–17; Seelig, "In Sickness and in Health: Donne's *Devotions upon Emergent Occasions*," *John Donne Journal* 8, nos. 1–2 (1989): 104–5.

34. Elena Levy-Navarro has made an intriguingly similar argument. In examining Donne's obsession with rumors in the *Devotions*, Levy-Navarro suggests that Donne wrote the work to preempt Catholic polemicists of the sort who claimed that John King, bishop of London, had converted to Catholicism on his deathbed in 1621. See "John Donne's Fear of Rumours in the *Devotions upon Emergent Occasions* and the Death of John King," *Notes and Queries* 47, no. 4 (2000): 481–83.

35. See Bald, *John Donne*, 451; Neil Rhodes, ed., *Selected Prose* (New York: Penguin, 1987), 13. The *Devotions* was entered in the Stationers' Register on January 9, 1623/4.

36. Robert M. Cooper, Kate Frost, and Dave Gray and Jeanne Shami have all argued that the *Devotions* was intended, at least in part, to administer political advice to

Charles. See Cooper, "The Political Implications of Donne's *Devotions*," *New Essays on Donne,* ed. Gary A. Stringer, Elizabethan and Renaissance Studies 57 (Salzburg: Institut für Englische Sprache und Literatur, 1977, 192–210); Frost, *Holy Delight,* 42–56; Gray and Shami, "Political Advice in Donne's *Devotions*," *Modern Language Quarterly* 50, no. 4 (1989), 337–56; and Shami, *Conformity,* 202–11.

37. Richard Strier, "Donne and the Politics of Devotion," in *Religion, Literature, and Politics in Post-Reformation England, 1540–1688,* ed. Donna B. Hamilton and Richard Strier (Cambridge: Cambridge University Press, 1996), 93–114.

38. For such readings see, for example, Joan Webber, *Contrary Music: The Prose Style of John Donne* (Madison: University of Wisconsin Press, 1963), 185, and A. C. Partridge, *John Donne: Language and Style* (London: André Deutsch, 1978), 199–201, 208.

39. Mary Arshagouni Papazian has also suggested that Donne may not have intended for his devotions to be read as purely private or individual prayers. See Arshagouni, "John Donne's *Devotions upon Emergent Occasions*," 10, 18–21, and "The Latin 'Stationes' in John Donne's *Devotions upon Emergent Occasions*," *Modern Philology* 89 (1991): 204. In emphasizing the sermonic aspects of the *Devotions,* Janel M. Mueller also gestures in this direction in "The Exegesis of Experience: Dean Donne's *Devotions upon Emergent Occasions*," *Journal of English and Germanic Philology* 67 (1968): 1–19.

40. Strier, "Politics of Devotion," 103.

41. Webber, *Contrary Music,* 184. See also Narveson, "Piety," 126–29, and Mueller, "Exegesis," 4.

42. Donne makes similar remarks in Prayers 3, 4, and 20 and in Expostulation 21.

43. Strier has argued that Donne's tone toward those who would abolish bell-ringing is "militant," and that he "is as unaccommodating as he can be to those whom he sees as 'schismatical.'" Although I think Strier's phrasing is a bit too strong, I generally agree with his assessment. See "Politics of Devotion," 106–7.

44. See Rosendale, *Liturgy and Literature,* 93–97; Ramie Targoff, *Common Prayer: The Language of Public Devotion in Early Modern England* (Chicago: University of Chicago Press, 2001), 33–35. The prayer book confessional rite is extremely general—the priest simply asks those who "do truly and earnestly repent" to "make [their] humble confession to almightie God, and to his holy church here gathered together in hys name, mekely kneyling upon your knees," and he then pronounces general absolution. See *The First and Second Prayer Books of Edward VI,* ed. E. C. Ratcliff (London: J. M. Dent, 1949), 224. Of course, there is nothing preventing an individual believer from confessing his sins to God, whatever his denomination, but as Thomas N. Tentler notes, the whole thrust of the Reformation critique of confession was that it forced the believer to dwell upon his sins—his deeds—rather than focusing on his justification through faith. *Sin and Confession on the Eve of the Reformation* (Princeton: Princeton University Press, 1977), 349–63.

45. Donne uses strikingly similar language in a sermon from 1627: "*I date my life from my Ministry; for I received mercy,* as I received the ministry, as the *Apostle* speaks." George R. Potter and Evelyn M. Simpson, eds., *Complete Sermons,* 10 vols. (Berkeley: University of California Press, 1953–62), 7: 403.

46. Hezekiah is mentioned in the line following the last one I cited, as well as at three other points in the *Devotions* proper. Although Hezekiah's son Manasseh is not mentioned by name, Frost argues—I think rightly—that the counterexample of Manasseh, as a bad king to Hezekiah's good king, is an implied warning to Charles about the sort of ruler he should *not* be. Frost, *Holy Delight,* 44–48.

47. As Frost has pointed out, there are significant details of Donne's life during his illness—such as the marriage that Donne hastened for his daughter Constance in the belief that he would otherwise die before seeing her settled—that he omits from the *Devotions* (Frost, *Holy Delight,* 17). It is also worth remembering that Donne's mother, who remained a Roman Catholic all her life, died only two months before Donne and lived for an unspecified number of her declining years in her son's home. See Bald, *John Donne,* 427.

CHAPTER 3. MILTON AND AUTOBIOGRAPHY IN CRISIS

1. *Fides Publica* (1654). Translated from the Latin by Paul W. Blackford and excerpted in *Complete Prose Works of John Milton,* 8 vols., ed. Don M. Wolfe et al. (New Haven: Yale University Press, 1953–1982), 4:1106. Unless otherwise noted, all quotations from Milton's prose are also from this edition, hereafter designated *YP* and cited parenthetically.

2. *YP* 4:1109.

3. Quoted by Milton in *Pro Se Defensio* (trans. Blackford), *YP* 4:772. The original can be found on p. 66 of *Fides Publica.*

4. Among the studies that make such a case are Stanley Fish, "Reason in *The Reason of Church Government,*" in Fish's *Self-Consuming Artifacts: The Experience of Seventeenth-Century Literature* (Berkeley: University of California Press, 1972), 298–300; Joseph Anthony Wittreich Jr., "'The Crown of Eloquence': The Figure of the Orator in Milton's Prose Works," in *Achievements of the Left Hand: Essays on the Prose of John Milton,* ed. Michael Lieb and John T. Shawcross (Amherst: University of Massachusetts Press, 1974), 3–54; David Loewenstein, "Milton and the Poetics of Defense," in *Politics, Poetics, and Hermeneutics in Milton's Prose,* ed. David Loewenstein and James Grantham Turner (Cambridge: Cambridge University Press, 1990), 171–92; chapter 3, "Humanist Individualism and the Puritan Polity in Milton's Antiprelatical Tracts," of Kevin Dunn's *Pretexts of Authority: The Rhetoric of Authorship in the Renaissance Preface* (Stanford: Stanford University Press, 1994), 51–81; Joseph Shub, "Milton's Prose Exordia and the Persuasion Through Character," *Prose Studies* 21, no. 1 (1998): 1–31. The obvious exception is Stephen Fallon's *Milton's Peculiar Grace.*

5. In *The Rise of Puritanism,* the historian William Haller refers to Milton's autobiographical passages, collectively, as Milton's "spiritual autobiography," and he sees little difference between Milton's narrative and those of his near-contemporaries. See *The Rise of Puritanism: or the way to the New Jerusalem as set forth in pulpit and press from Thomas*

Cartwright to John Lilburne and John Milton, 1570–1643 (New York: Columbia University Press, 1938), 296. Joan Webber, on the other hand, believes that Milton has adapted the conventions of the spiritual autobiography for his own literary purposes. See *The Eloquent "I,"* 217. Other scholars have likewise looked for echoes of the spiritual autobiography in both Milton's poetry and prose, beginning as early as the *Nativity Ode.* See, for example, Arthur E. Barker, "The Pattern of Milton's *Nativity Ode*," *University of Toronto Quarterly* 10 (1941): 167–81 (but for a persuasive refutation of Barker, see J. Martin Evans, "A Poem of Absences," *Milton Quarterly* 27, no. 1 [1993]: 31–35); Sharon Desmond Paradiso, "'Now Hear Mee Relate': Narrative Emplotment and Autobiography in *Paradise Lost*," *English Language Notes* 35, no. 2 (1997): 9–17; and Alinda Sumers-Ingraham, "John Milton's *Paradise Regained* and the Genre of the Puritan Spiritual Biography" (Ph.D. diss., George Washington University, 1984).

6. Fallon describes at length the differences between Milton's autobiographies and the spiritual autobiographies of his near-contemporaries. See *Peculiar Grace,* 21–44.

7. Christopher Hill, *Milton and the English Revolution* (New York: Viking, 1978), 9, 451–58.

8. The divorce pamphlets—which inspired attacks both in Parliament and in the press—are the most obvious case, but *Eikonoklastes* and *A Defence of the English People* also provoked attacks of a more or less personal nature.

9. See Alexander Leighton, *An Appeal to the Parliament; or Sions Plea Against the Prelacie* (Holland, 1628), 11.

10. It is widely assumed that Milton wrote the postscript to the Smectymnuans' first pamphlet, *An Answer to a Booke Entitled an Humble Remonstrance* (c. March 1641), but *Of Reformation* represents his first solo effort. See Barbara K. Lewalski, *The Life of John Milton: A Critical Biography* (Oxford: Blackwell, 2000), 128.

11. See, for example, Thomas Corns, *Uncloistered Virtue: English Political Literature, 1640–1660* (Oxford: Oxford University Press, 1992), 30–32.

12. Richard Strier—who similarly sees Milton's autobiographical passage in *Church-Government* as the result of "some powerful impulsion"—argues that this tension is the result of Milton's attempting to fuse Christian humility with Classical magnanimity. See "Milton Against Humility," in *Religion and Culture in Renaissance England,* ed. Claire McEachern and Debora Shuger (Cambridge: Cambridge University Press, 1997), 265–66.

13. See, for example, William Kerrigan, *The Prophetic Milton* (Charlottesville: University of Virginia Press, 1974), 176–77, 183–84; Louis L. Martz, "Milton's Prophetic Voice: Moving Toward Paradise," in *Of Poetry and Politics: New Essays on Milton and His World,* ed. P. G. Stanwood (Binghamton, NY: Medieval and Renaissance Texts and Studies, 1995), 1–16; Reuben Sánchez Jr., *Persona and Decorum in Milton's Prose* (Cranbury, NJ: Fairleigh Dickinson University Press, 1997), esp. 60–66; Dunn, *Pretexts of Authority,* 52, 58; Paul Stevens, "Discontinuities in Milton's Early Public Self-Representation," *Huntington Library Quarterly* 51, no. 4 (1988): 269. On the other hand, Richard Helgerson, noting that Milton was a member of the establishment for most of his prose-writing career, argues that although Milton "may have felt" some kinship with the Hebrew

prophets, he saw himself as "a figure neither of exile nor of opposition." *Self-Crowned Laureates: Spenser, Jonson, Milton and the Literary System* (Berkeley: University of California Press, 1983), 242.

14. Martz, "Milton's Prophetic Voice," 2.

15. See John T. Shawcross, *John Milton: The Self and the World* (Lexington: University Press of Kentucky, 1993), 93, and Helgerson, *Self-Crowned Laureates*, 249, 274–75. Milton does mention his ministerial ambitions in his later declaration that he was "destin'd of a child" to the ministry, until he was "Church-outed by the Prelats" (*YP* 1:822, 823), but this admission is deferred for many pages, until he has concluded his discussion of his poetic training and abilities.

16. See Dunn, *Pretexts of Authority*, 53–54, 59, and John Guillory, *Poetic Authority: Spenser, Milton, and Literary History* (New York: Columbia University Press, 1983), 95–98.

17. Both Milton and Hall, in fact, appear to have felt that there was a strong correlation between good style and good morals, but Milton's attacks are the fiercer and more constant. For a detailed consideration of Milton's and Hall's stylistic differences, and the possible moral valences that these differences may have suggested to Milton, see Henry S. Limouze, "Joseph Hall and the Prose Style of John Milton," *Milton Studies* 15 (1981): 121–42, and Thomas Kranidas, *Milton and the Rhetoric of Zeal* (Pittsburgh: Duquesne University Press, 2005), 88–162.

18. Although Milton sometimes implies that this work was written by Hall, most scholars believe that his role was, at most, only a minor collaborative one. Milton's second candidate for authorship, Hall's son, seems much more likely. See William Riley Parker, *Milton's Contemporary Reputation* (Columbus: Ohio State University Press, 1940), 15–16; Lewalski, *Life of John Milton*, 136.

19. John Guillory has suggested that Milton's anonymity in this tract is simply a practical acknowledgment of the fact that his name lacks sufficient reputation or recognition to advance his argument. Although Guillory provides a convincing reading of Milton's unwilling suppression of his name at various points throughout *An Apology*, I do not find his argument for the absence of Milton's name from the work's title page persuasive; as the counterexample of *Church-Government* demonstrates, the presence or absence of Milton's name on the title page of his early pamphlets admits no easy or single explanation. See *Poetic Authority*, 95–96.

20. *A Modest Confutation of a Slanderous and Scurrilous Libell, Entituled, Animadversions upon the Remonstrants Defense against Smectymnuus* (1642), A3 1r.

21. Ibid., 5–6.

22. It has been suggested that the Confuter's description of the author's being "vomited out" of "the brest of the University" (*Modest Confutation*, A3 1v) may refer to Milton's rustication from Cambridge, but such a vague statement is a poor basis for building an argument one way or the other. As Parker notes, the very randomness of the Confuter's attacks on Milton suggest that he either *did not* make inquiries or that he was unable to discover much about him. *Contemporary Reputation*, 268–69.

23. *Modest Confutation*, A3 1v.

24. Ibid.

25. Hugh M. Richmond, "Personal Identity and Literary Personae: A Study in Historical Psychology," *PMLA* 90, no. 2 (1975): 212–13. In Richmond's prose translation, the passage runs: "You complain moreover that my life is licentious, over-burdened with luxury, sport, and vice. You lie maliciously: if you had followed me for two months you would know well the state of my life and now I intend to spell it out for you so that everyone will know you are a liar. When I wake each morning before I do anything I say a prayer to the Eternal Father of all Good. . . . When I get out of bed and am clothed I devote myself to study and learn virtue, writing and reading as my vocation requires since I have been inclined to the Muses since my childhood. I stay closeted for four or five hours; then when too much reading wearies my spirit I drop my book and go to church. Returning I devote an hour to recreation; then dine soberly, saying grace."

26. Earlier in his digression Milton goes out of his way to include wedded intercourse under the rubric of chastity (*YP* 1:892–93), and toward the end of the tract he will describe his ideal wife as "a virgin of mean fortunes honestly bred" (*YP* 1:929)—countering the Confuter's claim that he is on the lookout for a rich widow—which some scholars have taken as an allusion to Mary Powell, whom Milton surprised his friends and family by marrying approximately two months after penning *An Apology*.

27. According to Parker, copies of the first printing of Milton's 1645 *Poems* were still available twelve years later. *Contemporary Reputation*, 23.

28. Annabel Patterson, Stephen M. Fallon, and J. Michael Vinovich have each promoted different arguments for autobiographical readings of the divorce tracts, all interested in what they consider the significant *suppression* of autobiography in those works. See Patterson, "No Meer Amatorious Novel?" in Loewenstein and Turner, *Politics, Poetics and Hermeneutics*, 85–101; Fallon, "The Spur of Self-Concernment: Milton in His Divorce Tracts," *Milton Studies* 38 (2000): 220–42; and Vinovich, "Protocols of Reading: Milton and Biography," *Early Modern Literary Studies* 1, no. 3 (1995). The textual features of Milton's 1645 *Poems* have also inspired biographical readings from a number of scholars, among them Louis L. Martz in *Poet of Exile: A Study of Milton's Poetry* (New Haven: Yale University Press, 1980), 31–59; John K. Hale in "Milton's Self-Presentation in *Poems . . . 1645*," *Milton Quarterly* 25 (1991): 37–48; and Leah S. Marcus in "John Milton's Voice," in her *Unediting the Renaissance: Shakespeare, Marlowe, Milton* (London: Routledge, 1996), 177–227.

29. Milton was attacked both in Parliament and in print for the *Doctrine and Discipline of Divorce*. Admittedly, however, the "personal" attacks in, for example, *An Answer to the Doctrine and Discipline of Divorce* (1644) are less vicious than they are in the *Modest Confutation* or *Clamor*. As Parker notes, Milton's attackers appear to have been unaware of his marital circumstances, for no contemporary criticism of the divorce tracts contains any reference to them.

30. Unless otherwise indicated, the English translation used for both *Defences* is that of the Yale Prose edition. For the Latin I have consulted the bilingual Columbia University Press edition of the work, located in volume 8 of *The Works of John Milton*, 18 vols.,

ed. Frank Patterson et al. (New York: Columbia University Press, 1931–1938). Subsequent citations of this work are abbreviated *CW*.

31. The exception is the *Doctrine and Discipline of Divorce,* which went through four editions in three years. None of Milton's other works from the 1640s received more than a single printing in that decade, and some are known to have left enough unsold copies that they were repackaged for sale in the 1650s, after Milton had achieved notoriety. Parker, *Milton's Contemporary Reputation,* 18, 15–16. *Tenure of Kings and Magistrates* was not published until February 1649, while Charles was executed on January 30; *Eikonoklastes* was published in October of that same year. Although *Eikonoklastes* later gained some renown, according to Parker it did not do so until after its author was made famous by the *First Defence* (*Contemporary Reputation,* 30–31).

32. The full sentence reads, "Sic itaque existimabam, si illos Deus res gerere tam praeclaras voluit, esse itidem alios à quibus gestas dici pro dignitate atque ornari, & defensam armis veritatem, ratione etiam, (quod unicum est praesidium verè ac propriè humanum) defendi voluerit" (*CW* 8:10).

33. Blackford translation, excerpted in *YP* 4:1045. To confuse an already vexed issue, the epistle *is* believed to have been written by More and prefaced to Du Moulin's work. The quotation from the *Aeneid* comes from book III.

34. In his 1655 sonnet to Cyriack Skinner, Milton makes the same claim. He writes, "Cyriack, this three years' day, these eyes, though clear / To outward view of blemish or of spot, / Bereft of light thir seeing have forgot." *Complete Poems and Major Prose,* ed. Merritt Y. Hughes (New York: Macmillan, 1985), 170.

35. That Milton's blindness was a punishment from God was asserted by later Royalists, of course, most famously in Roger L'Estrange's *No Blinde Guides* (1660), and it may well have been whispered in Milton's presence before then, but no such accusation is made in the *Clamor* or any other published works of the mid-1650s.

36. Milton's other known discussions of his blindness from this period include the sonnet to Skinner, written in 1655; the sonnet on the death of one of his wives, written no earlier than 1652 and quite possibly after 1658; and his letter to Leonard Philaras in 1654.

37. More writes, "You would even appear more lofty than the very exalted Cromwell, whom you address familiarly, without any preface of honor, whom you advise under the guise of praising, for whom you dictate laws, set aside titles, and prescribe duties, and to whom you suggest counsels and even present threats if he should act in any other fashion." *Fides Publica,* quoted in *YP* 4:1109. For more recent responses see, among others, Austin Woolrych, "Milton and Cromwell: 'A Short but Scandalous Night of Interruption'?" in Lieb and Shawcross, *Achievements of the Left Hand,* 185–218; Hill, *Milton and the English Revolution,* 193–94. A dissenting opinion is that expressed by Robert Thomas Fallon in "*A Second Defence*: Milton's Critique of Cromwell?" in *Milton Studies* 39 (2000): 167–83.

38. The relevant part of the passage reads as follows, "Si postrema primis non satis responderint, ipsi viderint; ego quæ eximia, quæ excelsa, quæ omni laude propè majora fuere, iis testimonium, prope dixerim monumentum, perhibui, haud citò interiturum; & si aliud nihil, certè fidem meam liberavi" (*CW* 8:252).

39. Annabel Patterson, "The Civic Hero in Milton's Prose," in James D. Simmonds, ed., *Milton Studies* 8 (Pittsburgh: Pittsburgh University Press, 1975), 71–101, esp. 95–98; Stephen Fallon, "Alexander More Reads Milton: Self-Representation and Anxiety in Milton's *Defences*," in *Milton and the Terms of Liberty*, ed. Graham Parry and Joad Raymond (Cambridge: D. S. Brewer, 2002), 111–24. See also Fallon, *Peculiar Grace*, 172–76.

40. In the *Modest Confutation* the Confuter provides a very brief, very general description of his background and qualifications for speaking—he is a man entirely contented with his station in life, who is not speaking out of envy, and so on—before proceeding to defend Bishop Hall. See *Modest Confutation*, 6.

41. For this prayer, see *YP* 4:1127–28. For Milton's reaction to it, see 4:823–25.

CHAPTER 4. THOMAS BROWNE'S UNEASY CONFESSION OF FAITH

1. Thomas Browne, *Religio Medici: Edited from the Manuscript Copies and the Early Editions*, ed. Jean-Jacques Denonain (Cambridge: Cambridge University Press, 1953), 3–4. Quotations from the later versions of the *Religio* (i.e., not from the c. 1635 Pembroke manuscript, which I discuss in note 6) come from this edition. Subsequent quotations from all versions of the work are cited in the text by part and section numbers.

2. Johnson's strongest argument is the oddity of Browne's having employed for his authorized edition the same printer, Andrew Crook, who printed the unauthorized one. See "Dr. Johnson's Life of Sir Thomas Browne," in Simon Wilkin, ed., *Sir Thomas Browne's Works*, 4 vols. (London: William Pickering, 1835–1836), 1:xx–xxi. This essay was originally published as a preface to an edition of Browne's *Christian Morals*.

3. See Denonain, "Introduction: Manuscript Evidence," in Browne, *Religio Medici* (1953), ix–xxi.

4. According to Love, manuscripts may be considered "published" when they have moved "from a private realm of creativity to a public realm of consumption," evidence for which includes the existence of the work in a large number of manuscript copies; the knowing relinquishment of control over a text by its author; and the exhibition of a polished, public literary style. From the variations among the eight surviving manuscript copies of the *Religio*, it can be inferred that a sizable number of copies once existed, and in his prefatory letter Browne himself admits to "communicat[ing]" his work to at least one reader. Harold Love, *The Culture and Commerce of Texts: Scribal Publication in Seventeenth-Century England* (Amherst: University of Massachusetts Press, 1998), 36–43. Ironically, despite the *Religio*'s meeting his criteria, Love takes Browne's protestations at face value and repeatedly cites the *Religio* as an example of a manuscript composition that circulated *without* its author's permission (see pp. 41, 43, 81).

5. The most notable exception is Jonathan F. S. Post's "Browne's Revisions of *Religio Medici*," *Studies in English Literature* 25 (1985): 145–63, which compares the first two published editions of the work (although it does not look at the earlier manuscript copies).

6. In the prefatory letter to the 1643 edition, Browne claims that the work was composed "about seven yeares past," and there is internal evidence to indicate that it was indeed

written as Browne was approaching his thirtieth birthday, in 1635. This version is represented by two of the eight extant manuscript copies of the *Religio*, of which only that held by Pembroke College, Oxford, is complete (MS 17, McGowin Library; the partial copy is British Library MS Lansdowne 489, 132v–137r). Quotations from this version of the *Religio* are drawn from my transcription of the Pembroke manuscript. However, for the reader's ease of reference, for quotations from both this and the second version of the *Religio*, I shall cite the 1643 part and section numbers that have become standard.

7. Several critics have considered the *Religio* within its Civil War context. See, for example, Post, "Browne's Revisions," 145–63; Achsah Guibbory, *Ceremony and Community from Herbert to Milton: Literature, Religion, and Cultural Conflict in Seventeenth-Century England* (Cambridge: Cambridge University Press, 1998), 119–31; Balachandra Rajan, "Browne and Milton: The Divided and the Distinguished," in *Approaches to Sir Thomas Browne: The Ann Arbor Tercentenary Lectures and Essays*, ed. C. A. Patrides (Columbia: University of Missouri Press, 1982), 1–11; Michael Wilding, "*Religio Medici* and the English Revolution,*" also in Patrides, *Approaches to Sir Thomas Browne*, 100–114. To my knowledge, no one other than Michael Wilding has seriously questioned the mid-1630s as the period of the work's initial composition, and Wilding offers no evidence for his argument other than the topicality of the *Religio* for the early years of the Civil War.

8. See, for example, Frank J. Warnke, "A Hook for Amphibium: Some Reflections on Fish," in Patrides, *Approaches to Sir Thomas Browne*, 54–56, 59; Anne Drury Hall, *Ceremony and Civility in English Renaissance Prose* (University Park: Pennsylvania State University Press, 1991), 174–76, 188–90 (and see also Hall's earlier and somewhat different version of her Browne chapter, "Epistle, Meditation, and Sir Thomas Browne's *Religio Medici*," *PMLA* 94, no. 2 [1979]: 243); Leonard Nathanson, *The Strategy of Truth: A Study of Sir Thomas Browne* (Chicago: University of Chicago Press, 1967), 8–9.

9. See, for example, Webber, *Eloquent "I,"* 149–83; Murray Roston, "The 'Doubting' Thomas," in Patrides, *Approaches to Sir Thomas Browne*, 69–80; Warnke, "A Hook for Amphibium," 49–59; Jonathan F. S. Post, *Sir Thomas Browne* (Boston: Twayne, 1987), esp. pp. 77, 85, 89–90; Victoria Silver, "Liberal Theology and Sir Thomas Browne's 'Soft and Flexible' Discourse," *English Literary Renaissance* 20, no. 1 (1990): 69–76, 86ff.; Guibbory, *Ceremony and Community*, 128–30; Debora Shuger, "The Laudian Idiot," in *Sir Thomas Browne: The World Proposed*, ed. Reid Barbour and Claire Preston (Oxford: Oxford University Press, 2008), 36–62.

10. As Fish writes toward the end of his chapter on Browne, "It becomes obvious that Browne doesn't feel anything, except the impulse to *amplificatio*." "The Bad Physician: The Case of Sir Thomas Browne," in *Self-Consuming Artifacts*, 368.

11. I believe that Claire Preston is exactly right in describing *Religio Medici* as messy, disorganized, and inconsistent (in contrast to other scholars, who insist that the work follows an elaborate and intentional pattern). See Claire Preston, *Thomas Browne and the Writing of Early Modern Science* (Cambridge: Cambridge University Press, 2005), 51, 53.

12. Green, *Christian's ABC*, 68, 76–77.

13. Ibid. The figure from the English Short Title Catalogue includes three different translations of the catechism found in the Book of Common Prayer (one in English, one in Welsh, and one in Greek and Latin).

14. Julian Davies, *The Caroline Captivity of the Church: Charles I and the Remoulding of Anglicanism 1625–1641* (Oxford: Clarendon Press, 1992), 24–26, 62–65.

15. Publication dates and other figures are based on information in the ESTC.

16. This is the familiar name of Robert Openshaw's *Short Questions and Answeares Conteining the Summe of Christian Religion*, first published in 1579.

17. Most of Browne's biographers have assumed that he studied first at Montpellier and then at Padua, partly because this is a more geographically logical route and partly because more advanced medical training (especially in anatomy) was available at both Padua and Leiden, and it seems logical that he would proceed from more elementary to more advanced studies. However, as there is no record or Browne's registration at either Montpellier or Padua, there is no way to be certain. Jeremiah S. Finch, *Sir Thomas Browne: A Doctor's Life of Science and Faith* (New York: Henry Schuman, 1950), 54–86; Frank Livingstone Huntley, *Sir Thomas Browne: A Biographical and Critical Study* (Ann Arbor: University of Michigan Press, 1962), 57–71. See also Reid Barbour's forthcoming *Sir Thomas Browne: A Life* (Oxford: Oxford University Press, 2013).

18. For the climate of religious tolerance at these universities, see Finch, *Sir Thomas Browne*, 57, 67, 75–76; Antonino Poppi, *Ricerche sulla teologia e la scienza nella Scuola padovana del Cinque e Seicento* (Soveria Mannelli: Rubbettino, 2001), 23–34, 101–23; Christine Kooi, *Liberty and Religion: Church and State in Leiden's Reformation, 1572–1620* (Leiden: Brill, 2000), 134, 155.

19. Notable antitrinitarians associated with Padua include Michael Servetus (1511–1553), the Catholic whom Calvin eventually had burned at the stake in Geneva, and both Laelius and his nephew Faustus Socinus, who studied in Padua off and on throughout the 1540s, 1550s, and 1560s, and whose beliefs would develop into Socinianism. See George Huntston Williams, *The Radical Reformation* (Philadelphia: Westminster Press, 1962), 21–24, 567–70, 621, 630–35.

20. From the introduction to Denonain's later edition of the *Religio*. Jean-Jacques Denonain, ed., *Religio Medici: A New Edition with Biographical and Critical Introduction* (Cambridge: Cambridge University Press, 1955), viii–ix. See also Finch, *Sir Thomas Browne*, 67.

21. Kooi, *Liberty and Religion*, 28, 162–63.

22. As Kooi writes, "Although one of the academy's *raisons d'être* was the training of Reformed ministers, the patricians who administered it jealously shielded it from local ecclesiastical control, and this had allowed a variety of religious opinions to flourish inside its lecture halls," *Liberty and Religion*, 134.

23. C. W. Schoneveld, "Sir Thomas Browne and Leiden University in 1633," *English Language Notes* 19, no. 4 (1982): 354.

24. During this period, Browne was beginning to practice medicine as a preliminary step toward receiving his M.D. from Oxford in 1637 (which he would need in order to continue practicing medicine in England), and it is conceivable that the prospect of

resubscribing to the Thirty-Nine Articles when he took his Oxford M.D. provided the immediate catalyst for Browne's reflections upon the articles of his own belief.

25. See Jeremiah S. Finch, ed., *A Catalogue of the Libraries of Sir Thomas Browne and Dr. Edward Browne, His Son: A Facsimile Reproduction* (Leiden: Leiden University Press, 1986), 26, 85. The edition in Browne's library, however, was in Latin and Greek.

26. Alexander Nowell, *A Catechisme, or first Instruction and Learning of Christian Religion. Translated out of Latine into Englishe* (London: John Daye, 1570), B.i.r–B.ii.r. Guibbory sees echoes of a different work in the opening sections of the *Religio*: the controversial *Appello Caesarum* (1625), which was written by Richard Montagu and associated with a ceremonialist, Arminian position. See *Ceremony and Community*, 120–25.

27. Nowell, *Catechisme*, B.ii.r.

28. In the second version of the work, Browne is slightly less coy, inserting, after "I am" the phrase, "of that reformed new-cast Religion, wherein I mislike nothing but the name."

29. Davies, *Caroline Captivity*, 61–65.

30. Ibid., 108–17.

31. Silver, "Liberal Theology," 84–85. Although I disagree that the *Religio* (at least in its earliest version) is intended as an embodiment of this sort of liberal theology, it seems perfectly possible to me that Browne might in certain places be drawing upon the works of such divines and intentionally trying to recast his doubts and anxieties as simple adiaphora. See also Hall, *Ceremony and Civility*, 179–84; and Guibbory, *Ceremony and Community*, 120–31. Debora Shuger, building on Guibbory, argues that Browne's theology is essentially Laudian. See "The Laudian Idiot," 36–62.

32. Silver, "Liberal Theology," 84*n*.24, 85*n*.27 (the quotation is from Taylor's *Ductor Dubitantium*). For further comparisons between Browne and Chillingworth and Taylor, see Nathanson, *The Strategy of Truth*, 116–28. For a more detailed discussion of the attitude of the latitudinarian divines toward reason, see Martin I. J. Griffin Jr., *Latitudinarianism in the Seventeenth-Century Church of England* (Leiden: Brill, 1992), especially chapter 5, "The Latitudianarians' Conception of Reason."

33. Williams, *Radical Reformation*, 104; Maurice Kelley, *Complete Prose*, 6:91–95. In his discussion of the popularity of various kinds of psychopannychism in the mid-seventeenth century, Kelley mentions in passing Browne's early attraction to mortalism and also notes the large number of attacks on the heresy that were published in the 1640s.

34. Kelley, *Complete Prose*, 92; Williams, *Radical Reformation*, 22.

35. See Anthony Levi, *Renaissance and Reformation: The Intellectual Genesis* (New Haven: Yale University Press, 2002), 164–65; Williams, *Radical Reformation*, 24; and the "Pomponazzi" entry in *The Catholic Encyclopedia* (New York: Robert Appleton, 1912; also available online at www.newadvent.org/cathen). Further evidence for the enduring popularity of psychopannychism among Englishmen of Browne's social and intellectual circles may be seen in a letter Browne received in 1648 from Henry Power, with whom he appears to have had a close, mentoring relationship. Power, then studying medicine at

Oxford, often wrote Browne for advice about his studies and for opinions on the nature of natural phenomena. In a letter of February 10, 1647/8, Power discusses "the re-individualling of an incinerated plant," which he urges as "not only an ocular demonstration of our resurrection, but a notable illustration of that Psychopannchy, wch. Antiquity so generally received, how these Formes of ours, may be lulled & ly asleepe after the Separation . . . untill that great & generall Day, when . . . it shall be resuscitated into its former selfe" (British Library MS Sloane 1911, f. 78).

36. See Levi, *Renaissance and Reformation*, 11, 32; "Origen," *The Catholic Encyclopedia*. Browne's library also contained a two-volume folio of Origen's complete works published in Basel in 1571. See Finch, *Catalogue*, 23.

37. *The Oxford Companion to the Bible* lists only two New Testament passages that seem to argue for a Trinity of three distinct persons (2 Cor. 13:13 and Matt. 28:19) and none that argues for the perfect equality of the three persons. The opening of the Gospel of John asserts the coeternality of only the first two persons (New York: Oxford University Press, 1993), 782–83. For a detailed consideration of the persistence of antitrinitarianism in Renaissance England, see Paul C. H. Lim, *Mystery Unveiled: The Crisis of the Trinity in Early Modern England* (Oxford: Oxford University Press, 2012).

38. See, for example, *Religio,* I.21 and I.22.

39. "Origen," *Catholic Encyclopedia*. Origen was never charged with any heresies during his own lifetime (and he is today considered a major theologian), but for hundreds of years some of his writings were considered heretical by the institutional church.

40. The section now numbered I.8 was added by Browne for the 1643 version and does not exist in any form in the earlier two versions.

41. In the *Religio*'s later two versions the first part of this line is revised to read—less controversially, although also less comprehensibly—"There is no attribute adds more difficulty *to* the mystery of the trinity" (emphasis added).

42. Kenelm Digby, *Observations on Religio Medici* (London, 1643), 19–20.

43. Fish, *Self-Consuming Artifacts*, 364–68. Fish's criticisms of Browne, of course, are no more shortsighted or potentially condescending than the attempted excuses made by many of Browne's defenders: according to Hall, for example, Browne's religion is "happily irrational," and Brown himself, though a great writer, is "complacent" and "not a great thinker" (*Ceremony and Civility*, 188, 189, 190).

44. Also known as Monarchism.

45. In the second-stage revision of the work Browne will add an entirely new section, I.32, which contains a second (and quite lengthy) discussion of the Holy Spirit—although he arrives at this only after discussing the Platonic notion of a shared spirit.

46. See Nathanson, *Strategy of Truth*, 93; Shuger, "Laudian Idiot," 55–56.

47. Browne mentions baptism twice in passing and communion once, also in passing. See I.45 and II.7.

48. See R. W. Sharples, *Stoics, Epicureans and Sceptics* (London: Routledge, 1996), 94–99; A. A. Long, *Hellenistic Philosophy: Stoics, Epicureans, Sceptics* (London: Duckworth, 1974), 41ff. For more on Browne and Stoicism, see Reid Barbour, *English Epicures and*

Stoics: Ancient Legacies in Early Stuart Culture (Amherst: University of Massachusetts Press, 1998), 226–27; Preston, *Thomas Browne*, 67–72.

49. Near the end of the *Religio*, Browne will again mention his age, characterizing his life as "but a miracle of 30 yeares" (II.11).

50. In the second-stage version of the work, Browne will expand upon this idea: "It is not, I confesse, an unlawfull Prayer to desire to surpasse the dayes of our Saviour, or wish to out-live that age wherein he thought fittest to dye, yet if (as Divinity affirmes,) there shall be no gray hayres in Heaven, but all shall rise in the perfect state of men, we doe but out-live those perfections in this world. . . . But age doth not rectife, but incurvate our natures, turning bad dispositions into worser habits . . . for every day as we grow weaker in age, we grow stronger in sinne, and the number of our dayes doth but make our sinnes innumerable" (I.42).

51. The lines are spoken by Volteius, a captain in Caesar's army during the civil war, who is trying to encourage his outnumbered and surrounded men by reminding them of the nobleness of their cause and the happiness of their death for that cause, regardless of whether they die at the hands of their enemies or kill themselves in order to avoid a dishonorable captivity. In a nineteenth-century English translation, the passage and its preceding lines are rendered: "Those alone whose end / Inspires them, know the happiness of death, / Which the high gods, that men may bear to live, / Keep hid from others." *Pharsalia*, bk. IV, ll. 579–82. Translation by Sir Edward Ridley, 1896. Online Medieval and Classical Library: http://omacl.org/Pharsalia/book4.html.

52. The extreme intensity of the feelings Browne claims to have for his friend have not attracted much scholarly notice—and neither has the fact that one of Browne's revisions to the *Religio* was to change nearly all of his references to "friend," singular, to "friends," plural. (See especially the passages in II.5, II.6, II.11.) However, both Hall and Huntley have discussed the ways in which the *Religio* reads like a communication between friends, with Huntley suggesting that the first version of the work was intended, specifically, for Browne's friend John Power of Halifax. See *Sir Thomas Browne*, 95–97; Hall, *Ceremony and Civility*, 172–73.

53. Denonain, introduction to Browne, *Religio Medici* (1953), xiv.

54. Milton's work is divided into two parts, while Taylor's *Holy Living* includes a third part, duties to self, to accompany the sections on duties to God and duties to neighbor. Catechisms vary in the number of their sections, but virtually all catechisms give special emphasis to the separate but related sections on faith and charity. See, e.g., Nowell's *Complete Catechisme*.

55. The imposition of the Book of Common Prayer provoked riots in Scotland in 1637 and led to the Scottish Assembly's abolition of bishops in 1638. Charles then initiated the first Bishop's War to bring Scotland into forcible conformity with the English Church.

56. There is some dispute as to whether Browne is responsible for the work's title. Nearly all of the manuscripts that bear the title have it added in a second, presumably later hand (likewise, many of the manuscripts have marginal or interlineated additions or

corrections that appear to have been the result of a later comparison with the printed version). Regardless of whether the title *Religio Medici* originated with Browne, however, he chose to retain it.

57. The fullest discussion of the changes between the 1642 and the 1643 printings is Post, "Browne's Revisions," 145–63.

58. A fragmentary copy of the 1642 *Religio* containing Browne's autograph corrections, apparently made in the process of preparing the 1643 version for the press, is held by the Princeton University Library (Robert Taylor Collection—17th Century—56). For a fuller description of this item, see my "Sir Thomas Browne's Annotated Copy of his 1642 *Religio Medici*," *Princeton University Library Chronicle* 67, no. 3 (2006): 595–610.

59. The new sections are those now identified as I.8, I.28, I.43, I.56. For a more detailed discussion of Browne's smaller changes, see Denonain, introduction to Browne, *Religio Medici* (1953), xxvii–xxviii.

60. For example, in the third version Browne adds yet another new passage shifting attention away from his heresies. Immediately after his catalogue of heresies comes an entirely new section in which he discusses the unavoidability of heresies in any church (I.8). Although by the third version he has more than doubled the total number of lines devoted to heresy, he has radically diminished the autobiographical impact of those lines by obscuring their personal component.

61. Immediately after an original section in which Browne has expressed his willingness to believe in miracles—even, just possibly, "that [which] is reported of the Jesuites and their Miracles in the Indies" (I.27)—he inserts an entirely new section in which he decries the efficacy of relics and ridicules some specific stories of their powers (I.28).

CHAPTER 5. JOHN BUNYAN'S DOUBLE AUTOBIOGRAPHY

1. John Bunyan, *Grace Abounding to the Chief of Sinners,* ed. Roger Sharrock (Oxford: Clarendon Press, 1962). All subsequent quotations from *Grace Abounding* are also from this edition.

2. For this version of Bunyan, see especially Roger Sharrock, *John Bunyan* (London: Macmillan, 1968), 41–42, 54–55, and Christopher Hill, *A Tinker and a Poor Man: John Bunyan and His Church* (New York: Knopf, 1989), 74, 106–9. Even Richard Greaves, who treats the depression of Bunyan's early years in sensitive detail, believes that his state of mind during the years he wrote *Grace Abounding* "was generally positive." *Glimpses of Glory: John Bunyan and English Dissent* (Stanford: Stanford University Press, 2002), 207–8.

3. William James famously described Bunyan as "a typical case of the psychopathic temperament." See *The Varieties of Religious Experience* (New York: Penguin Classics, 1985), 157. While few contemporary scholars would go so far as to call Bunyan a psychopath, the obsessive nature of his religious anxiety and his apparently deeply depressive temperament are widely recognized. For detailed discussions of Bunyan's depression and

general psychology, see Greaves, *Glimpses*, esp. 35–41, 56–60, 232–41, and Leopold Damrosch, *God's Plot and Man's Stories* (Chicago: University of Chicago Press, 1985), 124–36. More occasional discussions can be found in Hill, *Tinker*, 184–87, and Sharrock, *John Bunyan*, 27–28, 57–58, 63–67.

4. The title is an allusion to St. Paul's statement in 1 Timothy 1:15 that he himself is the chief of sinners. As the first Christian convert to write the story of his conversion, Paul is a model for many Christian spiritual autobiographers.

5. Many scholars have noted the ways in which *Grace Abounding* differs from the "typical" early modern spiritual autobiography, including Roger Sharrock in the introduction to his Clarendon Press edition of the work (1962), pp. xxix–xxxi. See also Michael Davies, *Graceful Reading: Theology and Narrative in the Works of John Bunyan* (Oxford: Oxford University Press, 2002), 97–98, 159–62; Felicity A. Nussbaum, "'By These Words I Was Sustained': Bunyan's *Grace Abounding*," *ELH* 49, no. 1 (1982): 18–34; Vera J. Camden, "'Most Fit for a Wounded Conscience': The Place of Luther's 'Commentary on Galatians' in *Grace Abounding*," *Renaissance Quarterly* 50 (1997): 819–49. *Grace Abounding* did become a model for later spiritual autobiographies, however, which perhaps accounts for the belief that it is typical of the genre. See D. Bruce Hindmarsh, *The Evangelical Conversion Narrative: Spiritual Autobiography in Early Modern England* (Oxford: Oxford University Press, 2005), 50–51.

6. To be sure, "straightforward," in this context, is a relative term: it is common for seventeenth-century spiritual autobiographies to recount a long series of struggles, with no single, definitive moment of conversion, and a greater focus on inward states rather than external events is also common. See, for example, Roger Sharrock, "Spiritual Autobiography: Bunyan's Grace Abounding," in Anne Laurence, W. R. Owens, and Stuart Sim, eds., *John Bunyan and His England, 1628–1688* (London: Hambledon Press, 1990), 99.

7. For a detailed discussion of the psychological aspects of *Grace Abounding*, see especially the essays in Vera J. Camden, ed., *Trauma and Transformation: The Political Progress of John Bunyan* (Stanford: Stanford University Press, 2008).

8. See Frank Kermode, *The Sense of an Ending* (Oxford: Oxford University Press, 1967); Peter Brooks, *Reading for the Plot: Design and Intention in Narrative* (New York: Knopf, 1984).

9. See John Bunyan, *A Relation of the Imprisonment of Mr. John Bunyan* (London, 1765), reprinted in Sharrock's Clarendon edition of *Grace Abounding*, 118–20. All subsequent quotations from the *Relation* refer to this edition and are cited parenthetically in the text.

10. These letters to his congregation were later published as *A Relation of the Imprisonment of Mr. John Bunyan* (see previous note). For a more detailed discussion of this work and its authenticity, see Roger Sharrock, "The Origin of *A Relation of the Imprisonment of Mr. John Bunyan*," *Review of English Studies*, new series 10 (1959): 250–56.

11. See N. H. Keeble, *The Literary Culture of Nonconformity in Late Seventeenth-Century England* (Athens: University of Georgia Press, 1987), 82–86.

12. See Keeble, "John Bunyan's Literary Life," in *The Cambridge Companion to Bunyan*, ed. Anne Dunan-Page (Cambridge: Cambridge University Press, 2010), 15–18; Sharon Achinstein, *Literature and Dissent in Milton's England* (Cambridge: Cambridge University Press, 2003), 101–3.

13. Bunyan wrote numerous tracts that take issue with the Quakers and the Ranters, but even there he rarely explicitly identifies those groups with the beliefs and practices that he is warning his reader away from. *Grace Abounding* is even less overtly polemical.

14. John Bunyan, *The Miscellaneous Works of John Bunyan*, ed. Roger Sharrock et al., 13 vols. (Oxford: Clarendon Press, 1976–1994), 1:11–16. All citations from this series are indicated in the text by the abbreviation *MW* followed by the volume and page number.

15. See *GA* §§229–30.

16. Richard Greaves has laid out the parallel parts of *Law and Grace* and *Grace Abounding* in his introduction to vol. 2 of the *Miscellaneous Works*. Interestingly, although there are some parallels with both the beginning and the ending of *Grace Abounding*, there are virtually none with the vast middle section, which deals with Bunyan's temptations. See *MW* 2:xxxii–xxxiv.

17. This seems to have been a Ranter belief, for, like the Quakers, the Ranters believed that divinity resided within the individual believer and denied that Christ acted as a personal savior. See Hill, *Tinker*, 80, and *MW* 1:xvi–xxi.

18. See Chapter 1.

19. Bunyan also omits this fact from the first edition of *Grace Abounding*, although he adds it in that work's third edition. In that edition, he admits to having read "some *Ranters* books"; he describes a once-close friend who fell under the Ranters' influence; and finally he explains that he was attracted to the Ranters because of their claim that they "had attained to perfection [and] could do what they would and not sin." "O," says Bunyan, "these temptations were suitable to my flesh, I being but a young man and my nature in its prime" (*GA* §§43, 44, 45).

20. Hill, *Tinker*, 75. See also 58–60, 74–84. For further discussion of Bunyan's relationship with the Ranters, see Greaves, *Glimpses*, 67–74.

21. Bunyan quotes the judge as saying, "You must be had back again to prison, and there lie for three months following; at three months end, if you do not submit to go to church to hear divine service, and leave your preaching, you must be banished the realm: And if, after such a day as shall be appointed you to be gone, you shall be found in this realm, &c. or be found to come over again without special license from the King, &c. you must stretch by the neck for it." Bunyan, *A Relation*, 118.

22. Over the course of those years Bunyan's treatment varied considerably, and he was occasionally allowed to leave prison for short periods, and sometimes even returned to his preaching. See Hill, *Tinker*, 121–22; Sharrock, *John Bunyan*, 42–43.

23. The manuscript version of this work no longer survives, but to the best of my knowledge no one has questioned the work's authenticity; Sharrock argues persuasively for Bunyan's authorship in "The Origin," 250–56.

24. The fourth letter is quite insistent that Bunyan was *not* seeking a royal pardon (as he was entitled to do, in a coronation year), because he did not admit that he had confessed to any guilt. He was appealing, instead, the legality of his conviction itself.

25. For further details on Bunyan's wife's appeal on his behalf, see Greaves, *Glimpses,* 142–45.

26. Ibid., 174–76.

27. Bunyan's contempt for the prayer book and his unwillingness to accept it as apostolic was one of the main issues raised at his trial. See *A Relation,* 114–18.

28. Although *The Holy City* is indebted to millenarian thought, scholars disagree about how revolutionary Bunyan's account of the apocalypse actually is. For two contrasting views, see Sears McGee's introduction to the work (*MW* 3: xxxix) and Greaves (*Glimpses,* 185–86).

29. See, for example, Achinstein, *Literature and Dissent,* 90–93.

30. For more on Bunyan's affection for Paul's epistles, see Dayton Haskin, "Bunyan's Scriptural Acts," in *Bunyan in Our Time,* ed. Robert G. Collmer (Kent, OH: Kent State University Press, 1989), 73–74.

31. For more on the violence latent in this comparison—and, Achinstein argues, much of Bunyan's oeuvre—see Achinstein, *Literature and Dissent,* 84–86, 101–14.

32. Keeble, *Literary Culture,* 84.

33. Ibid.

34. Many critics see this distinction as operating throughout the work. See, for example, John N. Morris, *Versions of the Self: Studies in English Autobiography from John Bunyan to John Stuart Mill* (New York: Basic Books, 1966), 96; Joan Webber, *Eloquent "I,"* 39. Others, such as Roger Pooley, noting the frequent intrusion of the present tense into the work, disagree that there is any such distinction. See "*Grace Abounding* and the New Sense of the Self," in Laurence, *John Bunyan and His England,* 109. I would argue that Bunyan *attempts* to make a distinction between his past and his present self, and this distinction is important to his project, but it is not consistently successful.

35. Tipcat is a game that involves striking an oblong piece of wood, pointed at both ends (the "cat"), with a stick. One stroke is intended to send the cat up and into the air, and the second, made while the cat is aloft, is meant to send it spinning around in the air.

36. See, for example, Sharrock, *John Bunyan,* 56–58; Hill, *Tinker,* 63–64; Morris, *Versions of the Self,* 91; Anne Hawkins, "The Double-Conversion in Bunyan's *Grace Abounding,*" *Philological Quarterly* 61, no. 3 (1982): 260.

37. The passage that Bunyan cites is Psalm 109:6–8, which he apparently understands as Christ's prayer against Judas.

38. See Dan G. Blazer, *The Age of Melancholy: "Major Depression" and Its Social Origins* (New York: Routledge, 2005), 44–45; Joel Rosenberg, "1 and 2 Samuel," in *The Literary Guide to the Bible,* ed. Robert Alter and Frank Kermode (Cambridge, MA: Belknap Press of Harvard University Press, 1987), 127–28.

39. There are two different biblical accounts of Saul's rejection by God. Twentieth-century scholars of the Bible have theorized that part of the original story may be missing, but in any case it is clear that the now-canonical text of 1 Samuel is the work of multiple authors who appear to have had very different attitudes toward monarchy. See John J. Collins, *Introduction to the Hebrew Bible* (Minneapolis: Fortress Press, 2004), 217–25, and the entry on Saul in *The Oxford Companion to the Bible*, 679–80.

40. "Whosoever speaketh a word against the Son of man, it shall be forgiven him: but whosoever speaketh against the Holy Ghost, it shall not be forgiven him, neither in this world, neither in the world to come." Matthew 12.32. See also Luke 12:10 and Mark 3:29.

41. John Bunyan, *The Pilgrim's Progress*, ed. J. B. Wharey and Roger Sharrock (Oxford: Oxford University Press, 1960), 2nd ed., 38.

42. For a reading of Bunyan's temptation to "sell Christ" that interprets that terminology as a troubled response to the economic language of Puritan covenant theology, see Lori Branch, "'As Blood Is Forced Out of Flesh': Spontaneity and the Wounds of Exchange in *Grace Abounding* and *The Pilgrim's Progress*," *ELH* 74, no. 2 (2007): 271–99.

43. Bunyan first explicitly voices his fear that "selling" Christ is the sin against the Holy Ghost in §148, but it seems implicit from §141 onward.

44. It also echoes Bunyan's discussion in *Resurrection of the Dead* of the punishments awaiting those who turn their backs on Christ.

45. Christopher Hill has also remarked on the prominence of this temptation and the oddity of Bunyan's declining to specify just what he was tempted to sell his birthright *for*. Hill argues, following a suggestion made by Jack Lindsay in *John Bunyan, Maker of Myths,* that Bunyan's association of this sin with Esau's sale of his birthright might represent Bunyan's fretting over "his family's sale of lands in the sixteenth and early seventeenth centuries," a sale that brought about "the wandering life of tinkers" (*Tinker,* 69–70). Although this is an intriguing suggestion, the parallels seem too distant; it seems unlikely that Bunyan would be so obsessed with the possibility of his committing a sin (if in fact he would have regarded the sale of the family lands as a sin) that had actually been committed by his ancestors two or three generations earlier.

46. Both of the biblical passages to which Bunyan refers have to do with murderers seeking shelter in the temple—rather than men who are officiants at the temple—but as it is clear that Bunyan does not think himself a murderer, the notion of being torn from God's altar sounds very much like a reference to Bunyan's parting from his congregation at his arrest.

47. *MW* 2:157–58. See the discussion earlier in this chapter.

48. In the 1666 version of *Grace Abounding*, this section leads directly into Bunyan's account of his arrest and imprisonment. In the third edition (c. 1674) Bunyan adds five new section that expand on this theme of humility, while in the fifth edition (1680), following the scandal involving Agnes Beaumont, Bunyan adds twelve more sections to those five, in which he defends himself against charges of licentiousness.

49. None of Bunyan's subsequent treatises contain anything like the autobiographical passages to be found in *Law and Grace* (or even *I Will Pray with the Spirit*). The 1672 *Confession of my Faith and a Reason of my Practice* begins with a creed-like section in which Bunyan outlines the specifics of his faith, but these specifics do little more than show a reader how unexceptional are the beliefs for which Bunyan was apparently sent to jail, and for which he has served twelve long years. For this interpretation of the work, see T. L. Underwood's discussion in *MW* 4:xxviii–xxix.

50. Roger Sharrock is the only scholar I am aware of who has discussed Bunyan's additions in any detail. See *John Bunyan*, 61–62, and "Spiritual Autobiography: Bunyan's *Grace Abounding*," *John Bunyan and His England*, 100.

CHAPTER 6. JAMES II AND THE END OF THE CONFESSION OF FAITH

1. This would become less true for both Milton and Browne as they aged (in the 1650s and after), but it was very much the case in the 1630s and 1640s.

2. The date of this speech is February 6, 1684/5. See James II, *Royal Tracts* (Paris, 1692), B r–B v. This volume, which is in two parts, contains "Select speeches, orders, messages, letters, &c." during James's reign, the Glorious Revolution, and immediately afterward, as well as "Imago Regis," a devotional work written during his exile. All subsequent quotations from this volume are cited in the text as *Royal Tracts*.

3. See, for example, W. A. Speck, *James II* (London: Longman, 2002), and Steve Pincus, *1688: The First Modern Revolution* (New Haven: Yale University Press, 2009), 96–99.

4. *Copies of two papers written by the Late King Charles II* (London: H. Hills, 1685), 1–5.

5. Under the title "Imago Regis," these meditations can be found in the second half of *Royal Tracts*.

6. These manuscripts have a complicated history. See James Stanier Clarke, ed., *Life of James the Second, King of England, Collected out of Memoirs Writ of His Own Hand* (London, 1816).

7. There is considerable disagreement among contemporary historians about the nature of James's support for toleration. Many have argued that James was sincere (even if he hoped that toleration, by removing the penalties for recusancy, would "naturally" bring most of his countrymen into the light of the truth of the Church of Rome), while others believe that it was simply a ploy. See, for example, John Miller, "James II and Toleration," in *By Force or by Default? The Revolution of 1688–89*, ed. Eveline Cruickshanks (Edinburgh: J. Donald, 1989), 8–27; Pincus, *1688*, 6, 143–217; Speck, *James II* (and see also Speck's *Reluctant Revolutionaries: Englishmen and the Revolution of 1688* [Oxford: Oxford University Press, 1989]).

8. Of course, the Revolution of 1688 also led to the law against Catholics inheriting the throne (as well as new penal laws against ordinary Catholics), so it was certainly not

a decisive blow for toleration. See Pincus, *1688*, 4, 456–58, 465–71; Miller, "James II," 23–24; and Clement Fatovic, "The Anti-Catholic Roots of Liberal and Republican Conceptions of Freedom in English Political Thought," *Journal of the History of Ideas* 66, no. 1 (2005): 37–58.

9. See, for example, Sidonie Smith, "Performativity, Autobiographical Practice, Resistance," in *Women, Autobiography, Theory: A Reader*, ed. Sidonie Smith and Julia Watson (Madison: University of Wisconsin Press, 1998), 110.

BIBLIOGRAPHY

Achinstein, Sharon. *Literature and Dissent in Milton's England.* Cambridge: Cambridge University Press, 2003.

An Act for the better discovering and repressing of Popish recusants. London, 1606.

Akrigg, G. P. V. *Jacobean Pageant, or, the Court of King James I.* Cambridge, MA: Harvard University Press, 1962.

Akrigg, G. P. V., ed. *Letters of King James VI and I.* Berkeley: University of California Press, 1984.

Alighieri, Dante. *The Vita Nuova.* Trans. Mark Musa. Bloomington: Indiana University Press, 1973.

Alter, Robert, and Frank Kermode, eds. *The Literary Guide to the Bible.* Cambridge, MA: Belknap Press of Harvard University Press, 1987.

Anastasii Bibliothecari. *Historia de vitis Romanorum Pontificum.* Venice, 1729.

Arshagouni, Mary. "John Donne's *Devotions upon Emergent Occasions*: A Puritan Reading." Ph.D. diss., UCLA, 1988.

———. "The Latin 'Stationes' in John Donne's *Devotions upon Emergent Occasions.*" *Modern Philology* 89, no. 2 (1991): 196–210.

Askew, Anne. *The first examinacyon of Anne Askewe: latelye martyred in Smythfelde, by the Romysh popes upholders, with the elucydacyon of Johan Bale.* Germany, 1546.

———. *The lattre examinacyon of Anne Askewe: latelye martyred in Smythfelde, by the wycked Synagoge of Antichrist, with the Elucydacyon of Johan Bale.* Germany, 1547.

Augustine. *The confessions of the incomparable doctour S. Augustine.* Trans. Sir Tobie Matthew. St. Omer, 1620.

———. *Saint Augustines Confessions translated.* Trans. William Watts. London, 1631.

Bald, R. C. *John Donne: A Life.* Oxford: Oxford University Press, 1970.

Barbour, Reid. *English Epicures and Stoics: Ancient Legacies in Early Stuart Culture.* Amherst: University of Massachusetts Press, 1998.

———. *Sir Thomas Browne: A Life.* Oxford: Oxford: University Press, 2013.

Barker, Arthur E. "The Pattern of Milton's *Nativity Ode.*" *University of Toronto Quarterly* 10 (1941): 167–81.

Barlow, William. *An Answer to a Catholike English-man.* London, 1609.

Barroll, J. Leeds. *Anna of Denmark, Queen of England: A Cultural Biography.* Philadelphia: University of Pennsylvania Press, 2001.

Bedford, Ronald, Lloyd Davis, and Philippa Kelly, eds. *Early Modern Autobiography: Theories, Genres, Practices.* Ann Arbor: University of Michigan Press, 2006.

Bellarmine, Cardinal. *Responsio Matthaei Torti.* 1608.

Black, Joseph L., ed., *The Martin Marprelate Tracts: A Modernized and Annotated Edition.* Cambridge: Cambridge University Press, 2008.

Blazer, Dan G. *The Age of Melancholy: "Major Depression" and Its Social Origins.* New York: Routledge, 2005.

Bottrall, Margaret. *Every Man a Phoenix: Studies in Seventeenth-Century Autobiography.* London: John Murray, 1958.

Branch, Lori. "'As Blood Is Forced Out of Flesh': Spontaneity and the Wounds of Exchange in *Grace Abounding* and *The Pilgrim's Progress.*" *ELH* 74, no. 2 (2007): 271–99.

Brooks, Peter. *Reading for the Plot: Design and Intention in Narrative.* New York: Knopf, 1984.

Browne, Thomas. Early manuscript copy of *Religio Medici.* Pembroke College (Oxford) Special Collections, MS 17.

———. Early manuscript copy of *Religio Medici.* British Library, MS Lansdowne 489, 132v–137r.

———. *Religio Medici: Edited from the Manuscript Copies and the Early Editions.* Ed. Jean-Jacques Denonain. Cambridge: Cambridge University Press, 1953.

———. *Religio Medici: A New Edition with Biographical and Critical Introduction.* Ed. Jean-Jacques Denonain. Cambridge: Cambridge University Press, 1955.

———. *Sir Thomas Browne's Works.* 4 vols. Ed. Simon Wilkin. London: William Pickering, 1835–1836.

Bunyan, John. *Grace Abounding to the Chief of Sinners.* Ed. Roger Sharrock. Oxford: Clarendon Press, 1962.

———. *The Miscellaneous Works of John Bunyan.* 13 vols. Ed. Roger Sharrock et al. Oxford: Clarendon Press, 1976–1994.

———. *The Pilgrim's Progress.* 2nd edition. Ed. J. B. Wharey and Roger Sharrock. Oxford: Oxford University Press, 1960.

Burckhardt, Jacob. *The Civilization of the Renaissance in Italy: An Essay.* New York: Modern Library, 1954.

Camden, Vera J. "'Most Fit for a Wounded Conscience': The Place of Luther's 'Commentary on Galatians' in *Grace Abounding.*" *Renaissance Quarterly* 50, no. 3 (1997): 819–49.

Camden, Vera J., ed. *Trauma and Transformation: The Political Progress of John Bunyan.* Stanford: Stanford University Press, 2008.

Carey, John. *John Donne: Life, Mind, and Art.* Oxford: Oxford University Press, 1981.

The Catholic Encyclopedia. New York: Robert Appleton, 1912. www.newadvent.org /cathen.

Charles II. *Copies of Two Papers Written by the Late King Charles II. Together With a Copy of a Paper written by the late Duchess of York.* London, 1685.

Coleman, Patrick, Jayne Lewis, and Jill Kowalik, eds. *Representations of the Self from the Renaissance to Romanticism.* Cambridge: Cambridge University Press, 2000.

Collins, John J. *Introduction to the Hebrew Bible.* Minneapolis: Fortress Press, 2004.

Collinson, Patrick. *Birthpangs of Protestant England: Religious and Cultural Change in the Sixteenth and Seventeenth Centuries.* New York: St. Martin's Press, 1988.

―――. "Elizabeth I." In *Oxford Dictionary of National Biography.* Oxford: Oxford University Press, 2004; online edition, 2008.

Conti, Brooke. "Sir Thomas Browne's Annotated Copy of His 1642 *Religio Medici.*" *Princeton University Library Chronicle* 67, no. 3 (2006): 595–610.

Cooper, Robert M. "The Political Implications of Donne's *Devotions.*" In *New Essays on Donne,* ed. Gary A. Stringer, 192–210. Elizabethan and Renaissance Studies 57. Salzburg: Institut für Englische Sprache und Literatur, 1977.

Corns, Thomas. *Uncloistered Virtue: English Political Literature, 1640–1660.* Oxford: Oxford University Press, 1992.

Cromartie, Alan. "King James and the Hampton Court Conference." In *James VI and I: Ideas, Authority, and Government,* ed. Ralph Houlbrooke, 61–80. Aldershot: Ashgate, 2006.

Cummings, Brian. *The Literary Culture of the Reformation: Grammar and Grace.* Oxford: Oxford University Press, 2002.

Davies, Julian. *The Caroline Captivity of the Church: Charles I and the Remoulding of Anglicanism 1625–1641.* Oxford: Clarendon Press, 1992.

Davies, Michael. *Graceful Reading: Theology and Narrative in the Works of John Bunyan.* Oxford: Oxford University Press, 2002.

Delany, Paul. *British Autobiography in the Seventeenth Century.* London: Routledge and Kegan Paul, 1969.

De Man, Paul. "Autobiography as De-Facement." *Modern Language Notes* 94, no. 5 (1979): 919–30.

Digby, Kenelm. *Observations on Religio Medici.* London, 1643.

Doelman, James. "'A King of Thine Own Heart': The English Reception of King James VI and I's *Basilikon Doron.*" *Seventeenth Century* 9, no. 1 (1994): 1–9.

Donne, John. *Complete Poetry and Selected Prose of John Donne.* Ed. Charles M. Coffin. New York: Modern Library, 1994.

―――. *Devotions upon Emergent Occasions.* Ed. Anthony Raspa. Montreal: McGill-Queen's University Press, 1975.

―――. *The Divine Poems.* Ed. Helen Gardner. Oxford: Clarendon Press, 1952.

―――. *Letters to Severall Persons of Honor.* London, 1651. Facsimile edition, ed. Charles Edmund Merrill Jr. New York: Sturgis and Walton, 1910.

―――. *Pseudo-Martyr.* Revised edition. Ed. Anthony Raspa. Montreal: McGill-Queen's University Press, 1993.

―――. *Selected Prose.* Ed. Neil Rhodes. New York: Penguin, 1987.

―――. *Sermons.* 10 vols. Ed. George R. Potter and Evelyn M. Simpson. Berkeley: University of California Press, 1953–1962.

Dragstra, Henk, Sheila Ottway, and Helen Wilcox, eds. *Betraying Our Selves: Forms of Self-Representation in Early Modern English Texts*. New York: St. Martin's Press, 2000.

Duffy, Eamon. *The Stripping of the Altars: Traditional Religion in England 1400–1580*. 2nd edition. New Haven: Yale University Press, 2005.

Dunn, Kevin. *Pretexts of Authority: The Rhetoric of Authorship in the Renaissance Preface*. Stanford: Stanford University Press, 1994.

Ebner, Dean. *Autobiography in Seventeenth-Century England: Theology and the Self*. The Hague: Mouton, 1971.

Elizabeth I. *Collected Works*. Ed. Leah S. Marcus, Janel Mueller, and Mary Beth Rose. Chicago: University of Chicago Press, 2000.

English Short Title Catalogue. London, British Library. http://estc.bl.uk.

Epiphanius. *The "Panarion" of Epiphanius of Salamis*. Trans. Frank Williams. Leiden: Brill, 2009.

Evans, J. Martin. "A Poem of Absences," *Milton Quarterly* 27, no. 1 (1993): 31–35.

Fallon, Robert Thomas. "*A Second Defence*: Milton's Critique of Cromwell?" *Milton Studies* 39 (2000): 167–83.

Fallon, Stephen M. "Alexander More Reads Milton: Self-Representation and Anxiety in Milton's *Defences*." In *Milton and the Terms of Liberty*, ed. Graham Parry and Joad Raymond, 111–24. Cambridge: D. S. Brewer, 2002.

———. *Milton's Peculiar Grace: Self-Representation and Authority*. Ithaca: Cornell University Press, 2007.

———. "The Spur of Self-Concernment: Milton in His Divorce Tracts." *Milton Studies* 38 (2000): 220–42.

Fatovic, Clement. "The Anti-Catholic Roots of Liberal and Republican Conceptions of Freedom in English Political Thought." *Journal of the History of Ideas* 66, no. 1 (2005): 37–58.

Finch, Jeremiah S., ed. *A Catalogue of the Libraries of Sir Thomas Browne and Dr. Edward Browne, His Son: A Facsimile Reproduction*. Leiden: Leiden University Press, 1986.

———. *Sir Thomas Browne: A Doctor's Life of Science and Faith*. New York: Henry Schuman, 1950.

The First and Second Prayer Books of Edward VI. Ed. E. C. Ratcliff. London: J. M. Dent, 1949.

Fish, Stanley. "One University Under God?" *Chronicle of Higher Education*, January 7, 2005. http://chronicle.com/article/One-University-Under-God-/45077.

———. *Self-Consuming Artifacts: The Experience of Seventeenth-Century Literature*. Berkeley: University of California Press, 1972.

Flynn, Dennis. "Donne's Politics, 'Desperate Ambition,' and Meeting Paolo Sarpi in Venice." *Journal of English and Germanic Philology* 99, no. 3 (2000): 334–55.

———. *John Donne and the Ancient Catholic Nobility*. Bloomington: Indiana University Press, 1995.

Frost, Kate Gartner. *Holy Delight: Typology, Numerology, and Autobiography in Donne's "Devotions upon Emergent Occasions."* Princeton: Princeton University Press, 1990.

Fumerton, Patricia. *Cultural Aesthetics: Renaissance Literature and the Practice of Social Ornament.* Chicago: University of Chicago Press, 1991.

———. *Unsettled: The Culture of Mobility and the Working Poor in Early Modern England.* Chicago: University of Chicago Press, 2006.

Goldberg, Jonathan. *James I and the Politics of Literature: Jonson, Shakespeare, Donne, and Their Contemporaries.* Stanford: Stanford University Press, 1989 (reprint; original Baltimore: Johns Hopkins University Press, 1983).

———. "The Understanding of Sickness in Donne's *Devotions*." *Renaissance Quarterly* 24, no. 4 (1971): 507–17.

Gray, Dave, and Jeanne Shami. "Political Advice in Donne's *Devotions*." *Modern Language Quarterly* 50, no. 4 (1989): 337–56.

Greaves, Richard. *Glimpses of Glory: John Bunyan and English Dissent.* Stanford: Stanford University Press, 2002.

Green, Ian. *The Christian's ABC: Catechisms and Catechizing in England c. 1530–1740.* Oxford: Clarendon Press, 1996.

Griffin, Martin I. J., Jr. *Latitudinarianism in the Seventeenth-Century Church of England.* Leiden: Brill, 1992.

Guibbory, Achsah. *Ceremony and Community from Herbert to Milton: Literature, Religion and Cultural Conflict in Seventeenth-Century England.* Cambridge: Cambridge University Press, 1998.

Guillory, John. *Poetic Authority: Spenser, Milton, and Literary History.* New York: Columbia University Press, 1983.

Haigh, Christopher. *English Reformations: Religion, Politics, and Society Under the Tudors.* Oxford: Clarendon Press, 1993.

———. *The Plain Man's Pathways to Heaven: Kinds of Christianity in Post-Reformation England, 1570–1640.* Oxford: Oxford University Press, 2007.

Haigh, Christopher, ed. *The English Reformation Revised.* Cambridge: Cambridge University Press, 1987.

Hale, John K. "Milton's Self-Presentation in *Poems . . . 1645*." *Milton Quarterly* 25, no. 2 (1991): 37–48.

Hall, Anne Drury. *Ceremony and Civility in English Renaissance Prose.* University Park: Pennsylvania State University Press, 1991.

———. "Epistle, Meditation, and Sir Thomas Browne's *Religio Medici*." *PMLA* 94, no. 2 (1979): 234–46.

Hall, Joseph. *The shaking of the olive tree: The remaining works of that incomparable prelate, Joseph Hall.* London, 1660.

Haller, William. *The Rise of Puritanism.* New York: Columbia University Press, 1939.

Hanson, Elizabeth. *Discovering the Subject in Renaissance England.* Cambridge: Cambridge University Press, 1998.

Haskin, Dayton. "Bunyan's Scriptural Acts." In *Bunyan in Our Time,* ed. Robert G. Col-
    lmer, 61–92. Kent, OH: Kent State University Press, 1989.

Hawkins, Anne. "The Double-Conversion in Bunyan's *Grace Abounding.*" *Philological
    Quarterly* 61, no. 3 (1982): 259–76.

Hayward, John. *An answer to the first part of a certain conference, concerning succession.*
    London, 1603.

Helgerson, Richard. *Self-Crowned Laureates: Spenser, Jonson, Milton and the Literary Sys-
    tem.* Berkeley: University of California Press, 1983.

Herman, Peter C. "Authorship and the Royal 'I': King James VI/I and the Politics of
    Monarchic Verse." *Renaissance Quarterly* 54, no. 4 (2001): 1495–1530.

Hester, M. Thomas, ed. *John Donne's "Desire of More": The Subject of Anne More Donne in
    His Poetry.* Newark: University of Delaware Press, 1996.

Higgons, Theophilus. *The Apology of Theophilus Higgons Lately Minister, Now Catholique.*
    1609. Facsimile edition, *English Recusant Literature 1558–1640,* vol. 57. Menston:
    Scolar Press, 1971.

Hill, Christopher. *Milton and the English Revolution.* New York: Viking, 1978.

———. *A Tinker and a Poor Man: John Bunyan and His Church.* New York: Knopf, 1989.

Hindmarsh, D. Bruce. *The Evangelical Conversion Narrative: Spiritual Autobiography in
    Early Modern England.* Oxford: Oxford University Press, 2005.

Houliston, Victor. "An Apology for Donne's *Pseudo-Martyr.*" *Review of English Studies* 57
    (September 2006): 474–86.

Huntley, Frank Livingstone. *Sir Thomas Browne: A Biographical and Critical Study.* Ann
    Arbor: University of Michigan Press, 1962.

Irenaeus. *Against Heresies.* In *Ante-Nicene Fathers,* vol. 1, ed. Alexander Roberts http://
    www.gnosis.org/library/advh1.htm.

Jackson, Ken, and Arthur Marotti. "The Turn to Religion in Early Modern English
    Studies." *Criticism* 46, no. 1 (2004): 167–90.

James VI and I. *An apologie for the oath of allegiance.* [2nd edition.] London, 1609.

———. *The Basilicon Doron of King James VI.* 2 vols. Ed. James Craigie. Edinburgh:
    Scottish Text Society, 1944.

———. *James VI and I: Political Writings.* Ed. Johann P. Sommerville. Cambridge:
    Cambridge University Press, 1994.

———. *To the Ministers Church-Wardens* [i.e., *Directions to Preachers*]. Oxford, 1622.

———. *Triplici nodo, triplex cuneus. Or An apologie for the Oath of allegiance.* London, 1607.

James II. *Life of James the Second, King of England, Collected out of Memoirs Writ of His
    Own Hand.* Ed. James Stanier Clarke. London, 1816.

———. *Royal Tracts.* Paris, 1692.

James, William. *The Varieties of Religious Experience.* New York: Penguin Classics, 1985.

Keeble, N. H. "John Bunyan's Literary Life." In *The Cambridge Companion to Bunyan,*
    ed. Anne Dunan-Page, 13–25. Cambridge: Cambridge University Press, 2010.

———. *The Literary Culture of Nonconformity in Later Seventeenth-Century England.*
    Athens: University of Georgia Press, 1987.

Kermode, Frank. *The Sense of an Ending: Studies in the Theory of Fiction.* Oxford: Oxford University Press, 1967.

Kerrigan, William. *The Prophetic Milton.* Charlottesville: University of Virginia Press, 1974.

Kooi, Christine. *Liberty and Religion: Church and State in Leiden's Reformation, 1572–1620.* Leiden: Brill, 2000.

Kranidas, Thomas. *Milton and the Rhetoric of Zeal.* Pittsburgh: Duquesne University Press, 2005.

Lake, Peter. *Anglicans and Puritans? Presbyterianism and English Conformist Thought, Whitgift to Hooker.* New York: HarperCollins, 1988.

Lander, Jesse. *Inventing Polemic: Religion, Print, and Literary Culture in Early Modern England.* Cambridge: Cambridge University Press, 2006.

A large examination taken at Lambeth, according to his Majesties direction, point by point, of M. G. Blakwell. London, 1607.

Leighton, Alexander. *An Appeal to the Parliament; or Sions Plea Against the Prelacie.* [Amsterdam?] 1628.

Lemon, Rebecca. *Treason by Words: Literature, Law, and Rebellion in Shakespeare's England.* Ithaca: Cornell University Press, 2006.

L'Estrange, Roger. *No Blinde Guides: in answer to a seditious pamphlet of J. Milton's.* London, 1660.

Levi, Anthony. *Renaissance and Reformation: The Intellectual Genesis.* New Haven: Yale University Press, 2002.

Levy-Navarro, Elena. "John Donne's Fear of Rumours in the *Devotions upon Emergent Occasions* and the Death of John King." *Notes and Queries* 47, no. 4 (2000): 481–83.

Lewalski, Barbara K. *The Life of John Milton: A Critical Biography.* Oxford: Blackwell, 2000.

Lilburne, John. *The Christian Mans Triall: or, A true relation of the first apprehension and severall examinations of John Lilburne.* 2nd edition. London, 1641.

———. *A worke of the Beast or A relation of a most unchristian censure, executed upon Iohn Lilburne.* Amsterdam, 1638.

Lim, Paul C. H. *Mystery Unveiled: The Crisis of the Trinity in Early Modern England.* Oxford: Oxford University Press, 2012.

Limouze, Henry S. "Joseph Hall and the Prose Style of John Milton." *Milton Studies* 15 (1981): 121–41.

Lindsay, Jack. *John Bunyan: Maker of Myths.* London: Methuen, 1937.

Loewenstein, David. "Milton and the Poetics of Defense." In *Politics, Poetics, and Hermeneutics in Milton's Prose*, ed. David Loewenstein and James Grantham Turner, 171–192. Cambridge: Cambridge University Press, 1990.

Long, A. A. *Hellenistic Philosophy: Stoics, Epicureans, Sceptics.* London: Duckworth, 1974.

Loomie, Albert J. "King James I's Catholic Consort." *Huntington Library Quarterly* 34, no. 4 (1971): 303–16.

Love, Harold. *The Culture and Commerce of Texts: Scribal Publication in Seventeenth-Century England.* Amherst: University of Massachusetts Press, 1998.

Lucan, *Pharsalia*. Trans. Sir Edward Ridley. London: Longmans, Green, 1896. Online Medieval and Classical Library: http://omacl.org/Pharsalia.

Luther, Martin. *Luther's Works*. 55 vols. Ed. Jaroslav Pelikan et al. Philadelphia: Fortress Press, 1955–1986.

Maltby, Judith. *Prayer Book and People in Elizabethan and Early Stuart England*. Cambridge: Cambridge University Press, 2000.

Marcus, Leah S. *Unediting the Renaissance: Shakespeare, Marlowe, Milton*. London: Routledge, 1996.

Marotti, Arthur. *John Donne, Coterie Poet*. Madison: University of Wisconsin Press, 1986.

———. "John Donne's Conflicted Anti-Catholicism." *Journal of English and Germanic Philology* 101, no. 3 (2002): 358–79.

Martz, Louis L. "Milton's Prophetic Voice: Moving Toward Paradise." In *Of Poetry and Politics: New Essays on Milton and His World*, ed. P. G. Stanwood, 1–16. Binghamton, NY: Medieval and Renaissance Texts and Studies, 1995.

———. *Poet of Exile: A Study of Milton's Poetry*. New Haven: Yale University Press, 1980.

———. *The Poetry of Meditation: A Study in English Religious Literature of the Seventeenth Century*. New Haven: Yale University Press, 1954.

Maus, Katharine Eisaman. *Inwardness and Theatre in the English Renaissance*. Chicago: University of Chicago Press, 1995.

Miller, John. "James II and Toleration." In *By Force or by Default? The Revolution of 1688–89*, ed. Eveline Cruickshanks, 8–27. Edinburgh: J. Donald, 1989.

Milton, John. *Complete Poems and Major Prose*. Ed. Merritt Y. Hughes. New York: Macmillan, 1985.

———. *Complete Prose Works of John Milton*. 8 vols. Ed. Don M. Wolfe et al. New Haven: Yale University Press, 1953–1982.

———. *The Works of John Milton*, 18 vols. Ed. Frank Patterson et al. New York: Columbia University Press, 1931–1938.

Modest confutation of a scandalous and scurrilous libell, entituled, Animadversions upon the remonstrants defense against Smectymnuus. London, 1642.

Montaigne, Michel de. *The Complete Essays of Montaigne*. Ed. and trans. Donald M. Frame. Stanford: Stanford University Press, 1998.

More, Thomas. *Complete Works of St. Thomas More*. 15 vols. New Haven: Yale University Press, 1961–1997.

Morris, John N. *Versions of the Self: Studies in English Autobiography from John Bunyan to John Stuart Mill*. New York: Basic Books, 1966.

Morrissey, Thomas J. "The Self and the Meditative Tradition in Donne's *Devotions*." *Notre Dame English Journal* 13, no. 1 (1980): 29–49.

Mueller, Janel M. "The Exegesis of Experience: Dean Donne's *Devotions upon Emergent Occasions*." *Journal of English and Germanic Philology* 67 (1968): 1–19.

———. "'To My Very Good Brother the King of Scots': Elizabeth I's Correspondence with James VI and the Question of Succession." *PMLA* 115, no. 5 (2000): 1063–71.

Murray, Molly. *The Poetics of Conversion in Early Modern English Literature: Verse and Change from Donne to Dryden.* Cambridge: Cambridge University Press, 2009.

Narveson, Kate. "Piety and the Genre of Donne's *Devotions.*" *John Donne Journal* 17 (1998): 107–36.

Narveson, Katherine Ruth. "The Soul's Society: Genre, Community, and Identity in Early Stuart Devotional Literature." Ph.D. diss., University of Chicago, 1996.

Nathanson, Leonard. *The Strategy of Truth: A Study of Sir Thomas Browne.* Chicago: University of Chicago Press, 1967.

Ng, Su Fang. *Literature and the Politics of the Family in Seventeenth-Century England.* Cambridge: Cambridge University Press, 2007.

Nitchie, George. "Donne in Love: Some Reflections on 'Loves Alchymie.'" *Southern Review* 15 (1979): 16–21.

Norbrook, David. "The Monarchy of Wit and the Republic of Letters: Donne's Politics." In *Soliciting Interpretation: Literary Theory and Seventeenth-Century English Poetry,* ed. Elizabeth D. Harvey and Katharine Eisaman Maus, 3–36. Chicago: University of Chicago Press, 1990.

North, Marcy L. "Anonymity's Subject: James I and the Debate over the Oath of Allegiance." *New Literary History* 33, no. 2 (2002): 215–32.

Nowell, Alexander. *A Catechisme, or first Instruction and Learning of Christian Religion. Translated out of Latine into Englishe.* London, 1570.

Nussbaum, Felicity A. "'By These Words I Was Sustained': Bunyan's *Grace Abounding.*" *ELH* 49, no. 1 (1982): 18–34.

Openshaw, Robert. *Short questions, and answeares conteyning the summe of Christian religion.* London, 1579.

Orgel, Stephen. "The Royal Theatre and the Role of the King." In *Patronage in the Renaissance,* ed. Guy Fitch Lytle and Stephen Orgel, 261–73. Princeton: Princeton University Press, 1981.

The Oxford Companion to the Bible. Ed. Bruce M. Metzger and Michael D. Coogan. New York: Oxford University Press, 1993.

Papazian, Mary Arshagouni. "Donne, Election, and the *Devotions upon Emergent Occasions.*" *Huntington Library Quarterly* 55, no. 4 (1992): 603–19.

———. "Literary 'Things Indifferent': The Shared Augustinianism of Donne's *Devotions* and Bunyan's *Grace Abounding.*" In *John Donne's Religious Imagination,* ed. Raymond-Jean Frontain and Frances M. Malpezzi, 324–49. Conway, AR: UCA Press, 1995.

Paradiso, Sharon Desmond. "'Now Hear Mee Relate': Narrative Emplotment and Autobiography in *Paradise Lost.*" *English Language Notes* 35, no. 2 (1997): 9–17.

Parker, William Riley. *Milton's Contemporary Reputation.* Columbus: Ohio State University Press, 1940.

Partridge, A. C. *John Donne: Language and Style.* London: André Deutsch, 1978.

Patterson, Annabel. "All Donne." In *Soliciting Interpretation: Literary Theory and Seventeenth-Century Poetry,* ed. Elizabeth D. Harvey and Katharine Eisaman Maus, 37–67. Chicago: University of Chicago Press, 1990.

———. "The Civic Hero in Milton's Prose." *Milton Studies* 8 (1975): 71–101.

———. "John Donne, Kingsman?" In *The Mental World of the Jacobean Court*, ed. Linda Levy Peck, 251–72. Cambridge: Cambridge University Press, 1991.

———. "No Meer Amatorious Novel?" In *Politics, Poetics and Hermeneutics in Milton's Prose*, ed. David Loewenstein and James Grantham Turner, 85–101. Cambridge: Cambridge University Press, 1990.

Patterson, W. B. *King James VI and I and the Reunion of Christendom*. Cambridge: Cambridge University Press, 1997.

Peck, Linda Levy, ed. *The Mental World of the Jacobean Court*. Cambridge: Cambridge University Press, 1991.

Pelikan, Jaroslav. *Credo: Historical and Theological Guide to Creeds and Confessions in the Christian Tradition*. New Haven: Yale University Press, 2003.

Perry, Curtis. *The Making of Jacobean Culture: James I and the Renegotiation of Elizabethan Literary Practice*. Cambridge: Cambridge University Press, 1997.

Persons, Robert. [R. Doleman, pseud.] *A Conference about the Next Succession to the Crowne of Ingland*. [Antwerp?] 1594.

———. *The judgment of a Catholike English-man*. St. Omer, 1608.

———. [N. D., pseud.] *A Treatise of Three Conversions of England from Paganisme to Christian Religion*. St. Omer, 1603.

Petition Apologeticall, presented to the Kinges most excellent Majesty, by the lay Catholikes of England. Doway [English Secret Press], 1604.

Petrarch, Francesco. *The Secret*. Ed. Carol E. Quillen. Boston: Bedford/St. Martin's, 2003.

Pincus, Steve. *1688: The First Modern Revolution*. New Haven: Yale University Press, 2009.

Pomponazzi, Pietro. *De Immortalitate Animae*. Messina: Giuseppe Principato, 1925.

Pooley, Roger. "*Grace Abounding* and the New Sense of the Self." In *John Bunyan and His England 1628–88*, ed. Anne Laurence, W. R. Owens, and Stuart Sim, 105–14. London: Hambledon Press, 1990.

Poppi, Antonino. *Ricerche sulla teologia e la scienza nella Scuola padovana del Cinque e Seicento*. Soveria Mannelli: Rubbettino, 2001.

Post, Jonathan F. S. "Browne's Revisions of *Religio Medici*." *Studies in English Literature* 25, no. 1 (1985): 145–63.

———. *Sir Thomas Browne*. Boston: Twayne, 1987.

Power, Henry. Letter to Thomas Browne, February 10, 1648. British Library MS Sloane 1911, f. 78.

Preston, Claire. *Thomas Browne and the Writing of Early Modern Science*. Cambridge: Cambridge University Press, 2005.

Pricket, Robert. *Unto the most high and mightie prince, his soveraigne lord King* James. London, 1603.

Prince, Gerald. "The Disnarrated." *Style* 22, no. 1 (1988): 1–8.

Questier, Michael. "Catholic Loyalism in Early Stuart England." *English Historical Review* 123 (October 2008): 1132–65.

————. *Conversion, Politics and Religion in England 1580–1625.* Cambridge: Cambridge University Press, 1996.

————. "Loyalty, Religion, and State Power in Early Modern England: English Romanism and the Jacobean Oath of Allegiance." *Historical Journal* 40, no. 2 (1997): 311–29.

Rajan, Balachandra. "Browne and Milton: The Divided and the Distinguished." In *Approaches to Sir Thomas Browne: The Ann Arbor Tercentenary Lectures and Essays*, ed. C. A. Patrides, 1–11. Columbia: University of Missouri, 1982.

Richmond, Hugh M., "Personal Identity and Literary Personae: A Study in Historical Psychology." *PMLA* 90, no. 2 (1975): 209–21.

Rickard, Jane. *Authorship and Authority: The Writings of James VI and I.* Manchester: Manchester University Press, 2007.

Rollin, Roger B. "John Donne's *Holy Sonnets*—The Sequel: *Devotions upon Emergent Occasions.*" *John Donne Journal* 13, nos. 1–2 (1994): 51–59.

Rosendale, Timothy. *Liturgy and Literature in the Making of Protestant England.* Cambridge: Cambridge University Press, 2007.

Roston, Murray. "The 'Doubting' Thomas." In *Approaches to Sir Thomas Browne: The Ann Arbor Tercentenary Lectures and Essays*, ed. C. A. Patrides, 69–80. Columbia: University of Missouri, 1982.

Sánchez, Reuben, Jr. *Persona and Decorum in Milton's Prose.* Cranbury, NJ: Associated University Presses, 1997.

The Satisfactorie Epistle of a Late Converted English Protestant, unto Catholyke Religion. 1630. Facsimile edition, ed. D. M. Rogers, *English Recusant Literature 1558–1640*, vol. 153. Menston: Scolar Press, 1973.

Schoneveld, C. W. "Sir Thomas Browne and Leiden University in 1633." *English Language Notes* 19, no. 4 (1982): 335–59.

Seelig, Sharon Cadman. *Autobiography and Gender in Early Modern Literature: Reading Women's Lives 1600–1680.* Cambridge: Cambridge University Press, 2006.

————. "In Sickness and in Health: Donne's *Devotions upon Emergent Occasions.*" *John Donne Journal* 8, nos. 1–2 (1989): 103–13.

Shami, Jeanne. *John Donne and Conformity in Crisis in the Late Jacobean Pulpit.* Cambridge: D. S. Brewer, 2003.

Sharples, R. W. *Stoics, Epicureans and Sceptics.* London: Routledge, 1996.

Sharrock, Roger. *John Bunyan.* London: Macmillan, 1968.

————. "The Origin of *A Relation of the Imprisonment of Mr. John Bunyan.*" *Review of English Studies*, New Series 10 (1959): 250–56.

————. "Spiritual Autobiography: Bunyan's *Grace Abounding.*" In *John Bunyan and His England 1628–1688*, ed. Anne Laurence, W. R. Owens, and Stuart Sim. London: Hambledon Press, 1990.

Shawcross, John T. *John Milton: The Self and the World.* Lexington: University Press of Kentucky, 1993.

Shub, Joseph. "Milton's Prose Exordia and the Persuasion Through Character." *Prose Studies* 21, no. 1 (1998): 1–31.

Shuger, Debora. *Habits of Thought in the English Renaissance: Religion, Politics, and the Dominant Culture.* Berkeley: University of California Press, 1990.

———. "The Laudian Idiot." In *Sir Thomas Browne: The World Proposed*, ed. Reid Barbour and Claire Preston, 36–62. Oxford: Oxford University Press, 2008.

Shumaker, Wayne. *English Autobiography: Its Emergence, Materials, and Form.* Berkeley: University of California Press, 1954.

Sidney, Philip. *The Oxford Authors: Sir Philip Sidney.* Ed. Katherine Duncan-Jones. Oxford: Oxford University Press, 1989.

Silver, Victoria Silver. "Liberal Theology and Sir Thomas Browne's 'Soft and Flexible' Discourse." *English Literary Renaissance* 20, no. 1 (1990): 69–105.

Skura, Meredith Anne. *Tudor Autobiography: Listening for Inwardness.* Chicago: University of Chicago Press, 2008.

Smectymnuus [pseud.]. *An answer to a booke entitled, An humble remonstrance.* London, 1641.

Smith, Sidonie. "Performativity, Autobiographical Practice, Resistance." In *Women, Autobiography, Theory: A Reader*, ed. Sidonie Smith and Julia Watson, 108–15. Madison: University of Wisconsin Press, 1998.

Smyth, Adam. *Autobiography in Early Modern England.* Cambridge: Cambridge University Press, 2010.

Speck, W. A. *James II.* London: Longman, 2002.

———. *Reluctant Revolutionaries: Englishmen and the Revolution of 1688.* Oxford: Oxford University Press, 1989.

Staines, John D. *The Tragic Histories of Mary Queen of Scots, 1560–1690: Rhetoric, Passions, and Political Literature.* Burlington, VT: Ashgate, 2009.

Starr, G. A. *Defoe and Spiritual Autobiography.* Princeton: Princeton University Press, 1965.

Stevens, Paul. "Discontinuities in Milton's Early Public Self-Representation." *Huntington Library Quarterly* 51, no. 4 (1988): 261–80.

Stewart, Alan. *The Cradle King: The Life of James VI and I.* New York: St. Martin's, 2003.

Strier, Richard. "Donne and the Politics of Devotion." In *Religion, Literature, and Politics in Post-Reformation England, 1540–1688*, ed. Donna B. Hamilton and Richard Strier, 93–114. Cambridge: Cambridge University Press, 1996.

———. "Milton Against Humility." In *Religion and Culture in Renaissance England*, ed. Claire McEachern and Debora Shuger, 258–86. Cambridge: Cambridge University Press, 1997.

Sumers-Ingraham, Alinda. "John Milton's *Paradise Regained* and the Genre of the Puritan Spiritual Biography." Ph.D. diss., George Washington University, 1984.

Targoff, Ramie. *Common Prayer: The Language of Public Devotion in Early Modern England.* Chicago: University of Chicago Press, 2001.

Taylor, Jeremy. *The Rule and Exercises of Holy Living.* London, 1651.

Tentler, Thomas N. *Sin and Confession on the Eve of the Reformation.* Princeton: Princeton University Press, 1977.

Teresa of Avila. *The Book of Her Life.* Ed. and trans. Kieran Kavanaugh and Otilio Rodriguez. Indianapolis: Hackett, 2008.

To the Kinges most excellent Majestie: The humble petition of two and twentie preachers in London and the suburbs thereof. [Secret press? 1605?]

Trevor, Douglas. "*Pseudo-Martyr* and the Oath of Allegiance Controversy." *Reformation* 5 (2001): 103–37.

Valbuena, Olga. "Casuistry, Martyrdom, and the Allegiance Controversy in Donne's *Pseudo-Martyr*." *Religion and Literature* 32, no. 2 (2000): 49–80.

Van Laan, Thomas F. "John Donne's *Devotions* and the Jesuit Spiritual Exercises." *Studies in Philology* 60 (1963): 191–202.

Vinovich, J. Michael. "Protocols of Reading: Milton and Biography." *Early Modern Literary Studies* 1, no. 3 (1995): 2.1–15. www.library.ubc.ca/emls/01-3/vinomilt.html.

Walsham, Alexandra. *Charitable Hatred: Tolerance and Intolerance in England 1500–1700*. Manchester: Manchester University Press, 2006.

———. *Church Papists: Catholicism, Conformity, and Confessional Polemic in Early Modern England*. Suffolk: Boydell Press, 1993.

Walton, Isaak. *The Lives of John Donne, Sir Henry Wotton, Richard Hooker, George Herbert, and Robert Sanderson*. London: Oxford University Press, 1966.

Warnicke, Retha M. *Mary Queen of Scots*. New York: Routledge, 2006.

Warnke, Frank J. "A Hook for Amphibium: Some Reflections on Fish." In *Approaches to Sir Thomas Browne: The Ann Arbor Tercentenary Lectures and Essays,* ed. C. A. Patrides, 49–59. Columbia: University of Missouri, 1982.

———. *John Donne*. Boston: Twayne, 1987.

Webber, Joan. *Contrary Music: The Prose Style of John Donne*. Madison: University of Wisconsin Press, 1963.

———. *The Eloquent "I": Style and Self in Seventeenth-Century Prose*. Madison: University of Wisconsin Press, 1968.

Wilding, Michael. "*Religio Medici* and the English Revolution." In *Approaches to Sir Thomas Browne: The Ann Arbor Tercentenary Lectures and Essays*, ed. C. A. Patrides, 100–114. Columbia: University of Missouri, 1982.

Williams, George Huntston. *The Radical Reformation*. Philadelphia: Westminster Press, 1962.

Willson, D. Harris. *King James VI and I*. New York: Henry Holt, 1956.

Wittreich, Joseph Anthony, Jr. "'The Crown of Eloquence': The Figure of the Orator in Milton's Prose Works." In *Achievements of the Left Hand: Essays on the Prose of John Milton,* ed. Michael Lieb and John T. Shawcross, 3–54. Amherst: University of Massachusetts Press, 1974.

Woolrych, Austin. "Milton and Cromwell: 'A Short but Scandalous Night of Interruption'?" In *Achievements of the Left Hand: Essays on the Prose of John Milton*, ed. Michael Lieb and John T. Shawcross, 185–218. Amherst: University of Massachusetts Press, 1974.

Wormald, Jenny. "'Basilikon Doron' and 'The Trew Law of Free Monarchies': The Scottish Context and the English Translation." In *The Mental World of the Jacobean Court*, ed. Linda Levy Peck, 36–54. Cambridge: Cambridge University Press, 1991.

ACKNOWLEDGMENTS
──────────

The chief article of my own confession of faith is a belief in the generosity of the scholarly community: without the support, advice, and timely interventions of dozens of people this book would never have been completed. Annabel Patterson, who believed in this project from the beginning, put up with my early drafts, my vague conviction that I was onto something, and periodically nudged me in more profitable directions. Others who helped me clear my earliest intellectual and conceptual hurdles include Linda Peterson, Jim Kearney, John Rogers, and especially Jason Shaffer.

The generosity of more recent intellectual interlocutors allowed the project to reach its current form. Three anonymous reviewers saw the manuscript over various stages of revision and provided wonderfully detailed feedback; although I can't name them, I am grateful for their thoughtful engagement with my work. Ryan Netzley, John Staines, Austin Busch, and Eric Song each provided nonanonymous readings of large portions of the project and also made crucial interventions—saving me both from actual error and from mere foolishness. Ayesha Ramachandran, Andrea Walkden, Emily Hodgson Anderson, and Jessica Leiman also read parts of the project, and David Randall gave me the perspective of a historian. The Texas Institute for Literary Studies 2009 summer symposium, "Literature and Religious Conflict," run by Frank Whigham and Wayne Rebhorn, profoundly affected my thinking about the larger context of my work. I am grateful to Wayne and Frank and all the symposium's participants, but especially Todd Butler and Dan Gibbons, who have proven valuable sounding boards in the years since then.

Other conferences and professional societies played a significant role in the development of this project. The John Donne Society allowed me to test out many of the readings in Chapters 1 and 2 in preliminary form, and its members were among my earliest intellectual champions (and my earliest professional friends); I am especially grateful to Jeanne Shami and Tom Hester. A 2005 conference in Leiden introduced me to a core group of scholars working on Thomas Browne, including Reid Barbour and Claire Preston, whose advice and support since then have meant so much. A 2011 MLA panel chaired by Richard Strier also provided me with valuable audience feedback on the general shape of my argument.

Portions of this book appeared elsewhere in different forms, and I am grateful to these journals, presses, and editors for their permission to republish. Part of Chapter 2 was published as "Donne, Doubt, and the *Devotions upon Emergent Occasions*," *John Donne Journal* 22 (2003): 145–64; it appears here by permission of that journal. A version of Chapter 3 was published as " 'That Really Too Anxious Protestation': Crisis and Autobiography in Milton's Prose," *Milton Studies* 45 (2006): 149–86; it appears by permission of Duquesne University Press. Finally, a greatly condensed version of Chapter 4 was published as "*Religio Medici*'s Profession of Faith," in Reid Barbour and Claire Preston, eds., *Sir Thomas Browne: The World Proposed*, 149–67 (Oxford: Oxford University Press, 2008). Reprinted by permission of Oxford University Press.

Many institutions also supported my research. The Beinecke Rare Book and Manuscript Library provided me with research fellowships at both the beginning and the end of this project; the Princeton Rare Book Room and the Harry Ransom Humanities Research Center also awarded me fellowships at crucial junctures; the staff at the British Library and the Pembroke College Library at Oxford were unfailingly patient and helpful; and research and travel funds from the College at Brockport made additional travel possible. Finally, a pre-tenure research leave awarded by the State University of New York and my faculty union, United University Professions, enabled my most sustained period of revision.

Others who provided words of support or advice—or simply a round of drinks at the right moment—include my colleagues at Brockport and in the greater Rochester area. I particularly thank Joe Ortiz, Megan Obourn, Alissa Karl, Elizabeth Mazzolini, Katie Mannheimer, June Hwang, and all the current and former members of my Early Modern reading group. I'm also grateful to the friends and colleagues I've encountered through social media and academic channels on the Internet (some of whom I've still never met in person) for making the profession a warmer, kinder place. My editor at Penn Press, Jerry Singerman, also deserves note in the "warmer, kinder" category: I can't thank Jerry enough for his enthusiasm for this project and his taking it on when he did. Indeed, everyone at Penn has been a delight to work with.

Finally I thank my family: my parents, Rodney and Lani, and my brother, Reid. A deep fascination with *other people*—what they say, what they don't say, and how their behaviors do or don't align with their self-declarations—is a shared family trait, and years of dinner-table dissections surely contributed to my interest in matters of rhetorical self-presentation. Above all, I thank Jim Marino, to whom this book is dedicated.